AF568154

Rural Women Empowerment and Development Banking

Rural Women Empowerment and Development Banking

Dr. Richa Dewani

Rural Women Empowerment and Development Banking

ISBN 978-93-5111-808-4

Published in 2016 in India by

RANDOM PUBLICATIONS

4376-A/4B, Gali Murari Lal, Ansari Road
New Delhi-110 002
Phone : +9111-43580356, 011-23289044, 011-43142548
e-mail: sales@randompublications.com,
info@randompublications.com, randomexports@gmail.com

Reprinted 2023

Type Setting by : Friends Media, Delhi-110089
Printed at : Replika Press Pvt. Ltd.

Preface

Empowerment is now increasingly seen as a process by which the one's without power gain greater control over their lives. This means control over material assets, intellectual resources and ideology. It involves power to, power with and power within. Some define empowerment as a process of awareness and conscientization, of capacity building leading to greater participation, effective decision-making power and control leading to transformative action.

Therefore, the changes in women's labour patterns were mixed, and not as positive as along other dimensions. There was little indication that women's control over their labour had undergone a marked change, and the evaluation noted that many women may simply have gone from undertaking paid work outside the home to becoming unpaid family labourers (in male-managed enterprises). At least self-employment allows women the possibility to have better working conditions, save on travel time, and be able to more effectively combine reproductive and productive roles.

In India, the trickle down effects of macroeconomic policies have failed to resolve the problem of gender inequality. Women have been the vulnerable section of society and constitute a sizeable segment of the poverty-struck population. Women face gender specific barriers to access education health, employment etc. Micro finance deals with women below the poverty line. Micro loans are available solely and entirely to this target group of women. There are several reason for this: Among the poor , the poor women are most disadvantaged -they are characterized by lack of education and access of resources, both of which is required to help them work their way out of poverty and for upward economic and social mobility. The problem is more acute for women in countries like India, despite the fact that women's labour makes a critical contribution to the economy. This is due to the low social status and lack of access to key resources. Evidence shows that groups of women are better customers than men, the better managers of resources. If loans are routed through women benefits of loans are spread wider among the household.

The present book investigates how far the social and development banking endeavours to benefit rural women who have long been relegated to background by tradition.

– Author

Contents

1

Women's Empowerment in Rural India

Since the 1990's women have been identified as key agents of sustainable development and women's equality and empowerment are seen as central to a more holistic approach towards establishing new patterns and processes of development that are sustainable.

The World Bank has suggested that empowerment of women should be a key aspect of all social development programmes. Although a considerable debate on what constitutes empowerment exists, in this document we find it useful to rely on Kabeer's definition: "The expansion in people's ability to make strategic life choices in a context where this ability was previously denied to them." For women in India, this suggests empowerment in several realms: personal, familial, economic and political.

Since the 1980's the Government of India has shown increasing concern for women's issues through a variety of legislation promoting the education and political participation of women. International organizations like the World Bank and United Nations have focused on women's issues especially the empowerment of poor women in rural areas. In the late 1980s and early 1990s, non-governmental organizations have also taken on an increased role in the area of women's empowerment. NGO's, previously catering to women's health and educational needs, have moved beyond this traditional focus to addressing the underlying causes of deprivations through promoting the economic and social empowerment of women.. There are many challenges that face NGOs who make it their goal to empower women. This document addresses one specific challenge that is faced by NGOs located in rural areas that wish to promote women's empowerment.

These NGOs have little or no access to skilled social workers. They must often depend on the local population for their employees, employees who may be vulnerable to the similar social pressures and are often equally marginalised as their clients. For rural NGOs to be successful they must attract employees who must at some level be relatively more empowered than the clients. They must have certain credibility to be able to effectively persuade their marginalised clients to alter their ways of thinking on many long-standing traditional issues, such as dowries, child labour, and patriarchal subjugation. The literature of behaviour change in the health field suggests that self-efficacy is one of the four most commonly cited constructs for behavioural change 1. Although stated for different purposes and from different perspectives, the literature on self-efficacy can be brought to bear on issues of empowerment. Self-efficacy determines when an individual will undertake new behaviours such as self-empowerment. Low self-efficacy beliefs of women in rural India often stem from the limited and disadvantaged positions women have in society.

This makes any behaviour change towards self-empowerment difficult if it merely relies on verbal persuasion. The best way by which self-efficacy is acquired is by combining persuasion with role modeling in a supportive and appreciative environment. NGO employees must model empowered behaviours in order to evoke sustained behaviour modification for the empowerment of women they serve. Rural NGOs, who have to often depend on the same local pool for clients and employees, find it difficult to promote empowerment effectively. Despite the training given to employees to promote empowerment among their clients, there may still be a gap between what the employees 'preach' and what they may 'practice' in their own lives. This, in turn, may make them less effective and impede the NGO from achieving its goals. In this document we seek to explore how a relatively small and isolated rural NGO in the foothills of the Himalayas has been successful in the empowerment of rural women living in highly patriarchal and traditional societies

BACKGROUND

Chinmaya Rural Training Centre is a successful rural NGO in India that has received accolades for its success in empowering the women of the region and drawing them out of the cycle of dependency. CRTC is located in an impoverished village of Sidhbari, in Himachal Pradesh, nestled in the foothills of the Himalayas. The vast majority of the population is made up of landless poor and unskilled people who have few opportunities for full-time employment. Villagers work the land, owned by a handful of upper caste families. As agricultural activity is seasonal and ceases in the winter months the employees are underemployed.

Hence many of them eke out a living through subsistence farming around their homes and are involved in local trade that is generally not profitable. They belong to many of the lower castes and tribes that are categorized by the Indian Government as 'Other Backward Classes'. CRTC was the founded by Swami Chinmayananda, a revered Hindu spiritual leader, who chose one of the most depressed areas of the Himachal Pradesh to start a religious centre to practice his beliefs as well as an NGO that would empower local women. Sustainable development of the region, he believed, was only possible if the women were uplifted and could contribute to the success of their family and community.

Dr. Kshama Metre, a follower in his religious centre and a practicing pediatrician in New Delhi, took on the leadership of this NGO in 1985. Starting in relatively small way with a donation of a few sewing machines, Dr. Metre, single-mindedly pursued the vision of empowering the women of the dismal rural area. From this humble beginning she infused energy and vision to make this organization into a large well funded NGO currently serving over 27,000 clients spanning 900 villages offering a variety of programmes that included literacy and health services to sanitation, micro-finance and legal aid.3 Though women are regarded as the primary focus, by extending their services to include the families of these women where relevant, CRTC ends up serving the entire village community. The effect of empowerment of women creates a powerful influence on the norms, values and finally the laws that govern these communities.

RESEARCH QUESTION

In this document we seek to explore how CRTC, a relatively small and isolated rural NGO in the foothills of the Himalayas, has been successful in the empowerment of rural women living in highly patriarchal and traditional societies. The Indian Government as well as CIDA profiles CRTC as a model NGO in the arena of women's empowerment. In particular we investigate the employees at CRTC, who come from the same villages as the clientele, and examine whether they are significantly different in their levels of empowerment than those they help.

Is a gap between the rhetoric and reality of empowerment among the employees? Are employees whose aim is to empower women, empowered themselves? Do they practice what they preach? We seek to uncover the reasons for their success. We organize this document as follows: a literature review on behaviour change and empowerment of women and concludes with empowerment measures we use in this research. This is followed by restates our research question and sets out the methodology. Our findings, quantitative and qualitative, are presented and discussed. In the conclusion, we offer some policy implications and some final comments.

BEHAVIOUR CHANGE

We first start with a review of the self-efficacy literature and focus on the criteria for successful behaviour change. Bandura suggests that a person's self-expectations determine whether or not certain behaviour will be undertaken, the extent of effort expended by the individual, and whether the individual can persist in the face of challenges encountered. This notion of self-efficacy is mediated by a person's beliefs or expectations about his/her ability to achieve certain tasks effectively or exhibit certain behaviours. For example, individuals with low self-efficacy regarding their behaviour limit their participation when making difficult behaviour changes and are more likely to give up when faced with obstacles.

Their efficacy beliefs about themselves serve as barriers to change, and in this case, their own empowerment. Furthermore, these authors state that self-efficacy is not necessarily an in-born trait and can be acquired and nurtured. This fact makes these concepts particularly relevant to our study. Bandura identifies four ways in which self-efficacy and self-efficacy expectations are acquired: performance accomplishments, vicarious learning, verbal persuasion and physical/affective status. Performance accomplishments are beliefs that stem from the reactions with which individual accomplishments are greeted. A negative assessment can lower confidence and self-efficacy beliefs; conversely a positive assessment encourages self-efficacy beliefs and the self-efficacy expectations that similar behaviours will be well received in the future.

Vicarious learning results in beliefs that are acquired by observing modeling behaviours. When the modeling behaviour is undertaken within similar contexts5 such as gender, economic and social class it presents a realistic option. Thus, one of the most effective strategies for enhancing self-efficacy beliefs and self-efficacy expectations is that modeling behaviour is context specific. It is of little use for a woman of low social class to observe the success of an entrepreneurial woman born to a family of high social standing with access to resources that are unavailable to the poor woman. Other ways such as 'verbal persuasion' and 'affective status6' encourage selfefficacy. Persuading women to attempt positive behaviour change and providing a supportive environment in which women can attempt change, further enhances self-efficacy. Changes based on verbal persuasion, affective status and modeling behaviour can lead to significant changes in self–beliefs and self-expectation.

These 'personal factors' according to Bandura and Pajares, from an integral part of a triadic relationship necessary for change. They suggest that there is a reciprocal relationship between 'personal factors', 'behaviour' and 'environmental factors', which result in social change. Changes in personal factors can affect an individuals' behaviour, which can impact on environmental factors.

These relationships are reciprocal and reinforce each other. This suggests that strategies purposefully introduced in order to enhance women's personal factors can lead to reinforcing behaviours which in turn can impact and reinforce environmental factors. The interaction and reciprocity of the triadic relationship can result in a positive and significant change for women.

WOMEN'S EMPOWERMENT

Although the notion of women's empowerment has long been legitimized by international development agencies7, what actually comprises empowerment, and how it is measured, is debated in the development literature.

Malhotra, Schuler and Boender, 2002 provide an excellent review of this debate. They review the many ways that empowerment can be measured and suggest that researchers pay attention to the process in which empowerment occurs. The frequently used Gender Empowerment Measure is a composite measure of gender inequality in three key areas: Political participation and decision-making, economic participation and decision-making and power over economic resources. It is an aggregate index for a population and does not measure Empowerment on an individual basis. It is made up of two dimensions: Economic participation and decision-making and political participation and decision-making. For our purposes GEM is limited and does not capture the multidimensional view of women's empowerment. It cannot be assumed that if a development intervention promotes women's empowerment along a particular dimension that empowerment in other areas will necessarily follow. A number of studies have shown that women may be empowered in one area of life while not in others. While we do not attempt to resolve this debate, we take the position, that women's empowerment can be measured by factors contributing to each of the following: their personal, economic, familial, and political empowerment.

We make a point to include household and interfamilial relations as we believe is a central locus of women's disempowerment in India. And by including the political, we posit that women's empowerment measures should include women's participation in systemic transformation by engaging in political action. Amin, Becker and Bayes split the concept of women's empowerment into three components each measured separately: Inter-spouse consultation index, which seeks to represent the extent to which husbands consult their wives in household affairs; Individual autonomy indexes which represents women's self-reported autonomy of physical movement outside the house and in matters of spending money; and the Authority index, which reports on actual decision-making power.

These indices are similar to those of used by Balk in her 1994 study. Comparable components of empowerment are included in the eight indicators by Hashemi: mobility, economic security, ability to make a small purchases, ability to make larger purchases, involvement in major decisions, relative freedom from domination by the family, political and legal awareness, and involvement in political campaigning and protests. Several different efforts have been made in recent years to develop comprehensive frameworks delineating the various dimensions along which women can be empowered. We construct four separate components of empowerment in Table that draw from many of the authors revealed earlier and especially rely on Hashemi and Amin Becker and Bayes, as their work seems most relevant for rural women in India. These measures in Table reflect our belief that to measure women's empowerment more fully and in the broadest sense, it is necessary to add an individualised component representing her political autonomy to the autonomy within the family. Given that the legislation in India reserves special seats for women in elected bodies, even at the village level, an empowerment index for rural women should include her awareness of political issues and participation in the political process.

Table. Empowerment Measures

Personal Autonomy Index	Generally(1) Occasionally (1/2) Never (0)
Visiting respondents' parental home	
Visiting Hospital	
Visiting village market	
Helping a relative with money	
Setting money aside for respondent's use	
Family Decision Making Index	Wife Alone (1) Joint Decision (1/2)
Husband Alone (0)	
Children's education in school	
Family planning	
Family day-to-day expenditures	
Going outside of home	
Medical treatment	
Entertaining guests	
Buying respondent's traditionally	
Favourite things	
Economic Domestic Consultation Index	Generally(1) Occasionally (1/2) Never (0)
Buying household furniture and utensils	
Purchase of land	
Education/expense of children	
Purchasing Medical treatment of family	
Purchasing women's clothes	
Purchasing children's clothes	
Purchasing daily food	
Political Autonomy Index	Generally(1) Occasionally (1/2) Never (0)
Voting according to own decision	
Awareness of any political issue	
Participating in any public protest	
Campaigning politically	
Standing for elections	

METHODOLOGY

As this document seeks to explore how a relatively small and isolated rural NGO in the foothills of the Himalayas has become a model for the development and empowerment of rural disenfranchised women, a few words on the choice of the NGO are appropriate. Using a database from the directorate of NGOs in India9 we examined several successful women led NGOs in different parts of India.

The criteria for inclusion were that the NGO cater to rural women of lower castes who face traditional gender and class discrimination. We also stipulated that the NGO must be a successful grass roots organization that has the empowerment of women as its mission.

It should have received attention for its success both locally and internationally, and whose founder/director had time to meet with us and would allow us to survey the employees. After a limited search, based on telephone calls, we decided to use the Chinmaya Rural Training Centre as it met our criteria, and the Director assured us her cooperation. CRTC has received attention nationally; the Director has been given awards for her work on the empowerment of rural women. CRTC has also been identified by the Canadian International Development Agency as their 'flagship' NGO that dealt with women's empowerment. The Centre was identified in 1998 by the NABARD as a mother N.G.O. for training of N.G.O.s. CRTC empowers women by increasing their ability to contribute to their families' support as well. Concurrently it undertakes a variety of intervention strategies to attend to the psychological and social well being of women and encourages them to take part in the political process in their villages. CRTC is a successful NGO on a variety of scales. Whether using Korten's 'generational strategies', or Uvin et al's measures of 'scaling up', or Kassam and Handy's measures of 'vertical integration', CRTC rates high in meeting the goals of women's empowerment.

RESEARCH METHODS

Ethnographic and survey research was undertaken at CRTC. Face to face interviews were conducted with CRTC's employees, and participant observation of the meetings and activities that took place at CRTC during two weeks in January in 2003 followed by visit in March 2004 to present our findings and tie up some loose ends. We also observed and documented the various programmes at the village level where the women gathered at a prearranged time to participated in a variety of programmes. To document the levels of empowerment among women in the NGO we drew our data from the employees who were responsible for the services that were designed to empower the rural village women.

At the leadership level we interviewed nearly all of the ``Supervisors''' of the various programmes. These ``Supervisors'' administered the `Field workers' who went into the villages and worked directly with the village women. We interviewed 32 of the 57 ```Fieldworkers''' who assisted the ```Supervisors'''. We also chose to interview 25 local women living the area that the NGO served. They represented women who were eligible to be among the `Recipients' of the services of the NGO, by the fact they lived in the areas the NGO served. Although these are potential recipients we call them `Recipients' for convenience. We chose not to interview current recipients of services, as we wanted to establish a baseline of empowerment among the village women from whom the employees were drawn. As all of the employees lived in the neighbouring villages before seeking employment the findings on the empowerment indices of the `Recipients' may also be seen to reflect the those of the employees before coming to the NGO We chose to interview women employees and eligible women `Recipients' to ascertain the main research question, of whether the employees were 'walking the talk' and if the employees were significantly different from the recipients. In other words did the women employees who intervened to help promote the empowerment of women were themselves empowered. We were seeking to establish whether the employees own individual levels of empowerment were significantly different from the recipients of the services. Furthermore, we interviewed individuals at both levels of hierarchies in the organization to ascertain if all employees had same or differing levels of empowerment.

We decided to interview half of the `Fieldworkers'. We ended up with a sample of 32/57 of `Fieldworkers'. The latter was an opportunistic sample, in that we simply interviewed all the employees who happened to be present in the CRTC headquarters on the days we visited. During the period we visited the NGO, there was a rotation of the `Fieldworkers' assigned to duties at villages coming in to meet with the `Supervisors'.

We were thus able to interview 32 of the `Fieldworkers'. The sample of women eligible to be recipients was done by employing two of the NGO employees to visit every third house in the village and identify women who would be likely potential recipients. We were able to get a sample of 25 women who were willing to be interviewed. Two `Supervisors' helped us fine tune and translate our instrument for the `Recipients', which included the measures of women's empowerment used for the employees.

Additionally, we trained one local woman to undertake the interviews due to their fluency in the language12. To get a better understanding of how the NGO worked, and how the employees were selected and trained, we conducted several interviews conducted with the Director, Dr. Kshama Metre, over the course of two weeks. These interviews ranged from short half an hour discussions to longer two-hour conversations. Dr Metre also invited us to visit the weekly meetings held with all staff so we could observe first hand the training and interactions. We also attended six meetings in the villages held by staff with the clients to observe their interactions as well.

DEMOGRAPHIC AND SOCIO ECONOMIC DATA

The women in our study are all from the district of Sidhbari, Himachal Pradesh. There is a wide age spread in the total number of respondents. They range in age from 21 to 65; most women are married and lived with their husbands and have an average of 2.74 children. Only five women in our study did not live with a spouse, 3 of the women are divorced and two are widowed.

Divorce is not common in the rural areas and the general tradition is to put up with an abusive spouse or a bad marriage. With reference to caste 89% of the women categorize themselves as low caste or 'OBC' or Other Backward

Classes. This is a 'catch all' category developed by the Government of India census to include some of the most marginalised caste segments of Indian society.

Four of the 'Supervisors' belong to the higher castes, as do two of the 'Fieldworkers' and one from the group of 'Recipients'. Family structure is relevant to discussion of empowerment. As many of the questions relate to domestic decisions making to establish empowerment levels family structures can influence the responses. The traditional family structure in India is not a nuclear family, it a joint family. In this system, when a son marries, he continues to reside with his parents with his wife and their children. The daughter on the other hand goes to her husband's home and lives with his parents, unmarried siblings, and the families of his married brothers. The parents of the husband, in a joint family, tend to hold decision-making authority that often overrides the authority of any of the married sons or their wives. Twenty-nine of the seventy two women in our study live in traditional joint families, whereas the rest lived in a nuclear family setting, which is far less than the norm in Himachal Pradesh of over 50%.

The women had an average of 6.13 years of education (The literacy rate in Himachal Pradesh is 77.13% which is much above the national average of 65.38%; Male literacy is 86% and female literacy is 68% (The Tribune, Chandigarh, India, Saturday, March 31, 2001) In this area where alcoholism is rampant, we asked our respondents if they had problems related to alcohol consumption. We find that half of the women suggested that they had experienced problems related to the alcohol consumption by their husbands. This ranged from beatings and the use of household money for alcohol to unemployment. The differences between the groups were striking, in that the least amount of alcoholism was present in the families of 'Fieldworkers' and the most in the 'Recipients', where as the half the 'Supervisors' experienced alcohol related problems.

Table. Comparison of Means of Socio Economic Data and Empowerment Index for 'Supervisors', 'Fieldworkers' and 'Recipients'

Mean	Supervisors	Fieldworkers Sig 2-tailed	Recipients	ANOVAF F Test 3 groups	T-Test for 2 groups S and F
Age	40	38.94	36.64	.818	.669
No. of Kids	3	2	3	5.117*	.048*
Income class	1.79	1.65	1.32	5.348*	.357
Years of Education	10.27	8.00	1.40	51.380**	.032*
Years in NGO	10.53	6.40	N/a	N/a	.008**
Empowerment Index	21.72	17.47	9.40	37.815**	.007**

Note: *Correlation is significant at the 0.05 level

** Correlation is significant at the 0.01 level

We then compared the differences of the means of several socio demographic variables and the means of the empowerment index between the three groups: 'Supervisors', 'Fieldworkers' and 'Recipients', to see if they differed significantly on any of the socio demographic variables and empowerment levels. While they appeared significantly different on the number of all counts with the exception of age, the Scheffe Post Hoc test showed that not all the differences were significant.

Scheffe Post Hoc tests reveals that for the variables Education and Income class there were no significant differences between the 'Supervisors' and 'Fieldworkers', but both groups of employees were significantly different from the 'Recipients'.

This is not surprising, as NGO employees need to be literate and have education to be hired as professional employees. The (income) class variable asked respondents to choose between three classes income: high, middle or low. The results show that respondents only chose either low or middle. This is expected given the poverty level in this area.

We find that there were no significant differences between the 'Supervisors' and 'Fieldworkers', but both groups of employees were significantly different from the 'Recipient' group. This may be explained by the fact that NGO employees earn a steady income while the 'Recipient' group do not have a steady income and are dependent on the local economy, Only six of the 'Recipient' group worked outside the home as compared to all the 'Fieldworkers' and 'Supervisors'. Finally the Scheffe Post Hoc test shows significant differences between all three groups on the empowerment index. Each group was significantly different from the other.

ECONOMIC EMPOWERMENT OF WOMEN

POVERTY ERADICATION

Since women comprise the majority of the population below the poverty line and are very often in situations of extreme poverty, given the harsh realities of intra -household and social discrimination, macro economic policies and poverty eradication programmes will specifically address the needs and problems of such women.

There will be improved implementation of programmes which are already women oriented with special targets for women. Steps will be taken for mobilization of poor women and convergence of services, by offering them a range of economic and social options, along with necessary support measures to enhance their capabilities

MICRO CREDIT

In order to enhance women's access to credit for consumption and production, the establishment of new, and strengthening of existing microcredit mechanisms and micro-finance institution will be undertaken so that the outreach of credit is enhanced. Other supportive measures would be taken to ensure adequate flow of credit through extant financial institutions and banks, so that all women below poverty line have easy access to credit.

WOMEN AND ECONOMY

Women's perspectives will be included in designing and implementing macro-economic and social policies by institutionalizing their participation in such processes. Their contribution to socio-economic development as producers and workers will be recognized in the formal and informal sectors (including home based workers) and appropriate policies relating to employment and to her working conditions will be drawn up. Such measures could include: Reinterpretation and redefinition of conventional concepts of work wherever necessary *e.g.* in the Census records, to reflect women's contribution as producers and workers. Preparation of satellite and national accounts Development of appropriate methodologies for undertaking (i) and (ii) above.

GLOBALIZATION

Globalization has presented new challenges for the realization of the goal of women's equality, the gender impact of which has not been systematically evaluated fully. However, from the micro-level studies that were commissioned by the Department of Women and Child Development, it is evident that there is a need for re -framing policies for access to employment and quality of employment.

Benefits of the growing global economy have been unevenly distributed leading to wider economic disparities, the feminization of poverty, increased gender inequality through often deteriorating working conditions and unsafe working environment especially in the informal economy and rural areas. Strategies will be designed to enhance the capacity of women and empower them to meet the negative social and economic impacts, which may flow from the globalization process.

WOMEN AND AGRICULTURE

In view of the critical role of women in the agriculture and allied sectors, as producers, concentrated efforts will be made to ensure that benefits of training, extension and various programmes will reach them in proportion to their numbers. The programmes for training women in soil conservation, social forestry, dairy development and other occupations allied to agriculture like horticulture, livestock including small animal husbandry, poultry, fisheries etc. will be expanded to benefit women workers in the agriculture sector.

WOMEN AND INDUSTRY

The important role played by women in electronics, information technology and food processing and agro industry and textiles has been crucial to the development of these sectors. They would be given comprehensive support in terms of labour legislation, social security and other support services to participate in various industrial sectors. Women at present cannot work in night shift in factories even if they wish to. Suitable measures will be taken to enable women to work on the night shift in factories. This will be accompanied with support services for security, transportation etc.

SUPPORT SERVICES

The provision of support services for women, like child care facilities, including crèches at work places and educational institutions, homes for the aged and the disabled will be expanded and improved to create an enabling environment and to ensure their full cooperation in social, political and economic life. Women-friendly personnel policies will also be drawn up to encourage women to participate effectively in the developmental process.

SOCIAL EMPOWERMENT OF WOMEN

EDUCATION

Equal access to education for women and girls will be ensured. Special measures will be taken to eliminate discrimination, universalise education, eradicate illiteracy, create a gender-sensitive educational system, increase enrolment and retention rates of girls and improve the quality of education to facilitate life-long learning as well as development of occupation/vocation/technical skills by women.

Reducing the gender gap in secondary and higher education would be a focus area. Sectoral time targets in existing policies will be achieved, with a special focus on girls and women, particularly those belonging to weaker parts including the Scheduled Castes/Scheduled Tribes/Other Backward Classes/Minorities. Gender sensitive curricula would be developed at all levels of educational system in order to address sex stereotyping as one of the causes of gender discrimination.

HEALTH

A holistic approach to women's health which includes both nutrition and health services will be adopted and special attention will be given to the needs of women and the girl at all stages of the life cycle.

The reduction of infant mortality and maternal mortality, which are sensitive indicators of human development, is a priority concern. This policy reiterates the national demographic goals for Infant Mortality Rate (IMR), Maternal Mortality Rate (MMR) set out in the National Population Policy 2000.

Women should have access to comprehensive, affordable and quality health care. Measures will be adopted that take into account the reproductive rights of women to enable them to exercise informed choices, their vulnerability to sexual and health problems together with endemic, infectious and communicable diseases such as malaria, TB, and water borne diseases as well as hypertension and cardio -pulmonary diseases.

The social, developmental and health consequences of HIV/AIDS and other sexually transmitted diseases will be tackled from a gender perspective. To effectively meet problems of infant and maternal mortality, and early marriage the availability of good and accurate data at micro level on deaths, birth and marriages is required. Strict implementation of registration of births and deaths would be ensured and registration of marriages would be made compulsory.

In accordance with the commitment of the National Population Policy (2000) to population stabilization, this Policy recognizes the critical need of men and women to have access to safe, effective and affordable methods of family planning of their choice and the need to suitably address the issues of early marriages and spacing of children. Interventions such as spread of education, compulsory registration of marriage and special programmes like BSY should impact on delaying the age of marriage so that by 2010 child marriages are eliminated. Women's traditional knowledge about health care and nutrition will be recognized through proper documentation and its use will be encouraged. The use of Indian and alternative systems of medicine will be enhanced within the framework of overall health infrastructure available for women.

NUTRITION

In view of the high risk of malnutrition and disease that women face at all the three critical stages *viz.*, infancy and childhood, adolescent and reproductive phase, focussed attention would be paid to meeting the nutritional needs of women at all stages of the life cycle. This is also important in view of the critical link between the health of adolescent girls, pregnant and lactating women with the health of infant and young children.

Special efforts will be made to tackle the problem of macro and micro nutrient deficiencies especially amongst pregnant and lactating women as it leads to various diseases and disabilities. Intra -household discrimination in nutritional matters *vis-à-vis* girls and women will be sought to be ended through appropriate strategies.

Widespread use of nutrition education would be made to address the issues of intra-household imbalances in nutrition and the special needs of pregnant and lactating women. Women's participation will also be ensured in the planning, superintendence and delivery of the system.

DRINKING WATER AND SANITATION

Special attention will be given to the needs of women in the provision of safe drinking water, sewage disposal, toilet facilities and sanitation within accessible reach of households, especially in rural areas and urban slums. Women's participation will be ensured in the planning, delivery and maintenance of such services.

HOUSING AND SHELTER

Women's perspectives will be included in housing policies, planning of housing colonies and provision of shelter both in rural and urban areas. Special attention will be given for providing adequate and safe housing and accommodation for women including single women, heads of househ olds, working women, students, apprentices and trainees.

ENVIRONMENT

Women will be involved and their perspectives reflected in the policies and programmes for environment, conservation and restoration. Considering the impact of environmental factors on their livelihoods, women's participation will be ensured in the conservation of the environment and control of environmental degradation. The vast majority of rural women still depend on the locally available non-commercial sources of energy such as animal dung, crop waste and fuel wood.

In order to ensure the efficient use of these energy resources in an environmental friendly manner, the Policy will aim at promoting the programmes of nonconventional energy resources. Women will be involved in spreading the use of solar energy, biogas, smokeless chulahs and other rural application so as to have a visible impact of these measures in influencing eco system and in changing the life styles of rural women.

SCIENCE AND TECHNOLOGY

Programmes will be strengthened to bring about a greater involvement of women in science and technology. These will include measures to motivate girls to take up science and technology for higher education and also ensure that development projects with scientific and technical inputs involve women fully.

Efforts to develop a scientific temper and awareness will also be stepped up. Special measures would be taken for their training in areas where they have special skills like communication and information technology. Efforts to develop appropriate technologies suited to women's needs as well as to reduce their drudgery will be given a special focus too.

WOMEN IN DIFFICULT CIRCUMSTANCES

In recognition of the diversity of women's situations and in acknowledgement of the needs of specially disadvantaged groups, measures and programmes will be undertaken to provide them with special assistance. These groups include women in extreme poverty, destitute women, women in conflict situations, women affected by natural calamities, women in less developed regions, the disabled widows, elderly women, single women in difficult circumstances, women heading households, those displaced from employment, migrants, women who are victims of marital violence, deserted women and prostitutes etc.

IMPACT ON POLITICAL EMPOWERMENT OF WOMEN AND WOMEN'S RIGHTS

Widespread political empowerment is a fairly rare outcome of most microfinance programmes. Although microfinance programmes offer services and products that can enhance individual women's abilities to participate effectively in politics, few microfinance organisations explicitly seek political mobilisation or structure their programmes in such a way as to deliberately nurture collective action. Nevertheless, many examples testify that women's participation in lending centers and groups increases their knowledge of political parties, processes, and channels of influence. Women clients of Opportunity Microfinance Bank in the Philippines have gained leadership experience and confidence as leaders of their Trust Banks and have gone on to be elected as leaders within their barangays.

Women clients of what is now FORA in Russia organised to campaign for democracy during recent Russian elections. Esmeralda Castaños, a former Trust Bank leader from Opportunity partner IDH in Honduras, recently ran for mayor of her small town of San Mateus. And a number of Trust Banks of AGAPE in Barranquilla, Colombia, helped organise a protest march to bring better sewage systems to their community. Some programmes, such as BRAC, offer training programmes with the specific aim of creating political and social awareness. In a study comparing the empowerment effects of participation in Grameen Bank and BRAC microfinance programmes, Hashemi, Schuler, and Riley found that participation in BRAC had a stronger effect on participation in political campaigns and public protests than did Grameen.

They believe that this "may be because BRAC provides more opportunities for its members to participate in training programmes, which give them an opportunity to travel outside their villages, and because of its greater emphasis on creating awareness of social and political issues." Other programmes such as Working Women's Forum (WWF) in India are very active politically. WWF has a union and advocacy branch as well as a lending programme and has been successful in mobilising very large numbers of women for political and legal changes that support women's rights and opportunities. According to WWF, over 89 percent of its members had taken up civic action for pressing problems in their neighbourhoods, showing that microfinance and political empowerment can be complementary processes.

And Human Development Initiatives Nigeria (HDI) has successfully combined education of widows about inheritance, legal, and property rights with training in business skills and microfinance. The education has allowed some widows to reclaim their husbands' property and to gain access to their bank accounts. HDI's counseling and mediation services have also helped them resolve conflicts with their husbands' families. Even programmes that are not explicitly addressing women's rights and political participation have had some impact on political and legal empowerment. By contributing to women's knowledge and self-confidence and by widening their social networks, many microfinance programmes give women the tools and skills they need to participate more effectively and successfully in formal politics and to informally influence decisions and policies that affect their lives.

For example, World Education, which focuses on literacy rather than political rights training, has found that women who have been through their literacy programme are more likely to stand for elected positions such as ward representative or health committee member. A study of Freedom From Hunger's Credit With Education clients in Bolivia found that clients were significantly more likely to have been a candidate for public office or to have been a member of the community's sindicato than non-clients.

Candidacy for public office can be a good indicator of women's self-confidence and efficacy and the community's respect for women as well as political empowerment; however, it is important to know the broader political conditions affecting their candidacy and role in office. For example, in Nepal, 96 women from CSD's programme were elected to village and district development committees, but the study also showed that women tended not to have any significant influence over decisions after being elected.

NEGATIVE IMPACTS ON WOMEN AND LIMITATIONS TO EMPOWERMENT

Both men and women assume risks when taking out a loan—which becomes debt with all of its accompanying stresses and responsibilities. In addition some studies of the impact of microfinance programmes have raised legitimate concerns about the potentially negative impact that programmes can have on women, particularly in highly restrictive environments. One often-reported concern is that clients' husbands or other household members take control of the woman's loans, yet the client herself retains responsibility for paying off the loans, thus increasing her level of stress and dependency. Other studies question the success of microfinance programmes in effecting lasting change in women's economic welfare or empowerment.

Some scholars, such as Linda Mayoux, argue that microfinance institutions cannot have more than a limited impact on women's empowerment unless there are changes in wider gender inequalities in the broader social and economic contexts in which they operate. In light of these limitations, Mayoux recommends that MFIs intentionally address women's empowerment as part of their goals, objectives, operations, and product design. Other common concerns raised include the increased burden that microenterprise activities place on women's time, MFIs' reinforcing rather than challenging gender inequalities, and the possibility that children will be kept out of school to help in their mother's business.

How does Women's Participation in Microfinance Programmes and Microenterprises Affect the use of their Time

Microfinance programmes can affect women's use of their time through two main channels: meeting time and expanded enterprise activity. Most methodologies that target women rely on women being able to spend time together to learn about effective financial management and to repay and disburse loans. Although time is precious and scarce for many poor women, it is one resource that most women can utilise to gain access to financial services. It is a key factor in facilitating cost-efficient delivery of services. There are concerns, however, that MFIs are increasing women's work burden by involving them in time-consuming meetings and income-generating activities without taking any action to reduce their traditional responsibilities.

Many women report an increased workload and responsibilities as a result of their loans. Several cases of women suffering ill health and exhaustion as a result of overwork have been reported. In other cases, though, women report that they are more than happy to assume the extra burden because of the respect, personal satisfaction, and improved standard of living they experienced as a result of their income-generating activities. In her study of the Small Enterprise Development Programme in Bangladesh, Naila Kabeer found that the majority of women who experienced an increased workload were happy and felt that the benefits outweighed the costs of participation. In the words of one Bangladeshi woman interviewed,

- My labour has increased, my husband can also see that.... I have less time to do the usual things so he is more tolerant. My labour has increased, but it means we are better off. You need to work. Now we

> have bought a loan and put it to work, if we have to work harder, that makes no difference to me, we do it with pleasure. The pleasure is that I do the work and I will make an extra bit of money. This was not the case before. The problem before was that I would think I need 500 takas for something, but where would I get the money from? We would have to borrow it. Now we are in position to lend.

Several women interviewed in Ghana also affirmed that in spite of their increased workload and responsibilities, they felt a great deal of pride and personal satisfaction in being able to make a substantial economic contribution to their household. In some cases, studies have revealed that other family members substantially increase their participation both in the business and with the household chores.

A study by Opportunity partner TSPI in the Philippines revealed that the percentage of women whose daughters participated in their businesses increased by 88 percent. Surprisingly, more sons started helping with housework after their mothers joined the programme. These findings suggest that it may be important to evaluate the impact of microenterprise not only on the women clients themselves but also on their adult and young children.

While the implications of microfinance for the demands on women's time vary considerably according to each individual's situation, MFIs need to be aware that their programmes do affect women's time, not always in positive ways, and should be prepared to assist them in negotiating a reasonable and sustainable balance between life and work.

Do Good Repayment Rates Depend, In Part, on Women's Disempowered Condition

Supporters of microfinance claim that solidarity groups, self-help groups, and village banks help build the social capital of their communities. Other scholars and development experts, however, worry that by using existing social capital in communities to ensure repayment, MFIs are introducing new stresses and pressures on community life and may damage important support relationships. They observe that MFIs may owe much of their high recovery rates to the lack of alternatives and powerlessness of their client base.

It has been well documented that microfinance figures into poor women's risk-management strategies and that continued access to credit is a major incentive for repayment. But, in this sense, incentives for repayment are little different from those for the formal financial markets. No one wants a bad credit record that could keep him or her from accessing financing in the future. The difference is that poor women have even fewer options and alternatives, so the incentive is even stronger. Because most microfinance approaches were developed to work with women in their disempowered condition, however, institutions need to be prepared to change and develop as the women and communities they serve change, become empowered, and have more options.

Do MFIs Reinforce Women's Traditional Roles Instead of Promoting Gender Equality

Some critics have argued that the majority of microfinance programmes are structured in such a way as to have their greatest impact in helping women perform traditional roles better. They argue that by emphasizing the benefits that women's families receive from their access to credit and helping them earn income in such a way that it does not interfere significantly with their traditional duties, microfinance institutions may reinforce traditional gender roles and relations rather than alter them. The reality that many of women's practical needs are closely linked to traditional gender roles, responsibilities, and social structures contributes to a tension between meeting women's practical needs in the short term and promoting long-term strategic change.

Yet by helping women meet their practical needs and increase their efficacy in their traditional roles, microfinance programmes can help women gain respect and achieve more in their traditional roles, which in turn can lead to increased esteem. Although improving women's ability to perform traditional roles is not sufficient to ensure empowerment, it may well be a necessary precondition. Enhancing women's sense of efficacy and financial security may contribute decisively to women's ability and willingness to challenge the social injustices and discriminatory systems that they face.

In the experience of ENDA Inter-Arabe in Tunisia, it is often an economic crisis such as divorce or the loss or illness of a wage earner that threatens a woman's ability to care for her family, draws her out of her submissive and dependent role, and leads her to take actions that surpass the expectations that others have of her.

ENDA Inter-Arabe finds that generating and controlling income is the starting point for other forms of empowerment. "Financial autonomy brings with it dignity. Their newly-gained knowledge and capacity to take and influence decisions provides them with self-confidence." Armed with the increased access to knowledge that the programme provides, combined with their new sense of self-confidence and dignity, many of ENDA Inter-Arabe's women clients are willing and able to take the next step by participating in public meetings, joining political parties, and assuming leadership roles in the community.

Although microfinance has helped empower many women in many different ways, empowerment is not an automatic outcome for all women. A closer look at the role that microfinance programmes play in women's empowerment and success in business will allow us to begin to understand the causes of both positive and negative outcomes and to develop programmes that can enhance the positive and minimize the risk and rate of negative outcomes.

WOMEN EMPOWERMENT IN INDIA

Empowerment is now increasingly seen as a process by which the one's without power gain greater control over their lives. This means control over material assets, intellectual resources and ideology. It involves power to, power with and power within. Some define empowerment as a process of awareness and conscientization, of capacity building leading to greater participation, effective decision-making power and control leading to transformative action.

This involves ability to get what one wants and to influence others on our concerns. With reference to women the power relation that has to be involved includes their lives at multiple levels, family, community, market and the state. Importantly it involves at the psychological level women's ability to assert themselves and this is constructed by the 'gender roles' assigned to her specially in a cultural which resists change like India. The questions surrounding women's empowerment the condition and position of women have now become critical to the human rights based approaches to development.

The Cairo conference in 1994 organized by UN on Population and Development called attention to women's empowerment as a central focus and UNDP developed the Gender Empowerment measure (GEM) which focuses on the three variables that reflect women's participation in society – political power or decision-making, education and health. 1995 UNDP report was devoted to women's empowerment and it declared that if human development is not engendered it is endangered a declaration which almost become a lei motif for further development measuring and policy planning. Equality, sustainability and empowerment were emphasized and the stress was, that women's emancipation does not depend on national income but is an engaged political process. Drawing from Amartya Sen's work on 'Human capabilities' — an idea drawn from Aristotle a new matrix was created to measure human development.

The emphasis was that we need to enhance human well being flourishing and not focus on growth of national income as a goal. People's choices have to be enlarged and they must have economic opportunities to make use of these capabilities. States and countries would consider developments in terms of whether its people lead a long healthy painless life or no are educated and knowledgeable and enjoy decent standards of living.

The intuitive idea behind the capability is twofold according to Martha Nussbaum (2003) first, that there are certain functions that are particularly central to human life. Second, that there is something do these in a truly human way, not a mere animal way. The list of capabilities that she draws is cross-cultural as necessary element of truly human functioning. They include:

- Life-being able to live to the end of human life of normal length: not dying prematurely, or before one's life is so reduced as to be not worth living.
- Bodily health – being able to have good health including reproductive health, to be adequately nourished, to have adequate shelter.
- Bodily integrity – Being able to move freely from place to place, to be secure against violent assault, including sexual assault and domestic violence; having opportunities for sex satisfaction and for choice in matters of reproduction.
- Senses, imagination and thought – Being able to use the sense, to imagine, think and reason in a truly human way including but not limited to literacy. Being able to use one's mind and imagination protected by freedom of expression.
- Emotions – being able to have attachments, to love, to grieve to experience longing gratitude and justified anger. Not having one's emotional development blighted by fear and anxiety.
- Practical Reason – Being able to form a conception of the good and to engage in critical reflection about planning of one's life's protected by liberty of conscience.
- Affiliation – Being able to live with and towards others to have social interactions, to have the capability of both justice and friendship. This would entail freedom of assembly and free speech. Having social bases for self-respect and non-humiliation, being protected against discrimination on the basis of race, sex sexual orientation religion caste or region.
- Other species – Being able to concern with nature.
- Play – being able to laugh, play and enjoy.
- Control over one's environment.
  - Political. Being able to participate effectively in political choices that govern one's life, having the right to political participation, protection of free speech and association.
  - Material. Being able to hold property to seek employment on equal bases and having freedom from unwarranted search and seizure. In work, being able to work as a human being, exercising practical reason and entering into meaningful relationships of mutual recognition with the workers.

These capabilities cover the so called "first generation rights" (political and civil liberties) as well as the "second generation rights" (economic and social rights0. It has been emphasized that women all over the world have been short shifted and have not found support for their central human functions. Women are capable of these functions given sufficient, nutrition, education and other support.

Women are most often not treated as subjects. Women are as capable as men of exercising will, controlling desires and taking decisions but males enjoy support of social institutions and women are excluded as the 'other'. Women are often not treated as "ends in themselves" persons with dignity who deserve respect from laws and institutions instead they are treated instrumentally as reproducers, caregivers, sexual receivers, agents of family's general prosperity. Human development report since 1999 demonstrate that practically no country in the world treats its women as well as men according to the measures of life expectancy wealth and education. Developing countries present especially urgent problems where caste and class result in acute failure of human capabilities of women. Women in this part of south East Asia lack essential support for fully functioning human lives. Within the country there are many issues to be addressed closely.

INTERNATIONAL EMPOWERMENT OF WOMEN

CHARTER OF UNO 1945

The Charter of the United Nations is the foundational treaty of the international organization called the United Nations. It was signed at the San Francisco War Memorial and Performing Arts Center in San Francisco, United States, on 26 June 1945, by 50 of the 51 original member countries (Poland, the other original member, which was not represented at the conference, signed it 2 months later). It entered into force on 24 October 1945, after being ratified by the five permanent members of the Security Council—the Republic of China (later replaced by the People's Republic of China), France, the Union of Soviet Socialist Republics (later replaced by the Russian Federation), the United Kingdom, and the United States—and a majority of the other signatories. Today, 193 countries are the members of the United Nations.

As a charter, it is a constituent treaty, and all members are bound by its articles. Furthermore, the Charter states that obligations to the United Nations prevail over all other treaty obligations. Most countries in the world have now ratified the Charter. One notable exception is the Holy See, which has chosen to remain a permanent observer state and therefore is not a full signatory to the Charter. The Charter consists of a *preamble* and a series of articles grouped into chapters. The preamble consists of two principal parts. The first part containing a general call for the maintenance of peace and international security and respect for human rights. The second part of the preamble is a declaration in a contractual style that the governments of the peoples of the United Nations have agreed to the Charter.

- Chapter I sets forth the purposes of the United Nations, including the important provisions of the maintenance of international peace and security.
- Chapter II defines the criteria for membership in the United Nations.
- Chapters III-XV, the bulk of the document, describe the organs and institutions of the UN and their respective powers.
- Chapters XVI and Chapter XVII describe arrangements for integrating the UN with established international law.
- Chapters XVIII and Chapter XIX provide for amendment and ratification of the Charter.

The following chapters deal with the enforcement powers of UN bodies:

- Chapter VI describes the Security Council's power to investigate and mediate disputes;
- Chapter VII describes the Security Council's power to authorize economic, diplomatic, and military sanctions, as well as the use of military force, to resolve disputes;
- Chapter VIII makes it possible for regional arrangements to maintain peace and security within their own region;
- Chapters IX and Chapter X describe the UN's powers for economic and social cooperation, and the Economic and Social Council that oversees these powers;
- Chapters XII and Chapter XIII describe the Trusteeship Council, which oversaw decolonization;
- Chapters XIV and Chapter XV establish the powers of, respectively, the International Court of Justice and the United Nations Secretariat.
- Chapters XVI through Chapter XIX deal respectively with XVI: miscellaneous provisions, XVII: transitional security arrangements related to World War II, XVIII: the charter amendment process, and XIX: ratification of the charter.

UNIVERSAL DECLARATION OF HUMAN RIGHTS 1948

The Universal Declaration of Human Rights (UDHR) is a declaration adopted by the United Nations General Assembly (10 December 1948 at Palais de Chaillot, Paris). The Declaration arose directly from the experience of the Second World War and represents the first global expression of rights to which all human beings are inherently entitled. It consists of 30 articles which have been elaborated in subsequent international treaties, regional human rights instruments, national constitutions and laws. The International Bill of Human Rights consists of the Universal Declaration of Human Rights, the International Covenant on Economic, Social and Cultural Rights, and the International Covenant on Civil and Political Rights and its two Optional Protocols. In 1966 the General Assembly adopted the two detailed Covenants, which complete the International Bill of Human Rights; and in 1976, after the Covenants had been ratified by a sufficient number of individual nations, the Bill took on the force of international law.

CONVENTION ON POLITICAL RIGHTS OF WOMEN

Desiring to implement the principle of equality of rights for men and women contained in the Charter of the United Nations, Recognizing that everyone has the right to take part in the government of his country, directly or indirectly through freely chosen representatives, and has the right to equal access to public service in his country, and desiring to equalize the status of men and women in the enjoyment and exercise of political rights, in accordance with the provisions of the Charter of the United Nations and of the Universal Declaration of Human Rights.

INTERNATIONAL COVENANT ON CIVIL AND POLITICAL RIGHTS

The International Covenant on Civil and Political Rights (ICCPR) is a multilateral treaty adopted by the United Nations General Assembly on December 16, 1966, and in force from March 23, 1976. It commits its parties to respect the civil and political rights of individuals, including the right to life, freedom of religion, freedom of speech, freedom of assembly, electoral rights and rights to due process and a fair trial. As of March 2012, the Covenant had 74 signatories and 167 parties.

The ICCPR is part of the International Bill of Human Rights, along with the International Covenant on Economic, Social and Cultural Rights (ICESCR) and the Universal Declaration of Human Rights (UDHR). The ICCPR is monitored by the Human Rights Committee (a separate body to the Human Rights Council), which reviews regular reports of States parties on how the rights are being implemented. States must report initially one year after acceding to the Covenant and then whenever the Committee requests (usually every four years). The Committee normally meets in Geneva and normally holds three sessions per year.

The ICCPR has its roots in the same process that led to the Universal Declaration of Human Rights. A "Declaration on the Essential Rights of Man" had been proposed at the 1945 San Francisco Conference which led to the founding of the United Nations, and the Economic and Social Council was given the task of drafting it. Early on in the process, the document was split into a declaration setting forth general principles of human rights, and a convention or covenant containing binding commitments. The former evolved into the UDHR and was adopted on December 10, 1948.

Drafting continued on the convention, but there remained significant differences between UN members on the relative importance of negative Civil and Political versus positive Economic, Social and Cultural rights. These eventually caused the convention to be split into two separate covenants, "one to contain civil and political rights and the other to contain economic, social and cultural rights." The two covenants were to contain as many similar provisions as possible, and be opened for signature simultaneously. Each would also contain an article on the right of all peoples to self-determination.

The first document became the International Covenant on Economic, Social and Cultural Rights and the second the International Covenant on Civil and Political Rights. The drafts were presented to the UN General Assembly for discussion in 1954, and adopted in 1966. As a result of diplomatic negotiations the International Covenant on Economic, Social and Cultural Rights was adopted shortly before the International Covenant on Civil and Political Rights. The Covenant follows the structure of the UDHR and ICESCR, with a preamble and fifty-three articles, divided into six parts.

- Part 1 (Article 1) recognises the right of all peoples to self-determination, including the right to "freely determine their political status", pursue their economic, social and cultural goals, and manage and dispose of their own resources. It recognises a negative right of a people not to be deprived of its means of subsistence, and imposes an obligation on those parties still responsible for non-self governing and trust territories (colonies) to encourage and respect their self-determination.
- Part 2 (Articles 2 – 5) obliges parties to legislate where necessary to give effect to the rights recognised in the Covenant, and to provide an effective legal remedy for any violation of those rights. It also requires the rights be recognised "without distinction of any kind, such as race, colour, sex, language, religion, political or other opinion, national or social origin, property, birth or other status," and to ensure that they are enjoyed equally by women. The rights can only be limited "in time of public emergency which threatens the life of the nation," and even then no derogation is permitted from the rights to life, freedom from torture and slavery, the freedom from retrospective law, the right to personhood, and freedom of thought, conscience and religion.
- Part 3 (Articles 6 – 27) lists the rights themselves. These include rights to

  - Physical integrity, in the form of the right to life and freedom from torture and slavery (Articles 6, 7, and 8);
  - Liberty and security of the person, in the form of freedom from arbitrary arrest and detention and the right to *habeas corpus* (Articles 9 – 11);
  - Procedural fairness in law, in the form of rights to due process, a fair and impartial trial, the presumption of innocence, and recognition as a person before the law (Articles 14, 15, and 16);
  - Individual liberty, in the form of the freedoms of movement, thought, conscience and religion, speech, association and assembly, family rights, the right to a nationality, and the right to privacy (Articles 12, 13, 17 – 24);
  - Prohibition of any propaganda for war as well as any advocacy of national or religious hatred that constitutes incitement to discrimination, hostility or violence by law (Article 20);
  - Political participation, including the right to join a political party and the right to vote (Article 25);
  - Non-discrimination, minority rights and equality before the law (Articles 26 and 27).
- Part 4 (Articles 28 – 45) governs the establishment and operation of the Human Rights Committee and the reporting and monitoring of the Covenant. It also allows parties to recognise the competence of the Committee to resolve disputes between parties on the implementation of the Covenant (Articles 41 and 42).
- Part 5 (Articles 46 – 47) clarifies that the Covenant shall not be interpreted as interfering with the operation of the United Nations or "the inherent right of all peoples to enjoy and utilize fully and freely their natural wealth and resources".
- Part 6 (Articles 48 – 53) governs ratification, entry into force, and amendment of the Covenant.

INTERNATIONAL COVENANT ON ECONOMIC, SOCIAL AND CULTURAL RIGHTS

The International Covenant on Economic, Social and Cultural Rights (ICESCR) is a multilateral treaty adopted by the United Nations General Assembly on 16 December 1966, and in force from 3 January 1976. It commits its parties to work towards the granting of economic, social, and cultural rights (ESCR) to individuals, including labour rights and the right to health, the right to education, and the right to an adequate standard of living. As of July 2011, the Covenant had 160 parties. A further six countries had signed, but not yet ratified the Covenant. The ICESCR is part of the International Bill of Human Rights, along with the Universal Declaration of Human Rights (UDHR) and the International Covenant on Civil and Political Rights (ICCPR), including the latter's first and second Optional Protocols. The Covenant is monitored by the UN Committee on Economic, Social and Cultural Rights.

The ICESCR has its roots in the same process that led to the Universal Declaration of Human Rights. A "Declaration on the Essential Rights of Man" had been proposed at the 1945 San Francisco Conference which led to the founding of the United Nations, and the Economic and Social Council was given the task of drafting it. Early on in the process, the document was split into a declaration setting forth general principles of human rights, and a convention or covenant containing binding commitments. The former evolved into the UDHR and was adopted on 10 December 1948.

Drafting continued on the convention, but there remained significant differences between UN members on the relative importance of negative civil and political versus positive economic, social and cultural rights. These eventually caused the convention to be split into two separate covenants, "one to contain civil and political rights and the other to contain economic, social and cultural rights."

The two covenants were to contain as many similar provisions as possible, and be opened for signature simultaneously. Each would also contain an article on the right of all peoples to self-determination. The first document became the International Covenant on Civil and Political Rights, and the second the International Covenant on Economic, Social and Cultural Rights. The drafts were presented to the UN General Assembly for discussion in 1954, and adopted in 1966. The Covenant follows the structure of the UDHR and ICCPR, with a preamble and thirty-one articles, divided into five parts.

- Part 1 (Article 1) recognises the right of all peoples to self-determination, including the right to "freely determine their political status", pursue their economic, social and cultural goals, and manage and dispose of their own resources. It recognises a negative right of a people not to be deprived of its means of subsistence, and imposes an obligation on those parties still responsible for non-self governing and trust territories (colonies) to encourage and respect their self-determination.
- Part 2 (Articles 2 – 5) establishes the principle of "progressive realisation" – see below. It also requires the rights be recognised "without discrimination of any kind as to race, colour, sex, language, religion, political or other opinion, national or social origin, property, birth or other status". The rights can only be limited by law, in a manner compatible with the nature of the rights, and only for the

purpose of "promoting the general welfare in a democratic society".

- Part 3 (Articles 6 – 15) lists the rights themselves. These include rights to
  - Work, under "just and favourable conditions", with the right to form and join trade unions (Articles 6, 7, and 8);
  - Social security, including social insurance (Article 9);
  - Family life, including paid parental leave and the protection of children (Article 10);
  - An adequate standard of living, including adequate food, clothing and housing, and the "continuous improvement of living conditions" (Article 11);
  - Health, specifically "the highest attainable standard of physical and mental health" (Article 12);
  - Education, including free universal primary education, generally available secondary education and equally accessible higher education. This should be directed to "the full development of the human personality and the sense of its dignity", and enable all persons to participate effectively in society (Articles 13 and 14);
  - Participation in cultural life (Article 15).
- Part 4 (Articles 16 – 25) governs reporting and monitoring of the Covenant and the steps taken by the parties to implement it. It also allows the monitoring body – originally the United Nations Economic and Social Council – now the Committee on Economic, Social and Cultural Rights – see below – to make general recommendations to the UN General Assembly on appropriate measures to realise the rights (Article 21)
- Part 5 (Articles 26 – 31) governs ratification, entry into force, and amendment of the Covenant.

THE DECLARATION OF MEXICO ON THE EQUALITY OF WOMEN

Aware that the problems of women, who constitute half of the world's population, are the problems of society as a whole, and that changes in the present economic, political and social situation of women must become an integral part of efforts to transform the structures and attitudes that hinder the genuine satisfaction of their needs.

Recognizing that international co-operation based on the principles of the Charter of the United Nations should be developed and strengthened in order to find solutions to world problems and to build an international community based on equity and justice.

Recalling that in subscribing to the Charter, the peoples of the United Nations undertook specific commitments: "to save succeeding generations from the scourge of war..., to reaffirm faith in fundamental human rights, in the dignity and worth of the human person, in the equal rights of men and women and of nations large and small, and to promote social progress and better standards of life in larger freedom".

Taking note of the fact that since the creation of the United Nations very important instruments have been adopted, among which the following constitute landmarks: the Universal Declaration of Human Rights, the Declaration on the Granting of Independence to Colonial Countries and Peoples, the International Development Strategy for the Second United Nations Development Decade, and the Declaration and Programme of Action for the Establishment of a New International Economic Order based on the Charter of Economic Rights and Duties of States.

Taking into account that the United Nations Declaration on the Elimination of Discrimination against Women considers that: "discrimination against women is incompatible with human dignity and with the welfare of the family and of society, prevents their participation, on equal terms with men, in the political, social, economic and cultural life of their countries and is an obstacle to the full development of the potentialities of women in the service of their countries and of humanity".

Recalling that the General Assembly, in its resolution 3010 (XXVII) of 18 December 1972, proclaimed 1975 as International Women's Year and that the Year was to be devoted to intensified action with a view to: promoting equality between men and women, ensuring the integration of women in the total development effort, and increasing the contribution of women to the strengthening of world peace.

Recalling further that the Economic and Social Council, in its resolution 1849 (LVI) of 16 May 1974, adopted the Programme for International Women's Year, and that the General Assembly, in its resolution 3275 (XXIX) of 10 December 1974, called for full implementation of the Programme.

Taking into account the role played by women in the history of humanity, especially in the struggle for national liberation, the strengthening of international peace, and the elimination of imperialism, colonialism,, neo-colonialism, foreign occupation,zionism, alien domination,racism and *apartheid*,
Stressing that greater and equal participation of women at all levels of decision-making shall decisively contribute to accelerating the pace of development and the maintenance of peace.

Stressing also that women and men of all countries should have equal rights and duties and that it is the task of all States to create the necessary conditions for the attainment and the exercise thereof.

Recognizing that women of the entire world, whatever differences exist between them, share the painful experience of receiving or having received unequal treatment, and that as their awareness of this phenomenon increases they will become natural allies in the struggle against any form of oppression, such as is practised under colonialism, neo-colonialism, zionism, racial discrimination and *apartheid*, thereby constituting an enormous revolutionary potential for economic and social change in the world today.

Recognizing that changes in the social and economic structure of societies, even though they are among the prerequisites, cannot of themselves ensure an immediate improvement in the status of a group which has long been disadvantaged, and that urgent consideration must therefore be given to the full, immediate and early integration of women into national and international life.

Emphasizing that under-development imposes upon women a double burden of exploitation, which must be rapidly eliminated, and that full implementation of national development policies designed to fulfil this objective is seriously hindered by the existing inequitable system of international economic relations.

Aware that the role of women in child-bearing should not be the cause of inequality and discrimination, and that child-rearing demands shared responsibilities among women, men and society as a whole.

Recognizing also the urgency of improving the status of women and finding more effective methods and strategies which will enable them to have the same opportunities as men to participate actively in the development of their countries and to contribute to the attainment of world peace.

Convinced that women must play an important role in the promotion, achievement and maintenance of international peace, and that it is necessary to encourage their efforts towards peace, through their full participation in the national and international organizations that exist for this purpose.

Considering that it is necessary to promote national, regional and international action, in which the implementation of the World Plan of Action adopted by the World Conference of the International Women's Year should make a significant contribution, for the attainment of equality, development and peace.

Decides to promulgate the following principles:

- Equality between women and men means equality in their dignity and worth as human beings as well as equality in their rights, opportunities and responsibilities.

- All obstacles that stand in the way of enjoyment by women of equal status with men must be eliminated in order to ensure their full integration into national development and their participation in securing and in maintaining international peace.
- It is the responsibility of the State to create the necessary facilities so that women may be integrated into society while their children receive adequate care.
- National non-governmental organizations should contribute to the advancement of women by assisting women to take advantage of their opportunities, by promoting education and information about women's rights, and by co-operating with their respective Governments.
- Women and men have equal rights and responsibilities in the family and in society. Equality between women and men should be guaranteed in the family, which is the basic unit of society and where human relations are nurtured. Men should participate more actively, creatively and responsibly in family life for its sound development in order to enable women to be more intensively involved in the activities of their communities and with a view to combining effectively home and work possibilities of both partners.
- Women, like men, require opportunities for developing their intellectual potential to the maximum. National policies and programmes should therefore provide them with full and equal access to education and training at all levels, while ensuring that such programmes and policies consciously orient them towards new occupations and new roles consistent with their need for self-fulfilment and the needs of national development.
- The right of women to work, to receive equal pay for work of equal value. to be provided with equal conditions and opportunities for advancement in work, and all other women's rights to full and satisfying economic activity are strongly reaffirmed. Review of these principles for their effective implementation is now urgently needed, considering the necessity of restructuring world economic relationships. This restructuring offers greater possibilities for women to be integrated into the stream of national economic, social, political and cultural life.
- All means of communication and information as well as all cultural media should regard as a high priority their responsibility for helping to remove the attitudinal and cultural factors that still inhibit the development of women and for projecting in positive terms the value to society of the assumption by women of changing and expanding roles.

- Necessary resources should be made available in order that women may be able to participate in the political life of their countries and of the international community since their active participation in national and world affairs at decision-making and other levels in the political field is a prerequisite of women's full exercise of equal rights as well as of their further development and of the national well-being.
- Equality of rights carries with it corresponding responsibilities; it is therefore a duty of women to make full use of opportunities available to them and to perform their duties to the family, the country and humanity.
- It should he one of the principal aims of social education to teach respect for physical integrity and its rightful place in human life. The human body, whether that of woman or man, is inviolable and respect for it is a fundamental element of human dignity and freedom.
- Every couple and every individual has the right to decide freely and responsibly whether or not to have children as well as to determine their number and spacing, and to have information, education and means to do so.
- Respect for human dignity encompasses the right of every woman to decide freely for herself whether or not to contract matrimony.
- The issue of inequality, as it affects the vast majority of the women of the world, is closely linked with the problem of under-development, which exists as a result not only of unsuitable internal structures but also of a profoundly unjust world economic system.
- The full and complete development of any country requires the maximum participation of women as well as of men in all fields: the under-utilization of the potential of approximately half of the world's population is a serious obstacle to social and economic development.
- The ultimate end of development is to achieve a better quality of life for all, which means not only the development of economic and other material resources but also the physical, moral, intellectual and cultural growth of the human person.
- In order to integrate women into development, States should undertake the necessary changes in their economic and social policies because women have the right to participate and contribute to the total development effort.
- The present state of international economic relations poses serious obstacles to a more efficient utilization of all human and material potential for accelerated development and for the improvement of living standards in developing countries aimed at the elimination of

hunger, child mortality, unemployment, illiteracy, ignorance and backwardness, which concern all of humanity and women in particular. It is therefore essential to establish and implement with urgency the New International Economic Order, of which the Charter of Economic Rights and Duties of States constitutes a basic element, founded on equity, sovereign equality, inter-dependence, common interest, co-operation among all States irrespective of their social and economic systems, on the principles of peaceful coexistence and on the promotion by the entire international community of economic and social progress of all countries, especially developing countries, and on the progress of States comprising the international community.

- The principle of the full and permanent sovereignty of every State over its natural resources, wealth and all economic activities, and its inalienable right of nationalization as an expression of this sovereignty constitute fundamental prerequisites in the process of economic and social development.
- The attainment of economic and social goals, so basic to the realization of the rights of women, does not, however, of itself bring about the full integration of women in development on a basis of equality with men unless specific measures are undertaken for the elimination of all forms of discrimination against them. It is therefore important to formulate and implement models of development that will promote the participation and advancement, of women in all fields of work and provide them with equal educational opportunities and such services as would facilitate housework.
- Modernization of the agricultural sector of vast areas of the world is an indispensable element for progress, particularly as it creates opportunities for millions of rural women to participate in development. Governments, the United Nations, its specialized agencies and other competent regional and international organizations should support projects designed to utilize the maximum potential and develop the self-reliance of rural women.
- It must be emphasized that, given the required economic, social and legal conditions as well as the appropriate attitudes conducive to the full and equal participation of women in society, efforts and measures aimed at a more intensified integration of women in development can be successfully implemented only if made an integral part of overall social and economic growth. Full participation of women in the various economic, social, political and cultural sectors is an important indication of the dynamic progress of peoples and their development.

Individual human rights can be realized only within the framework of total development.

- The objectives considered in this Declaration can be achieved only in a world in which the relations between States are governed, *inter alia*, by the following principles: the sovereign equality of States, the free self-determination of peoples, the unacceptability of acquisition or attempted acquisition of territories by force and the prohibition of recognition of such acquisition, territorial integrity, and the right to defend it, and non-interference in the domestic affairs of States, in the same manner as relations between human beings should be governed by the supreme principle of the equality of rights of women and men.
- International co-operation and peace require the achievement of national liberation and independence, the elimination of colonialism and neo-colonialism, foreign occupation, zionism, *apartheid*, and racial discrimination in all its forms as well as the recognition of the dignity of peoples and their right to self-determination.
- Women have a vital role to play in the promotion of peace in all spheres of life: in the family, the community, the nation and the world. Women must participate equally with men in the decision-making processes which help to promote peace at all levels,
- Women and men together should eliminate colonialism, neo-colonialism, imperialism, foreign domination and occupation, Zionism, *apartheid*, racial discrimination, the acquisition of land by force and the recognition of such acquisition, since such practices inflict incalculable suffering on women, men and children.
- The solidarity of women in all countries of the world should be supported in their protest against violations of human rights condemned by the United Nations. All forms of repression and inhuman treatment of women, men and children, including imprisonment, torture, massacres, collective punishment, destruction of homes, forced eviction and arbitrary restriction of movement shall be considered crimes against humanity and in violation of the Universal Declaration of Human Rights and other international instruments.
- Women all over the world should unite to eliminate violations of human rights committed against women and girls such as: rape, prostitution, physical assault, mental cruelty, child marriage, forced marriage and marriage as a commercial transaction.
- Peace requires that women as well as men should reject any type of

intervention in the domestic affairs of States, whether it be openly or covertly carried on by other States or by transnational corporations. Peace also requires that women as well as men should also promote respect for the sovereign right of a State to establish its own economic, social and political system without undergoing political and economic pressures or coercion of any type.

- Women as well as men should promote real, general and complete disarmament under effective international control, starting with nuclear disarmament. Until genuine disarmament is achieved, women and men throughout the world must maintain their vigilance and do their utmost to achieve and maintain international peace.

CONSTITUTIONAL EMPOWERMENTS OF WOMEN

RIGHT TO EQUALITY

Right to equality is an important right provided for in Articles 14, 15, 16, 17 and 18 of the constitution. It is the principal foundation of all other rights and liberties, and guarantees the following:

- Equality before law: Article 14 of the constitution guarantees that all citizens shall be equally protected by the laws of the country. It means that the State cannot discriminate any of the Indian citizens on the basis of their caste, creed, colour, sex,gender, religion or place of birth.
- Social equality and equal access to public areas: Article 15 of the constitution states that no person shall be discriminated on the basis of caste, colour, language etc. Every person shall have equal access to public places like public parks, museums, wells, bathing ghats and temples etc. However, the State may make any special provision for women and children. Special provisions may be made for the advancements of any socially or educationally backward class or scheduled castes or scheduled tribes.
- Equality in matters of public employment: Article 16 of the constitution lays down that the State cannot discriminate against anyone in the matters of employment. All citizens can apply for government jobs. There are some exceptions. The Parliament may enact a law stating that certain jobs can only be filled by applicants who are domiciled in the area. This may be meant for posts that require knowledge of the locality and language of the area. The State may also reserve posts for members of backward classes, scheduled castes or scheduled tribes which are not adequately represented in the services under the State to bring up the weaker sections of the

society. Also, there a law may be passed which requires that the holder of an office of any religious institution shall also be a person professing that particular religion. According to the *Citizenship (Amendment) Bill*, 2003, this right shall not be conferred to Overseas citizens of India.

- Abolition of untouchability: Article 17 of the constitution abolishes the practice of untouchability. Practice of untouchability is an offence and anyone doing so is punishable by law. The *Untouchability Offences Act* of 1955 (renamed to *Protection of Civil Rights Act* in 1976) provided penalties for preventing a person from entering a place of worship or from taking water from a tank or well.
- Abolition of Titles: Article 18 of the constitution prohibits the State from conferring any titles. Citizens of India cannot accept titles from a foreign State. The British government had created an aristocratic class known as *Rai Bahadurs* and *Khan Bahadurs* in India — these titles were also abolished. However, Military and academic distinctions can be conferred on the citizens of India. The awards of *Bharat Ratna* and *Padma Vibhushan* cannot be used by the recipient as a title and do not, accordingly, come within the constitutional prohibition". The Supreme Court, on 15 December 1995, upheld the validity of such awards.

CONSTITUTIONAL PROVISIONS

The Constitution of India not only grants equality to women but also empowers the State to adopt measures of positive discrimination in favour of women for neutralizing the cumulative socio economic, education and political disadvantages faced by them.

Fundamental Rights, among others, ensure equality before the law and equal protection of law; prohibits discrimination against any citizen on grounds of religion, race, caste, sex or place of birth, and guarantee equality of opportunity to all citizens in matters relating to employment. Articles 14, 15, 15(3), 16, 39(a), 39(b), 39(c) and 42 of the Constitution are of specific importance in this regard.

Constitutional Privileges

- Equality before law for women (Article 14)
- The State not to discriminate against any citizen on grounds only of religion, race, caste, sex, place of birth or any of them (Article 15 (i))
- The State to make any special provision in favour of women and children (Article 15 (3))
- Equality of opportunity for all citizens in matters relating to

employment or appointment to any office under the State (Article 16)

- The State to direct its policy towards securing for men and women equally the right to an adequate means of livelihood (Article 39(a)); and equal pay for equal work for both men and women (Article 39(d))
- To promote justice, on a basis of equal opportunity and to provide free legal aid by suitable legislation or scheme or in any other way to ensure that opportuni-ties for securing justice are not denied to any citizen by reason of economic or other disabilities (Article 39 A)
- The State to make provision for securing just and humane conditions of work and for maternity relief (Article 42)
- The State to promote with special care the educational and economic interests of the weaker sections of the people and to protect them from social injustice and all forms of exploitation (Article 46)
- The State to raise the level of nutrition and the standard of living of its people (Article 47)
- To promote harmony and the spirit of common brotherhood amongst all the people of India and to renounce practices derogatory to the dignity of women (Article 51(A) (e))
- Not less than one-third (including the number of seats reserved for women belonging to the Scheduled Castes and the Scheduled Tribes) of the total number of seats to be filled by direct election in every Panchayat to be reserved for women and such seats to be allotted by rotation to different constituencies in a Panchayat (Article 243 D(3))
- Not less than one- third of the total number of offices of Chairpersons in the Panchayats at each level to be reserved for women (Article 243 D (4))
- Not less than one-third (including the number of seats reserved for women belonging to the Scheduled Castes and the Scheduled Tribes) of the total number of seats to be filled by direct election in every Municipality to be reserved for women and such seats to be allotted by rotation to different constituencies in a Municipality (Article 243 T (3))
- Reservation of offices of Chairpersons in Municipalities for the Scheduled Castes, the Scheduled Tribes and women in such manner as the legislature of a State may by law provide (Article 243 T (4))

LEGAL PROVISIONS

To uphold the Constitutional mandate, the State has enacted various legislative measures intended to ensure equal rights, to counter social discrimination and various forms of violence and atrocities and to provide support services especially to working women.

Although women may be victims of any of the crimes such as 'Murder', 'Robbery', 'Cheating' etc, the crimes, which are directed specifically against women, are characterized as 'Crime against Women'. These are broadly classified under two categories.

The Crimes Identified Under the Indian Penal Code (IPC)

- Rape (Sec. 376 IPC)
- Kidnapping and Abduction for different purposes (Sec. 363-373)
- Homicide for Dowry, Dowry Deaths or their attempts (Sec. 302/304-B IPC)
- Torture, both mental and physical (Sec. 498-A IPC)
- Molestation (Sec. 354 IPC)
- Sexual Harassment (Sec. 509 IPC)
- Importation of girls (up to 21 years of age)

The Crimes identified under the Special Laws (SLL)

Although all laws are not gender specific, the provisions of law affecting women significantly have been reviewed periodically and amendments carried out to keep pace with the emerging requirements. Some acts which have special provisions to safeguard women and their interests are:

- The Employees State Insurance Act, 1948
- The Plantation Labour Act, 1951
- The Family Courts Act, 1954 The Special Marriage Act, 1954
- The Hindu Marriage Act, 1955
- The Hindu Succession Act, 1956 with amendment in 2005
- Immoral Traffic (Prevention) Act, 1956
- The Maternity Benefit Act, 1961 (Amended in 1995)
- Dowry Prohibition Act, 1961
- The Medical Termination of Pregnancy Act, 1971
- The Contract Labour (Regulation and Abolition) Act, 1976
- The Equal Remuneration Act, 1976
- The Prohibition of Child Marriage Act, 2006
- The Criminal Law (Amendment) Act, 1983
- The Factories (Amendment) Act, 1986
- Indecent Representation of Women (Prohibition) Act, 1986

- Commission of Sati (Prevention) Act, 1987
- The Protection of Women from Domestic Violence Act, 2005

SPECIAL INITIATIVES FOR WOMEN

- National Commission for Women: In January 1992, the Government set-up this statutory body with a specific mandate to study and monitor all matters relating to the constitutional and legal safeguards provided for women, review the existing legislation to suggest amendments wherever necessary, etc.
- Reservation for Women in Local Self -Government : The 73 Constitutional Amendment Acts passed in 1992 by Parliament ensure one-third of the total seats for women in all elected offices in local bodies whether in rural areas or urban areas.
- The National Plan of Action for the Girl Child (1991-2000): The plan of Action is to ensure survival, protection and development of the girl child with the ultimate objective of building up a better future for the girl child.
- National Policy for the Empowerment of Women, 2001: The Department of Women and Child Development in the Ministry of Human Resource Development has prepared a "National Policy for the Empowerment of Women" in the year 2001. The goal of this policy is to bring about the advancement, development and empowerment of women.

2

Entrepreneurship Development of Rural Women

ADVANTAGES OF ENTREPRENEURSHIP AMONG RURAL WOMEN

Empowering women particularly rural women is a challenge. Micro enterprises in rural area can help to meet these challenges. Micro – enterprises not only enhance national productivity, generate employment but also help to develop economic independence, personal and social capabilities among rural women.

Following are some of the personal and social capabilities, which were developed as result of taking up enterprise among rural women:

- Economic empowerment
- Improved standard of living
- Self confidence
- Enhance awareness
- Sense of achievement
- Increased social interaction
- Engaged in political activities
- Increased participation level in gram sabha meeting
- Improvement in leadership qualities
- Involvement in solving problems related to women and community
- Decision making capacity in family and community

Economic empowerment of women by micro entrep-reneurship led to the empowerment of women in many things such as socio-economic opportunity, property rights, political representation, social equality, personal right, family development, market development, community development and at last the nation development.

ENTREPRENEURSHIP DEVELOPMENT OF RURAL WOMEN THROUGH SELF HELP GROUPS

Women comprise half of human resources they have been identified as key agents of sustainable development and women's equality is as central to a more hoslistic approach towards estabilizing new patterns and process of development that are sustainable.. The contribution of women and their role in the family as well as in the economic development and social transformation are pivotal.

Women constitute 90 per cent of total marginal workers of the country. Rural women who are engaged in agriculture form 78 per cent of all women in regular work. Experience of NIRD action research projects reveal that, the operational aspects, such as the extent of enabling that goes into the community self help processes and sharpening the mind set of women.

Men and the project administrators are low or critical components that determine their extent to which empowerment may or may not take place. The role of micro-credit is to, improve the socio and economic development of women and improve the status of women in households and communities. The micro entrepreneurships are strengthening the women empowerment and remove the gender inequalities.

Self Help Group's micro credit mechanism makes the members to involve in other community development activities. Micro credit is promoting the small scale business enterprises and its major aim is to alleviate poverty by income generating activities among women and poor. Therefore, they could achieve self-sufficiency.

Now-a-days economic development is one of the factors that have changed the entire scenario of social and cultural environment within the country especially for the women. The rural women are engaged in small-scale entrepreneurship programme with the help of Self Help Groups. Through that they were economically empowered and attaining status in family and community. Rural women play a vital role in farm and home system. She contributes substantially in the physical aspect of farming, livestock management, post harvest and allied activities. Her direct and indirect contribution at the farm and home level along with livestock management operation has not only help to save their assets but also led to increase the family income. She performs various farm, livestock, post harvest and allied activities and possesses skills and indigenous knowledge in these areas.

The women were empowering themselves technically to cope with the changing times and productively using their free time and existing skills for setting and sustaining enterprises. They were engaged in starting individual or collective income generation programme with the help of self-help group.

This will not only generate income for them but also improve the decision-making capabilities that led to overall empowerment.

AREAS OF MICRO-ENTERPRISE DEVELOPMENT

Depending on number of factors ranging from landholdings, subsidiary occupations, agro climatic conditions and socio-personal characteristics of the rural women and her family member the areas of micro-enterprises also differ from place to place.

The micro enterprises are classified under three major heads:

- Micro Enterprise development related to agriculture and allied agricultural activities like cultivating to organic vegetables, flowers, oil seeds and seed production are some of the areas besides taking up mushroom growing and bee – keeping. Some more areas can be like dehydration of fruits and vegetables, canning or bottling of pickles, chutneys, jams, squashes, dairy and other products that are ready to eat.
- Micro-Enterprise development related to livestock management activities like diary farming, poultry farm, livestock feed production and production of vermi composting using the animal waste can be an important area in which women can utilise both her technical skills and raw materials from the farm and livestock to earn substantial income and small scale agro-processing units.
- Micro – Enterprise development related to household based operations like knitting, stitching, weaving, embroidery, bakery and flour milling, petty shops, food preparation and preservation.

PROMOTION OF RURAL LIVELIHOOD THROUGH WOMEN SELF HELP GROUPS

Most of the women Self Help Groups promoted under different development and microcredit programmes are involved in savings through periodic collection from the members, recycling of this money among the members as micro-credit for consumptive and productive purposes and training of women members for initiating various micro-enterprises.

Many Self Help Groups have progressed further to deal with various social issues such as education for girls, prevention of child marriages, struggle against liquor sale, promotion of community health, sanitation, establishment of community grain banks and protest against violence. Promotion of micro-enterprises and various income generation activities is an important aspect of women empowerment. Although it is extremely difficult to find remunerative selfemployment, there are enormous untapped opportunities in the rural sector. These include both on-farm and off-farm opportunities.

Advantages of Agro-Based Activities: While promoting various income generation activities, agro-based activities have advantages because of the following reasons:

- Target groups are acquainted with most of the basic skills.
- Easy access to inputs.
- No problems of marketing, as most of the outputs are locally consumed as food. Market outlets for even cash crops have been well established.
- As over 75-85% of the rural families own land and livestock, income generation activities can be initiated immediately without heavy capital investment.
- Risk of failure due to improper technology, poor quality, low demand and poor price recovery are very low. Hence, the chances of success are high.
- Infrastructure required for promotion of on-farm activities has been very well established. Hence, the entrepreneurs can progress even in backward regions, which are deprived of regular power supply and electronic information connectivity.

It is therefore advantageous to tap all the opportunities to promote various on-farm activities. The experience of BAIF has confirmed that the best strategy to promote income generation activities through SHGs is to analyse the on-going agro-based activities undertaken by the members and introduce suitable interventions to enhance the production. There are also excellent opportunities to improve post production management of the produce through grading, storage, processing and marketing. Establishment of direct linkage with the consumers through establishment of consumer stores and farmers. open markets in small and large towns will not only reduce the cost of marketing but also help in receiving feedback from the customers.

Such direct interaction with the customers will help the farmers to improve the quality and variety of produce and enhance the profitability. Most of the agricultural products have stable prices and steady demand. Hence, the risk of price fluctuation and market glut is limited. As these products have good local demand, marketing cost is low. Most of the surplus can be stored to ensure food security in the future. In case of non-farm activities, most of the skills and inputs will have to be brought from outside. There is very limited scope for marketing these products locally. As some of the activities are new to the local women, the cost of starting the enterprise is very high. As a result, chances of success and sustainable growth of these enterprises are also very high.

The non-farm enterprises are often affected due to glut in the market, fall in prices due to competition and poor market distribution and outlet network.

The enterpreneurs are not able to sustain such shocks and end up in deep financial crisis, which threaten their food security as well. It is therefore suggested that agro-based activities be promoted, followed by different non-farm activities, which will have greater chances of success and risk bearing ability. While the on-farm activities address food security, supplementary non-farm activities can contribute to rural prosperity.

OPPORTUNITIES FOR RURAL MICRO-ENTERPRISES THROUGH WOMEN SHGS

With careful planning, many opportunities can be created to generate gainful employment for the rural families, particularly for women.

Some of the important enterprises are listed below:

On-farm activities:

- Crop production
- Forestry, Sericulture
- Agro Service Centres
- Processing of food and forest products
- Production of Agricultural inputs
  - Bio-fertilizers
  - Bio-pesticides
  - Vermicompost
  - Mushroom spawn production
  - Seeds and Plants
  - Cattle feed

Off-farm activities:

- Cottage Industries
  - Pottery, Smithy, Carpentry
  - Textile
  - Production of building materials
- Services
  - Automobile hire and repairs
  - Electrical works
  - Civil construction
  - Consumer stores

BAIF has promoted various micro-enterprises through Self Help Groups in different parts of the country. Among these activities, trade is the most popular activity followed by agriculture, animal husbandry and food processing.

However, over a period of time, agriculture, animal husbandry and food processing supercede the trade as many individuals participate in enhancing their production at the family level and try to organise themselves to market them collectively. Other activities such as production of utility items, construction related activities, textile, handicrafts and pottery find it difficult to sustain due to poor marketing infrastructure, lack of proper feedback from the customers and competition from other sources.

SUPPORT NEEDED FOR PROMOTION MICRO-ENTERPRISES

Following support is needed to promote micro-enterprises through women SHGsL:

- Motivation of the target communities, particularly women
- Formation of Self Help Groups and their Federations
- Introduction of drudgery reduction activities
- Gender sensitization
- Training and capacity building
- Micro-finance. provision of credit facilities and linkage with banks
- Development of infrastructure, particularly through the SHG Federations to provide necessary support services and marketing
- Trade networking and establishment of market outlets
- Village level Information Centre/e-Chaupal for dissemination of useful information

A multi-disciplinary team can interact with the SHGs to explore the potentials for development of various enterprises and extend necessary support for dissemination of technologies, procurement of inputs, training of members and establishment of linkage with the market. There should be some agency to provide guidance to the entrepreneurs as and when needed.

AREAS FOR MICRO-ENTERPRISE DEVELOPMENT

Variations in role performance and direct and indirect contribution varied within the state depending on number of factors ranging from landholdings, subsidiary occupations, agroclimatic conditions, and socio-personal characteristics of the rural women and her family members. Based upon the results of the case studies the following areas for micro-enterprises development are suggested:

Micro-enterprise Development Related to Agriculture and Allied Agricultural Activities

Women have been performing agricultural operations and have been very actively participating in seed selection, seed treatment and vegetable growing.

They can be trained and motivated to adopt micro-enterprises in which her skill and patience can be exploited. Ali (1997) in his document on post harvest processing of agricultural produce stated that value addition includes processes like sorting, grading, cutting, seeding, shelling and quality packaging etc. Growing of organic vegetables, flowers, oilseeds and seed production are some of the areas beside taking up mushroom growing and bee-keeping. Some more areas can be like dehydration of fruits and vegetables, canning or bottling of pickles, chutneys, jams, squashes, dairy and other products which are ready to eat.

Micro-Enterprise Development Related to Livestock Management Activities

The major share of work is being handled by women in performance of livestock management operations. Hence this area needs to be exploited for microenterprise development. Empowerment of women through formation of self help groups and all women dairy and poultry cooperatives can help women to control the decision making and the financial aspects of livestock management.

Livestock feed production and production of vermi-compost using the animal waste can be an important area in which women can utilise both her technical skills and raw material from the farm and livestock to earn substantial income. Value addition to livestock based raw material and establishment of small scale agro-processing units can benefit the women.

Micro-enterprise Development Related to Household Based Operations

Women perform many household tasks besides looking after the needs of the family. This involves taking care of the children, cooking cleaning the house etc. but at the same time she is equipped with skills such as knitting, stitching, weaving, embroidery etc.

Bakery and flour milling are some more examples of the enterprises that can be taken up by women in this area of her activity.

EXTENSION STRATEGIES TO PROMOTE ENTREPRENEURSHIP

Creating Awareness

Awakening of rural women to the possibilities of the easily accessible micro-enterprises is the foremost task. The government, semi- government and nongovernment organizations should create awareness among the most productive age group of rural women. The printed media can be effectively put to use for the purpose.

Motivating Entrepreneurs

Psychological stimulation is the prerequisite for putting any idea virtually into action. For proper motivation of rural women, the economic, social and health benefits of various possible enterprises should be highlighted. The use of farm visits, video film shows, dramas, puppet shows, group meeting etc. will help in motivating the potential group.

Expertise Development

After awakening and motivating the next step in development and success of an enterprise is the acquisition of knowledge and skill up-gradation and polishing of existing knowledge and skills in production, processing, packaging and marketing techniques are the basic requirements.. Saha (1999) also emphasized the need of value addition as it ensures high premium to the producer.

He stated that India ranks second in food production but only two per cent of the produce is processed.In addition to this, knowledge regarding accessibility to loans, various funding agencies, procedures regarding certification etc, should be provided.

Lectures, printed material, discussions, institutional and non institutional skill trainings for imparting first hand technical knowledge in production, processing, procurement and management should be provided to rural women who are interested or already engaged in various enterprises. Education in direct and indirect marketing of the produce and finance management should be in-built component of future training programmes for women.

Continuous Follow-up

Constant follow-up should be ensured for the sustainability of a e micro-enterprises. During this phase various constraints such as personal, social, economic, marketing etc. faced by entrepreneurs should be addressed. Possible help in the form of knowledge, technical skills and inputs should be provided to enable them to solve their problems.

Table. Personal and Environmental Prerequisites for Entrepreneurial Development

Personal Prerequisites	Environmental prerequisites
Powerful urge	Availability of infrastructural facilities
Strong determination	Venture capital availability
Hard work	Technically skilled labour
Risk bearing capacity	Accessibility of suppliers.
Emotional maturity	Proximity of supporting organization/institution
Knowledge:	Attitude of the area population
• Technical	
• Legal	
• Marketing	
Administrative skills	

Far sightedness.
Innovativeness
Ability to use available resources
Previous experience/entre-preneurial parents
Education

RURAL WOMEN IN AGRICULTURAL COOPERATIVES

Women are represented in various forms and in various types of cooperatives in the Region. In most of the South-Asian countries women membership in mixed membership cooperatives is generally lower as compared with those from other countries in the Region. In societies where culture restricts women's membership in cooperatives, women-only cooperatives proliferate.

It is in women-only cooperatives that women feel freer and less restricted in their participation in cooperatives. In countries like India, Nepal, Bangladesh, Sri Lanka and Pakistan, women comprise just 7.5% as compared with men (92.5%) of the total membership. In Malaysia it is around 30.6%. In many of the Asian countries women's membership is low [ranging from 2 to 10.5%] in agricultural cooperatives. This reflects the age-old stereotype that men are the farmers and not the women, and the title of the farm property should be in the name of the man. This situation automatically prohibits women to be the members. Out of a total of 450,000 cooperatives with a total membership of 204.5 million in India, there were 8,171 women-only cooperatives with a total membership of 693,000.

It is also known that the women-only cooperatives *e.g.*, cooperative banks, consumer stores, fruits and vegetable vendors, have done exceedingly well and provided a whole range of services to their members. In India, with a view to involve women in the process of decision-making in local selfgovernment bodies including cooperatives, a 33% representation has been instituted and in a number of states all boards of directors have women serving on them. There has also been a discussion to have a similar representation in state and national legislatures as well.

The highest number of women in cooperatives in the Region comes from the credit and consumer sectors. In Japan the membership of women in agricultural cooperatives and in decision-making organs is low. No discriminatory provisions preventing women's participation in agricultural cooperatives are contained in the Agricultural Cooperative Law nor in the bylaws of the agricultural cooperatives.

In the majority of the bylaws, membership is based either on land ownership or work on the farm for more than 90 days a year. Despite this, women membership has not increased mainly due to the fact that most cooperatives have a membership policy that allows only one member per household, based on the idea that a household is the minimum unit for production.

In addition, it is customary that women follow their husbands in the village life and decision-making. Women themselves do not want to cause troubles by challenging such a tradition. Therefore, men became the majority of directors and delegates and women quietly accepted the situation. However, the concept of plural membership from households is being encouraged. There are still some prevailing laws which place barriers for women's participation in agricultural cooperatives and/or farmers' associations, like land ownership and head of the household. In many societies the very women who need to organise to cooperate and prosper, lack the time for participation due to multiple work demands. Cooperatives being people-centered movement had recognised these limitations place on women by the society and economic institutions.

Experiments made in different parts of the world clearly indicate that women's participation in cooperatives and other local government bodies not only provides them an opportunity to articulate their problems but it also helps them to be an active partner in decisionmaking process.

The relationship between women and their cooperatives in the context of gender integeration can be summarised as under:

- A cooperative being a social development agency should play an active role in advocating for gender equality;
- Since women have been active in development work, they should play central role in development;
- The cooperative can be a venue to improve women's social status and economic conditions; and
- Thus, cooperatives should promote women's empowerment by integrating gender concerns and formulating a strategy that would address gender issues.

In terms of the ratio of membership of women in agricultural cooperatives, the percentage is rather low, but they have a strong influence on them - through the heads of the household. Certain obvious barriers restrict their direct and formal entry in agricultural cooperatives. Agricultural cooperatives, in present times, everywhere have come under dark clouds due to heavy competitions and pressures of open market economy systems.

They are now expected to meet the challenges which they had never anticipated before. Their business methods remain traditional and they expect government support in the form of protection and subsidies. These are no longer available and will not be available in the near future. In several countries, agricultural cooperatives have either folded up or are under massive reorganisation.

The challenges faced by agricultural cooperatives can be enumerated as under:

- Assured supply of farm inputs [quality seeds, chemical fertilizer, farm chemicals, credit and extension services];
- Be aware of quality controls and standardisation of farm products to be able to compete effectively in the open market;
- Establishment of a marketing intelligence system within the Cooperative Movement to enable the farmer-producers follow market trends and plan their production and marketing strategies;
- Establishment of business federations through cooperative clusters to undertake primary agro-processing marketing of local products and to cover financial requirements;
- Need for providing information to the farmers and farmers' organisations on the implications of restructuring, globalisation and WTO agreements.
- Need to improve professional management skills of those who provide advisory or guidance services to cooperatives and of the managers and some key members of primary level cooperatives;
- Participate in efforts to conserve natural resources which directly and indirectly, influence farm production and rural employment;

CONSTRAINTS FACED BY RURAL FARM WOMEN

Based on the experiences of farm extension workers, field advisors and rural farm women in the Asia-Pacific Region, the following are the general constraints faced by them:

- Absence of property inheritance rights, restriction on acquiring membership of agricultural cooperatives consequently being deprived of farm credit etc.;
- High illiteracy rates and poor living conditions among rural women;
- Inadequate access to credit and agricultural inputs and other services;
- Inadequate health care services in rural areas;
- Inadequate water supply for household and farm operations;
- Lack of appropriate agricultural technology aimed at reducing the physical burden of farm women;
- Lack of female farm extension workers;
- Lack of leadership and inadequate participation in the organisational and economic affairs of their agricultural cooperatives;
- Lack of marketing facilities and opportunities;
- Lack of opportunities to improve socio-economic status of farm women;

- Lack of secretariat supporting functions for women's organisations and allocation of funds for them in cooperative organisations.
- Lack of skills and attitudes in leadership and management development; and
- Less participation in decision-making - even within the household;
- Male migration/urban drift which increases pressure on women;
- Traditional, religious, social and cultural obstacles;

FACILITATION ROLE OF THE ICA AND ITS DEVELOPMENT PARTNERS

Since the establishment of the ICA Regional Office in New Delhi in 1960, efforts have consistently been made to initiate and promote programmes aimed at emancipation of women and their involvement in the organisational and business activities of cooperatives.

This has been done through a long chain of seminars, discussions, conferences and technical assistance programmes which have been carried out with the collaboration of its Member-Organisations and development partners.

In the agricultural cooperatives sector some of the most recent initiatives have been as follows:

- A series of specialised training courses for rural women leaders in agricultural cooperatives, on an yearly basis, with the financial support of the Government of Japan and in collaboration with the JA-Zenchu and the IDACA;
- A series of technical meetings and conferences were held which had taken note of the recommendations of UN and other international conferences and initiatives on women in cooperative development;
- Development of training manuals and other supporting materials for the use of women leaders to develop women's associations and help increase women's participation in agricultural cooperatives.
- Three top level Asian and African Conferences on Farm Women Leaders in Agriculture and Agricultural Cooperatives during 1997 and 1998 [one more conference is planned in 1999] in collaboration with the JA-Zenchu, AARRO and the IDACA and with the full technical support of the Government of Japan in the Ministry of Agriculture, Forestry and Fisheries-MAFF;

ISSUES INVOLVED

In the background of the discussion and in view of the constraints faced by women with regard to their participation in agricultural cooperatives, the following issues need to be tackled by the concerned authorities and cooperative institutions:

- Accord due credibility to the achievements of women in agricultural cooperative development through publicity, exchange of visits, participation in meetings and conferences. Women need a platform through which they could justify their participation in cooperative action;
- Cooperatives to initiate education, training and extension programmes for women through vocational and literacy programmes [these also include home improvement activities *e.g.*, cooking classes, handcrafts, social interactions, environment related activities etc.];
- Creating conditions for women to market their products through outlets established by agricultural cooperatives. [Agricultural cooperatives in Japan set apart a space in their shopping areas exclusively for the Women's Associations and even for the individual farmers to sell their products, including organising Morning Markets etc.].
- Development of Plans of Action at all levels. Women's cooperative organisations at primary levels should try to federate themselves into higher federations or association so that their 'bargaining power' is strengthened. The cooperatives and women's associations should develop realistic plans of action to be followed for three-five years;
- Encouraging cooperatives to have special programmes and tasks for women to perform in the organisational and business affairs. It has been observed that in many of the countries of the Region more women are being taken in to undertake administrative and functional activities - they make very good, reliable and honest cashiers, sales girls, inventory controllers, secretaries, public relations officers and member contact persons;
- Identification of an appropriate mechanism which could provide development opportunities to women in rural areas;
- Replication of successful experiences. The work done by the Women's Associations of Japanese agricultural cooperatives and Han Groups has produced good results for the community and business of their cooperatives. Such experiences need a thorough study. They have a lot of good things to offer;
- Review, revision and reformation of cooperative legislation and government policies which facilitate and encourage women to become members of cooperatives and participate in decision-making processes. Cooperative institutions and their federations may take

the lead on their own to institute programmes for the participation of women in cooperatives. Voluntary initiatives by cooperatives themselves do not necessarily to be qualified by government approvals. Cooperatives should lobby with their governments to replace or suitably amend the restrictive laws;

EMPOWERMENT, ENTREPRENEURSHIP, AND EDUCATION

Clearly, the student learned much about community organization in social work practice. The purpose of this analysis is to relay the voices, actions, and messages of people living in northern rural villages in India per the observations and records of the student social worker. The majority of the people that talked to the student social worker were women. For example, the women told the student social worker about living with social and economic inequality. They discussed limited access to resources such as income and education. They said that resources were especially limited for women living in rural areas. Strengths of rural areas include informal community resources and leaders. In an often patriarchal and impoverished rural India, the student observed that informal community leaders included rural women who pooled their assets to improve village well being. These community organization efforts appeared to be directed towards empowerment, entrepreneurship, and education, particularly for women and youth. Empowerment, entrepreneurship, and education comprise the"three E's" of social change efforts of the rural Indian women described herein.

BACKGROUND LITERATURE

A global economy impacts people across the world within a"complex web of economic relationships" as people's lives are"linked to the lives of distant others through the clothes they wear, the energy that warms them, and even the food that they eat". As international corporations relocate to poorer nations to access cheaper sources of labour and less environmental constraints, people from developed countries can purchase less costly goods and services. People from underdeveloped countries are more likely to find jobs and their national economies demonstrate unprecedented rates of growth. At the same time, rapid development brings environmental damage and social justice challenges as human rights are often compromised with inhumane work environments, child labour, low wages, human trafficking, and inequitable distribution of wealth.

India's rapid growth of business-generated capital is hailed as an"economic miracle [that] bypasses" Indian people living in rural areas. Chatterjee says that India's economy is"surging", with large industry"growing at a frenetic pace" while most rural people are"desperately poor and vulnerable". The most recent national census taken by the government of India in 2001 indicates that the rural to urban population is 72.4% to 27.6%. The United Nations International Children's Fund, 35% of India's population lives on one dollar or less per day. Rural Indian people have inadequate access to health services, sanitation, nutrition, and safe drinking water.

For example, five per cent of children in a poor rural area of Bihar are immunized versus 90% of children in 42 wealthy urban districts. Singh reports that 250 million people in India are poor and 23 million people are unemployed. Poverty in India is further complicated by discrimination towards people with lower social class, lower status caste membership, tribal membership, disabilities, and gender. For example, O'Neil *et al.* found that women from lower caste/class and some tribal affiliations are more likely to be designated from early childhood to enter"traditional sex work." Sex trade workers increasingly come from"poor low-caste rural families...[that are] pressured to dedicate their daughters".

Indian women live with just laws but unjust application of the laws. India has long held cultural roots that used to include customs such as child marriage, burning the widow on the funeral pyre of her husband, female infanticide, marriage dowries, dowry murders, prohibited remarriage for widows, shunning of widows, rape, and female travel restrictions. Although outlawed, some of these customs appear to continue, *i.e.*, infanticide, aborting female fetuses, marriage dowries, dowry murders, rape, and sex trafficking. For example, 5,000 to 7,000 Indian women per year reportedly die in"bride burning" dowry deaths. Srinvasan and Bedi report that"dowry torture" and"daughter aversion" increase as the dowry tradition of the upper caste/ class becomes an"all caste/class phenomenon"; recent changes also include escalating rates of dowry payments.

Unlike the United States, the Constitution of India guarantees equality to Indian women including forbidding gender discrimination and requiring equal pay for equal work. Despite this law, women experience little access to social and economic resources. Most Indian women do not own property; they are frequently excluded from inheritance of property. Households headed by women comprise 35% of those below the Indian government poverty line. Violent crimes towards women are frequent, such as sexual harassment, rape, molestation, physical violence, emotional abuse, and even human trafficking. Pay for women is lower than for men and the jobs they obtain are often less desirable.

Women in rural areas of India experience serious risk factors that can impact their very survival and the survival of their family members, particularly young children. Aurora and Srinivasan report that women in rural India are on the"lowest rung of the socioeconomic ladder" with little capacity to take part in the economic opportunities afforded to others. Rural women are more likely to be impacted by traditional social customs. In rural India, 60% of young women are married before the age of 18. Rates of HIV are epidemic for women in rural areas of India. Maternal mortality is particularly high in rural areas where the majority of births are not supervised by a health care professional. In fact, there are far more men living in India than women. This is a reversal of birth trends worldwide, leading Menon-Sen and Kumar to call for an inquiry into"20-25 million missing women in India. Some are never born [female fetus abortions] and the rest die because they do not have the opportunity to survive".

While women in rural areas make up over half of the low paid agricultural labour and forestry, a broader workforce perspective reveals that rural areas overall are less likely to have people employed in high paying jobs and there are far less women in the paid workforce than men. Specifically, women are three times more likely than urban women to be employed in"informal workforces" found in agriculture, forestry, and fishing. The hours of work for women can be extreme. FOA reports,"in the Indian Himalayas, a pair of bullocks works 1064 hours, a man 1212 hours and a woman 3485 hours in a year on a one-hectare farm". Gender inequality also persists in the rural fishing industry where,"Men cast nets while women and children catch fish with hands".

Throughout India and particularly in rural areas, women are far less likely to be able to read and write. For example, 34% of women in the rural area of Bihar are able to read and write compared to 95% in the more wealthy area of Mizoram. UNDP reports that 62% of Indian women are illiterate compared to 34% of Indian men. FOA says,"Female literacy is substantially lower in rural areas than in urban areas". Park described widespread dissatisfaction of rural women with the top down management style of upper caste male teachers towards mostly lower caste and some tribal village residents. The women were more optimistic about the chances that their children would be able to read and write than for themselves. More than 50% of girls drop out of school by the time they are in middle school. They are often caring for children and siblings, helping with family work, and/or working in paid employment.

Strategies for improving female education rates include having toilets, free midday meals, free books and uniforms, childcare, more female teachers, and village computer training centers for distance learning. One strategy for improving the income of rural Indian women and their families is called micro financing. A number of Indian nongovernmental organizations are helping rural Indian village women to pool their assets in order to finance new businesses for members of their collective or self-help group. Singh explains that micro-finance, also called micro-credit, offers"a low rate of interest, easy and periodic repayments with a moratorium period, credit for income generating activities, easy process of disbursement, no collateral or security, and less paperwork."

American social work education and practice are beginning to address needs of international groups such as people living in underdeveloped areas of the world. Practice interventions include focusing on communities, understanding connections among people, using generalist practice skills, advocating for just programme and policy development, and respecting diversity.

METHODS

Data were drawn from a social work student's international placement in an organization in northern rural India. The social work student was a junior at a large public university in the Midwest. She volunteered within the university international office. The placement was coordinated through a collaborative agreement between the university and a grassroots Indian non-governmental organization. In this analysis, the Indian organization responsible for the student placement shall be called"the NGO" or"the organization" so as guard anonymity. The student spent 13 weeks in India. For six of these weeks, she lived in a village located in the north Himalayas as an intern for the NGO.

The organization had a mission to"explore, support, and provide opportunities a better quality of life to socially deprived and economically marginalized mountain people, especially regional women.". The organization trained and disseminated community organizers to help rural residents work to improve the social and economic conditions of their communities and families. Some of the organization's grassroots projects included a medicinal plant nursery, watershed development, a traditional health clinic, and a resource room for educators. The student worked separately with women's self-help groups and the education systems of villages in northern rural India. Self-help group participants and key stakeholder interviewees were part of two convenience samples of evaluation participants.

Self-help groups for rural women Upon arriving in India, the student and two colleagues met with the president of the NGO, a non-governmental grass roots community organization. He discussed community needs, internship parameters, and organizational programmes and approaches. Internship parameters excluded asking participants and interviewees about the Indian caste system. It was not culturally acceptable to discuss the caste system with non-Indian visitors. The student and one colleague were assigned to evaluate women's self-help groups through attending SHG meetings, interviewing organizational leaders, women SHG members, and village members on the impacts of self-help groups on their lives, families, and communities. For a total of six consecutive weeks, the student visited one to four self-help group meetings per day.

The organization leaders served as"guides" for the student and her colleagues to enter self-help group meetings. For example, they introduced the student to the self-help group participants and translated Hindi into English.

The self-help groups included intergenerational village women that met regularly to advocate, plan, and support each other socially and economically. Group members pooled their skills, time, and financial resources to assist members with financing social events, such as family weddings, and new business ventures intended to increase family income. A typical meeting began with the student's arrival.

Chai tea and biscuits were served to guests while waiting for members to arrive. In rural India, in accordance with their social and religious practices, guests are afforded utmost respect. The leader introduced the student as a visitor from the USA who wanted to learn about the women and their feelings of empowerment through self-help groups to assist the NGO in evaluating the groups. Then the student shared a few words in Hindi. Group leaders collected monthly savings from each member, recorded numbers, and began the group's song and dance. One, two, or a group of women responded; their responses were recorded in the student's field notes. The women were voluntary informants. They could choose not to answer any or all questions, particularly those that they appeared not to understand and those that contained content they did not wish to share. Interviews flowed as offered by participants, although a series of questions helped to guide the discussion.

These discussion questions centered on the women's lives, self-help group experiences, challenges, goals, and skills:

- How many members are in your self-help group?
- How often do you meet?
- What is your self-help group purpose?
- How much do save per month?
- What type of loans have your members taken out?
- What was your situation prior to the self-help group formation?
- What problems do you have?
- What goals do you have?
- What is different in your life now that you meet as a self-help group?
- Are men supportive?
- What is a normal day like for you?
- What is a normal day like for each of your family members?
- How do you make income?
- What income generating skills have you learned?
- Do you have any ideas to improve your life?

Depending on the guide's level of English, the guide clarified the question with the student or simply said"language problem" and continued to the next question. Most frequently, the student addressed the women with the question in English and waited for the guide to interpret the question for the women in Hindi. The social work student recorded the content and process of the discussions with the women as field notes within a project journal. For example, the student wrote field notes about the rituals, savings, number of group members, and the appearances and affect expressions of the groups. To the extent possible, the student captured the words of the women. Some examples of field note content illustrate the journaling process. The student noticed that some groups did not mention their husbands, or the way the women were being treated within the family. When asked,"What is a normal day like for each of your family members?" women sometimes inferred that their husbands were not around or talked about their children solely. Another field note record showed what appeared to be increased women's empowerment when the women responded to,"Are men supportive?" with"men have changed and become supportive and have even come to women to ask for loans."

RURAL EDUCATION

The organization president asked the student to go to area schools to assess community residents' perspectives of"what's lacking" in village education systems. In addition to assessing the"missing links," the student's assignment was to"design a model for the future institution of education in rural India" and"provide a module of a new idea" for teachers to change routine. One teacher defined"quality education" as accessible to low income families with"good" teachers who are dedicated to their work." Another asked for improved facilities,"The physical environment confines creativity." A woman from one self-help group said:

- We are illiterate, but we want our daughters and sons to have equal education. We want our daughters to have good character, intelligence, so we can send her any place, like you. You came here because you have education.

The social work student also visited primary schools in two rural districts within the northern Himalayas region of India. She observed curriculum content delivery, school procedures, and overall primary school learning environments. She talked to teachers, administrators, and parents about rural education in India. Many of these key informants were women parents. She asked these key informants about youth access to education, quality of education, and what they would like for the future of their educational systems. She asked key informants about access to education for girls and young women. The methodology for data collection was similar to that used for the women's self-help groups. Initial questions were also drawn from the practice literature, programme orientation sessions, and the social work student's observations. They included open-ended questions with flexible probes. Questioning followed the process and content of information offered by the key informants. Early interview data helped generate discussion questions for subsequent interviewees. Field notes were regularly recorded. They included many direct quotations of key informants and observational data.

ANALYSES

The social work student analysed field notes for topics offered most frequently by the key informants. The student engaged in iterative combing of the data with identification of themes offered by key informants that ranged from broad to specific. Thus data were sorted and assembled using an open, axial, and categorical method consistent with grounded theory analysis. Field note data were triangulated with student observations and literature. Main themes, with supportive data to illustrate each theme, were described within a summary course paper and three presentations to community organizers in India, university study abroad faculty, and American social work students, social work professors, and participants of the 2007 annual conference of the National Rural Social Work Caucus. The outcome themes and supporting data were reviewed by, and discussed at length with, a university social work professor. The data and findings of this study were literally built from the ground up.

OUTCOMES

Three main themes emerged from analysis of the key informant discussions and observational data. Two themes were drawn from the self-help group women. First, the women reported that self-help groups were a beginning step in the empowerment of women within a largely patriarchal society. Second, the women said that self-help group's micro-finance activities increased opportunities for women's entrepr-eneurship that generated income for the women and their families. A third theme was drawn from data about the rural education system reported by the women in the self-help groups, combined with data drawn from the student's school observations, and as reported by educational key informants, *i.e.*, teachers, school administrators, and parents of school age children. Most parents were mothers of the children. Key informants said there was a strong need for increased access to quality education within rural Indian communities, particularly for girls and young women.

EMPOWERMENT OF WOMEN

The development of mutual aid within self-help groups of rural women appeared to be part of a strengthening social action movement among women in rural India. Although the groups were originally encouraged by the grassroots nongovernmental organization, the data suggested that the women made largely autonomous local decisions about what events and enterprises they would support and to what extent. It appeared that the self-help groups were having a significant impact on the empowerment of women in rural areas per the following field note:

- Women repeatedly speak positively about their self-organization, support, and community. During marriage ceremonies, women joined in to help ease the workload. In village K., women expressed that they feel they can talk easily now, have something fun to do, and come out of their houses...Women also said they felt more"in control" after formation of the self-help group. They said they felt"very good" and"important."

Self-help groups provided opportunities for women to serve as models of leadership for the children that were often present in the background during group meetings. Girls and young women watched their mothers, aunts, and grandmothers serve as decision makers and persons that were listened to by others. Several poignant field notes recorded the enthusiasm of the women self-help group participants: Many of the women appeared eager to attend the groups even if they have to walk for hours to get there." [Within the groups], the women"were willing to try new things." The student recorded,"Every woman I talked to had positive feelings towards [the self-help group]" and,"They seem to have a sense of pride and ownership in their group organization."

It appeared that the self-help groups might take on some of the functions of supportive extended family kinship networks. For example, they provided a mechanism for group cohesion expressed through ritual:

- *Song and dance played an integral role in self-help groups*: They [taught] some songs, which appeared to be an effective method to communicate social messages and build cohesion within the group. At first, I was embarrassed and annoyed that the women insisted on me dancing for them. After weeks of Indian dancing in the center of the self-help group meetings, I started to enjoy the event. It made me feel part of the village and as one woman told me once, I felt"same, same."

Through the cultural communication of dance, the student was invited into Indian culture. The women's invitation impacted both the women and student. Women experienced a genuine interest from a person outside the self-help group, fostering an opportunity to share their story and to become part of the student's life and reality. The student learned how to be part of another culture, meeting people"where they are," as she shared a few moments of the rural women's lives. The nontraditional learning experience inspired the student to seek additional learning about Indian culture.

The groups appeared to provide a close bond for expression of feelings, including worry and frustration:

- During self-help group meetings, women expressed problems that

> affect their livelihood. Initially, women responded with"no problems" to every question I asked. After further probing, the first and foremost issue ...women expressed that there was no rain. [The women explained that] drought leads to shortage of drinking water, lower crop yields, and lower income. In S. village, wild animals were eating crops and lowering the production.

The self-help group participants said that migration of youth to the cities also affected agricultural production and cultural integrity:

- When families migrate to larger cities, the land is left barren and also looses percolation qualities. Not only could families in need of extra income use the land but it also affects the quality of the land around it, when it lies barren. Also, as families move to find better jobs, village traditions disperse and culture fades away.

In addition to rural youth drain, family distance, and cultural dissolution afforded by migration to urban areas, the rural women discussed gender role concerns and family issues. They complained of"hard labour from dawn to dusk and men do not recognize their labour as a source of income." The women said that,"Girls are required to drop education to learn domestic labour." Within the kinship-type networks of the self-help groups, the women shared information that is seldom discussed outside families:

- Alcoholism in men is overlooked in the villages, but families are affected especially when the ramifications include domestic violence. As a result [of domestic violence many] women do not appear to have a voice in the home or community.

Clearly the empowerment of women has far to go within rural northern Indian communities. However, the self-help group appears to be one way to begin.

RURAL WOMEN EMPOWERMENT AND ENTREPRENEURSHIP DEVELOPMENT

The emergence of women entrepreneurs and their contribution to the national economy is quite visible in India. The number of women entrepreneurs has grown over a period of time, especially in the 1990s.

Women entrepreneurs need to be lauded for their increased utilization of modern technology, increased investments, finding a niche in the export market, creating a sizable employment for others and setting the trend for other women entrepreneurs in the organized sector.

While women entrepreneurs have demonstrated their potential, the fact remains that they are capable of contributing much more than what they already are. Women's entrepre-neurship needs to be studied separately for two main reasons.

The first reason is that women's entrepreneurship has been recognised during the last decade as an important untapped source of economic growth. Women entrepreneurs create new jobs for themselves and others and also by being different.

They also provide the society with different solutions to management, organisation and business problems as well as to the exploitation of entrepreneurial opportunities. The second reason is that the topic of women in entrepreneurship has been largely neglected both in society in general and in the social sciences.

Not only have women lower participation rates in entrepreneurship than men but they also generally choose to start and manage firms in different industries than men tend to do. Development of the society is directly related with the Income Generation Capacity of its members with agriculture, as the key income generation activity the entrepreneurship on farm and home can directly affect the income of a major chunk of our population.

The growth of modernization processes such as indus-trialization, technical change; urbanization and migration further encourage it. Entrepreneurship on small scale is the only solution to the problems of unemployment and proper utilization of both human and non-human resources and improving the living condition of the poor masses in their book on entrepreneurship started that entrepreneurship is the dynamic process of creating incremental wealth.

This wealth is created by individuals who take the major risks in terms of equity, time and career commitment of providing value to some products or services the product or service itself may or my not be new or unique but value must some how be infused by the entrepreneur by securing and allocating the necessary skill and resources.

The delivery of micro finance to the poor is smooth; effective and less costly if they are organized into SHGs. SHG is promoting micro enterprise through micro-credit intervention. Micro enterprise is an effective instrument of social and economic development. The micro finance is agenda for empowering poor women.

Micro enterprises are an integral part of planned strategy for securing balanced development of the economy of the poor women. Rural women's participation in agro-based activities is much more than what statistics reveal. This is mainly due to the fact that most of the work done by the women at farm and home is disguised as daily chores.

Mechanization and easy availability of labour provide more time to energetic women to engage themselves in self-employment or entrepreneur ventures. Rural women are having human and nonhuman resources to take up an enterprise need one an innovative mind and motivation.

Entrepreneurship is the only solution to the growing employment among rural youth. It helps to generate employment for a number of people within their own social system. This is more beneficial for women in rural areas as it enables them to add to the family income while taking care of their own home and livestock centered task.

Rural women possess abundant resources to take up enterprises. She has the benefit of easy availability of arm and livestock based raw materials and other resources. Hence, she can effectively undertake both the production and processing oriented enterprises. Entrepreneurship development among rural women helps to enhance their personal capabilities and increase decision-making status in the family and society as a whole.

USE OF ICT FOR RURAL WOMEN IN INDIA

Information and Communication Technologies comprise a complex and heterogeneous set of goods, applications and services used to produce, process, distribute and transform information. Traditional technologies continue to be important for large numbers of people around the world, particularly in rural areas. However, new technologies have a vast potential for empowerment which needs to be fully exploited.

Over the past decade, there has been a growing understanding that these technologies can be powerful instruments for advancing economic and social development through the creation of new types of economic activity, employment opportunities, improvements in health-care delivery and other services, and the enhancement of networking, participation and advocacy within society. ICT also have the potential to improve interaction between Governments and citizens, fostering transparency and accountability in governance.

While the potential of ICT for stimulating economic growth, socioeconomic development and effective governance is well recognized, the benefits of ICT have been unevenly distributed within and between countries. The term "digital divide" refers to the differences in resources and capabilities to access and effectively utilise ICT for development that exist within and between countries, regions, sectors and socio-economic groups. The digital divide is often characterized by low levels of access to technologies. Poverty, illiteracy, lack of computer literacy and language barriers are among the factors impeding access to ICT infrastructure, especially in developing countries. Another hindrance pertains to ICT is lack of its access to women.

GENDER EQUALITY AND ICT

While there is recognition of the potential of ICT as a tool for the promotion of gender equality and the empowerment of women, a "gender divide" has also been identified, reflected in the lower numbers of women accessing and using ICT compared with men. Unless this gender divide is specifically addressed, there is a risk that ICT may exacerbate existing inequalities between women and men and create new forms of inequality. If, however, the gender dimensions of ICT—in terms of access and use, capacity-building opportunities, employment and potential for empowerment—are explicitly identified and addressed, ICT can be a powerful catalyst for political and social empowerment of women, and the promotion of gender equality.

In the past few years, the global community has seen the "gender issue" come onto the agenda. Despite economic and socio-cultural barriers to women's use of Information and Communication Technology (ICT), when women are able to use them productively, they can substantially improve their lives and increase their income. They have proved useful in: health care delivery; distance education; enhancing rural productivity through access to market information and access to finance; promoting empowerment and participation in national and international policy processes; improving service delivery by governments; improving environmental monitoring and response systems; and facilitating environmental activism.

In general, women make up a small percentage of internet and computer users. This is changing in some countries – generally those which have greater levels of development and gender equality. ICTs are potentially an important knowledge resource for women, but a focus on access is insufficient. We need also to consider what kind of information is being accessed? Who produced it? Who can use it?

What is it used for? In sum, we need to view women not as passive recipients of information, but active knowledge and technology developers. To orient ICT projects so that they address these areas, ICT project planning and implementation for social development and gender equality must take place in a context which consists of five main components:

- Creating an enabling environment which supports and encourages strategies to promote women's equal access to and opportunity to benefit from ICT projects, as well as creating a regulation and policy environment which supports women's use of ICTs;
- Developing content which speaks to women's concerns and reflects their local knowledge, and which is of value for their daily lives, business enterprises, and family responsibilities;
- Supporting increased representation of women and girls in scientific and technical education, and using ICTs to promote their increased participation in education at all levels;
- Promoting increased employment in the IT sector for women and the use of ICTs for women's SMEs.

- Implementing e-governance strategies which are accessible to women; and promoting women's lobbying and advocacy activities.

INTERNATIONAL TREATIES AND CONVENTIONS

The 20th century has witnessed the upsurge of women empowerment movement universally. The Universal Declaration of Human Rights (1948) reaffirming faith in the fundamental Human Rights, in the dignity and worth of the human person, and in the equal rights of men and women, contemplated the entitlement of all cherished freedoms to all human beings without any distinction of any kind, including discrimination based on sex. The World Conference on Human Rights at Vienna in 1993 had declared the human rights of women and the girl child to be "inalienable, integral and indivisible part of universal human rights" and eradication of any form of discrimination on the basis of sex, is the priority objective of the international community. The Convocation on the Elimination of All Forms of Discrimination Against Women (CEDAW), 1979 is the United Nations' landmark treaty marking the struggle for women's rights. Described as the Bill of Rights for women, it spells out what constitutes discrimination against women and propagates strategies based on "non-discriminatory" model, so that women's rights are seen to be violated, if women are denied the same rights as men.

INDIAN PERSPECTIVE

For centuries, women in this country have been socially and economically handicapped. They have been deprived of equal participation in the socio-economic activities of the nation. The Constitution of any country is supreme law of the land and is followed absolutely, subject to the limits provided in the solemn document itself. So much is the importance of the Constitution that if a statutory law is in conflict with it, the same would be "unconstitutional" and void in nature. The Constitution is organic and living in nature.

It is also well settled that the interpretation of the Constitution of India or statutes would change from time to time. Being a living organ, it is ongoing and with passage of time, law must change. New rights may have to be found out within the constitutional scheme. It is established that Fundamental Rights themselves have no fixed content; most of them are empty vessels into which each generation must pour its contents in the light of its experience. The attempt of the court should be to expand the reach and ambit of the Fundamental Rights by process of judicial interpretation.

There cannot be any distinction between the Fundamental Rights mentioned in Chapter III of the Constitution and the declaration of such rights on the basis of the judgments rendered by the Supreme Court. Thus, horizons of Constitutional law are expanding. Further, it is presumed that the Parliament intends the court to apply to an ongoing Act a construction that continuously updates its wordings to allow for changes since the Act was initially framed. While it remains law, it has to be treated as always speaking. This means that in its application on any day, the language of the Act though necessarily embedded in its own time, is nevertheless to be construed in accordance with the need to treat it as a current law. Thus, we cannot allow the dead hand of the past to stifle the growth of the living present.

Law cannot stand still; it must change with the changing social concepts and values. If the bark that protects the tree fails to grow and expand along with the tree, it will either choke the tree or if it is a living tree it will shed that bark and grow a living bark for itself. Similarly, if the law fails to respond to the needs of changing society, then either it will stifle the growth of the society and choke its progress or if the society is vigourous enough, it will cast away the law, which stands in the way of its growth.

Law must therefore constantly be on the move adapting itself to the fast-changing society and not lag behind. Thus, for conferring the strongest protection and to emancipate women, the provisions of the Constitution should be interpreted liberally and in a purposive manner. The Constitution of India recognises women as a class by itself and permits enactment of laws and reservations favouring them. Several articles in our Constitution make express provision for affirmative action in favour of women.

It prohibits all types of discrimination against women and lays a carpet for securing equal opportunity to women in all walks of life, including education, employment and participation. Article 51 of the Constitution obligates the State to honour international law and treaty obligations. Our natural obligation to renounce practices derogatory to the dignity of women has been elevated to the status of fundamental duty by Article 51-A. The Constitution of India recognises equality of the sexes and in fact provides for certain provisions under the Chapter on Fundamental Rights more favourable to women but in actual practice they are observed more in breach than in compliance. In our society the freedom of women to seek employment outside the family is a major issue. This freedom is denied in many cultures and this attitude in itself is a serious violation of women's liberty and gender equality.

The absence of this freedom militates against the economic empowerment of women, with many other deleterious consequences. Thus, these Constitutional ideal have by and large remained unaccomplished and we have to cover a long distance before the benefits of ICT can be reaped by women effectively. One of the ignored ICT issues in India is the "gender sensitisation" that must be adopted while formulating and implementing the ICT policies in India. It is commonly understood that men and women understand and use Computers and Internet differently.

Thus, the policy decisions must make sufficient provision for adopting itself with this aspect. Within India also we must understand that the training, use and adoption of ICT must be "gender neutral". For a gender neutral technology we have to first place the women on an equal platform. They cannot be put on an equal platform till they have equal capacity and opportunity to use ICT. They cannot also effectively use ICT till their "feedbacks and concerns" are incorporated in the National Policies including the E-governance plans. The position is worst when it comes to women that also rural women. In our society, whether they belong to the majority or the minority group, what is apparent is that there exists a great disparity in the matter of economic resourcefulness between a man and a woman.

Our society is male dominated both economically and socially and women are assigned, invariably, a dependant role, irrespective of the class of society to which she belongs. It must be appreciated that a nation that does not respect its women cannot be described as a civilised nation at all. Such a nation cannot grow and develop and will ultimately perish due to its own rudimentary and tyrannical dogma. Thus, the national consensus should concentrate on betterment of women by suitably empowering them. The plight of the women, however, cannot be improved till they are duly represented in the "power structure" of the nation. In a democratic country the voice of women can be heard only to the extent they are sharing the power structure in the supreme governance of the country. Thus, ICT can play a major role in women empowerment if they are provided employment opportunities at the village level after providing them suitable training. We have to open more village kiosks so that greater women participation can be there. This cannot happen till we first make the e-governance and ICT strategies and policies transparent and accountable. Mere computerisation is not e-governance.

3

Women Employment in Rural India

INTRODUCTION

Employment is critical for poverty reduction and for enhancing women's status. However, it is potentially empowering and liberating only if it provides women an opportunity to improve their well being and enhance their capabilities.

On the other hand, if it is driven by distress and is low-paying then it may only increase a woman's drudgery. To understand women's work status in India's rural areas and to examine the trends and nature of women's employment, this thesis analyses the data from large scale national surveys. The National Sample Survey Organisation carries out quinquennial surveys on employment and unemployment and covers more than 100,000 households and 500,000 individuals throughout the country. The survey covers socio-economic and demographic characteristics, employment and unemployment characteristics, and provides information on wages.

The latest year for which data is available for both surveys is 2004-05. The National Family Health Survey covers households with women in the reproductive age group of 15-49 and in the latest survey carried out in 2005-06; it covered 63,896 women in this age group. The authors' estimates from the NSS surveys of 1983, 1993-94, and 2004-05 and the NFHS survey of 2005-06 are based on analysis of unit level data. In addition, we have also drawn on data on women's control on agricultural holdings from the agricultural census, a large scale survey conducted by the Ministry of Agriculture, Government of India, as well as other sources of information such as national income data from the Central Statistical Organisation. The thesis is organised in six sections. The next section analyses work participation rates for women by socio economic characteristics such as caste, religion, education, and economic status.

The participation of women in the agricultural and nonagricultural sectors and their categorisation by employment status. Some of the correlates of workforce participation including education and poverty. The determinants of women's work participation and the factors that influence their participation in different kinds of employment are explored by means. The last section concludes with an overview and suggestions for improving the position of women workers in rural areas.

SOCIO-ECONOMIC CHARACTERISTICS

The notion of work and employment, especially for women, is complex. The reasons why women work in gainful activity, or whether they work part time or full time, can be diverse and may be rooted in a complex interplay of economic, cultural, social, and personal factors. In developing economies, workers combine multiple activities over different parts of the year. The NSSO defines a person who is employed for a major part of the year as being"Principal Status" employed. If gainfully employed only for a part of the year, she is described as being employed in the"Subsidiary Status".

A person employed either in"Usual Principal Status" or"Usual Subsidiary Status" is enumerated as being employed in the"Usual Status". Unless otherwise stated, the reference is to UPSS employment throughout this thesis. The industry associated with her employment is the one which she is associated for a major part of the employment. We focus for the most part on rural employment, but also provide data on urban employment in order to highlight the contrasts. As in most other parts of the world, fewer women participate in employment in India compared to men. In 2004-05, while in urban areas, 16.6 per cent women and 54.9 per cent men were employed, in rural areas, these percentages were 32.7 and 54.6 respectively. More women are employed only in the subsidiary status, than men, especially in rural areas. This can be explained by factors from the supply side as well as the demand side. Taking the former first, the rural economy has been largely stagnant over the years and employment opportunities have not grown.

Most women, therefore, are able to get work for only a few months in the year. This keeps them employed only in the'subsidiary status'. On the supply side, women's primary duties are supposed to be in the household. For economic reasons they have to work, but must do so in addition to their domestic responsibilities, and are therefore only able to enter the labour force as subsidiary workers. Over a thirty-two year span, the workforce participation rate of males and females shows no systematic variation despite a larger percentage of persons in the younger age groups joining education. The only notable changes appear to be a small increase in male WPR after 1987-88 and that urban females recorded a higher employment rate in 2004-05 over all preceding rounds of the survey. This also shows that globalisation appears to have enlarged work opportunities for women in urban areas, but has had no impact in rural areas.

Yet, there are large variations in women's participation in work across socio-economic groups and across regions and states in India which we shall presently discuss. While mainly economic factors determine a man's participation in employment, the forces that influence a woman's participation in work are many and diverse and include demographic, reproductive, social, religious and cultural factors. WPR is highest for scheduled tribe and scheduled caste women and lowest for women from the'other' caste. The SCs and STs are the most marginalised sections in the economy and the most impoverished. Women from these groups have higher WPRs because extreme poverty leaves them with little choice but to work, and because they do not face social taboos that disapprove of work.

The converse is true for women from'other' castes. When religious background is considered, Muslim women in rural areas have a significantly low WPR-nearly half the national rate for women of all religions. Once again it is social norms that restrict women's mobility and entry into the workforce that keep more Muslim women tied to hearth and home. Does education propel women into employment? The gender differences in this respect are interesting and stark. For male workers, higher levels of education are indeed associated with higher WPR, both in rural and urban areas.

But for women, WPR is higher for illiterate women than for women with higher levels of school education-a trend which reverses itself only for women with technical/vocational education or graduates. This again is a pattern which reveals itself both in rural and urban areas. Thus 51 per cent of illiterate men are employed but this percentage goes up to 71 per cent among men who have passed their higher secondary.

On the other hand, 39 per cent illiterate women are employed, but this percentage declines to just 25 per cent among women who have passed higher secondary. Why? Multiple factors such as the compulsion for men to earn, the greater availability of jobs for men, and the restrictive social norms operating for women, appear to explain this pattern. It is interesting that in urban areas by contrast, women's employment goes up at higher educational levels and shows a pattern similar to that for men showing the narrowing of gender gaps in urban areas.

How does economic status of women influence their participation in work? Indeed, the relationship between workforce participation and economic status of the household is critical for policy and programme interventions. While the NSSO does not collect data on incomes, it provides data on monthly per capita consumption expenditure; a measure that is widely used as a proxy for the economic status of households. The authors have computed participation in employment across MPCE deciles groups from NSS unit records. Workforce participation shows a consistently declining trend with rising economic status for rural women, clearly reflecting on the economic distress that compels poor women to work. In contrast, for urban women, work participation shows a skewed v-shape, declining as economic status improves, but rises again with the highest consumption decile. The latter reflects on higher educational attainments of women associated with higher incomes, and the greater availability of employment opportunities in urban areas. To conclude, women's participation in gainful work is lower compared to men; it is higher for scheduled caste and scheduled tribe women who are less restricted by social norms; among religious groups, work participation is lowest for Muslim women; education impacts differentially for men and women, with level of participation increasing with educational levels for men, but declining for rural women; as economic status improves, work participation declines for rural women suggesting that when there are no compelling economic reasons to earn, social taboos on women's mobility and participation in work exercise a strong influence. In general, while the gaps in work participation between men and women are clear and well recognised, the gaps between different classes of women hailing from different social and economic backgrounds are less well known and need to be understood for effective policy measures.

EMPLOYMENT GUARANTEE FOR RURAL WOMEN IN INDIA

The National Rural Employment Guarantee Act is one of the most progressive legislations enacted since independence. Its significance is evident from a variety of perspectives. First, it is a bold and unique experiment in the provision of rural employment – in India and indeed in the world at large. Second, it is the first expression of the right to work as an enforceable legal entitlement. In a country where labour is the only economic asset for millions of people, gainful employment is a prerequisite for the fulfilment of other basic rights – the right to life, the right to food, and the right to education.There is much that the NREGA promises from the perspective of women's empowerment as well.

Most boldly, in a rural milieu marked by stark inequalities between men and women – in the opportunities for gainful employment afforded as well as wage rates – NREGA represents action on both these counts. The act stipulates that wages will be equal for men and women. It is also committed to ensuring that at least 33% of the workers shall be women. By generating employment for women at fair wages in the village, NREGA can play a substantial role in economically empowering women and laying the basis for greater independence and self-esteem. Government figures indicate an impressive participation of women in the NREGA. It is above 33 per cent in 15 states. Tamil Nadu, with 82 per cent, shows the highest participation with Kerala and Rajasthan also showing impressive figures.

At an all-India level, women's employment as a percentage of total employment in NREGA works was 40 per cent in 2007-08. The first four months of 2008-09 have already seen this figure go up to 50 per cent.

Table. Women's Participation in NREGA (women workers as a percentage of all NREGA workers)

States	2008 – 09 (%)
Tamil Nadu	82.01
Kerala	71.39
Rajasthan	69.00
Andhra Pradesh	57.75
Karnataka	49.77
Gujarat	46.54
Tripura	44.51
Uttaranchal	42.77
Chattisgarh	42.05
Madhya Pradesh	41.67
Maharashtra	39.99
Sikkim	36.73
Orissa	36.39
Haryana	34.44
Mizoram	33.62
Manipur	32.80
Meghalaya	30.87
Assam	30.85
Himachal Pradesh	30.11
Arunachal Pradesh	29.58
Nagaland	29.36
Jharkhand	27.17
Bihar	26.62
West Bengal	16.99
Punjab	**16.29**
Uttar Pradesh	14.53
Jammu and Kashmir	1.08
All India	49.33

With this in mind, the National Federation of Indian Women (NFIW) carried out a survey to assess the impact of NREGA on women. The basic objective is to measure the tangible benefits that women have received from the implementation of the NREGA over a period of two years. A second aim of the study is to shed light on possible improvements that can be introduced to make NREGA more effective and responsive to the needs of women, particularly given its extension to all of rural India from April 2008.

The survey was carried out in one district each of four states where the NREGA had been in force since February 2006: Rajnandgaon (Chhattisgarh), Jhabua (Madhya Pradesh), Mayurbhanj (Orissa) and Cuddalore (Tamil Nadu). In each of the districts, two blocks and five Gram Panchayats per block were randomly selected.

A random sampling was also done to select women workers from completed worksites' muster rolls of 2007-2008. Two sets of questionnaires were used for the data collection. One was addressed to members of the Gram Panchayat and the second was addressed to women workers. The target number of sample workers was 800 (200 in each district). A total of 776 women workers and 40 Gram Panchayat members were actually interviewed.

Close to half (49%) of the interviewed women were Scheduled Tribes; the rest were SCs (20 per cent) and OBCs (27 per cent). Out of the total sample of women workers 68 per cent were illiterate. Half of the respondent households had less than 5 acres land, and 35 per cent had no land at all. Most respondents reported agriculture or manual labour as the households' main occupation.

Table. Sample Areas of the NFIW Study

State	District	Blocks
Chhattisgarh	Rajnandgaon	Rajnandgaon
Dungargarh		
Orissa	Mayurbhanj	Shamakhunta
Bangriposi		
Madhya Pradesh	Jhabua	Pethlawad Rama
Tamil Nadu	Cuddalore	Mel Bhuvanagiri
Kurinjipadi		

NUMBER OF DAYS WORKED AND WAGES

Employment at NREGA worksites seems to have raised both enthusiasm and expectations among women workers. Women workers unanimously affirmed that the benefits from NREGA employment were high and that they would like to get more days of work in a year. The challenge of the situation becomes clearer when we look at the small proportion of women surveyed (only 7 per cent) who got more than 75 days of work in the last year. Almost half of the respondents (43 per cent) reported that they had worked for fewer than 25 days in the previous year.

Regarding wage payments, we found, in Cuddalore district, that most women workers were receiving the stipulated minimum wage, *i.e.* Rs. 80 per day. In the other three districts, however, the average wage was generally around Rs. 60 per day (as compared to a minimum wage of Rs. 69 in Madhya Pradesh, Rs. 70 in Orissa and Rs. 66.70 in Chhattisgarh) in the financial year 2007 – 08. Nevertheless, even where the full minimum wage was not being received, it is clear that NREGA wages are far higher than the wages otherwise locally available.

For example, Bhagwati w/o Ram from Gram Panchayat Khaira of Dongargarh block in Rajnandgaon district said:

- "Before NREGA, we were forced to work as agricultural labourers or casual labourers in brick kilns for Rs. 25/- to 30/- per day. But under NREGA, we are getting Rs. 62 to 64 per day, more than double, which is almost an unexpected amount for us."

It is also clear that, by and large, men and women are paid equal wages at NREGA worksites as has been mandated by the Act. Given that wage gaps between the male and female casual workers have been the norm in rural India, this is an extremely significant development.

Table. Women Workers' Access to Minimum Wage and Days of Work

Districts	Statutory minimum wage* (Rs/day) (Rs/day)	Per cent women aware about min. wage workers	Average wage paid to women under NREGA getting the full	Proportion (%) of sample women mini. Wage
Rajnandgaon (Chhattisgarh)	66.70**	33	62	18
Jhabua (Madhya Pradesh)	69	25	60	10
Mayurbhanj (Orissa)	70	51	60	40
Cuddalore (Tamil Nadu)	80	84	80	93

CONTRIBUTION TO WOMEN'S INDEPENDENCE

By putting cash incomes into their hands, NREGA is beginning to create a greater degree of economic independence among women. This was one of NREGA's main aims: with the increased participation of women in household income-generation a positive contribution to gender relations can be made. The survey data (both qualitative and quantitative) suggest that women workers are more confident about their roles as contributors to family expenditure and their work decisions, and that they are also becoming more assertive about their space in the public sphere. More then half of the respondents felt that the NREGA has brought a significant change in their villages as well as in their own lives.

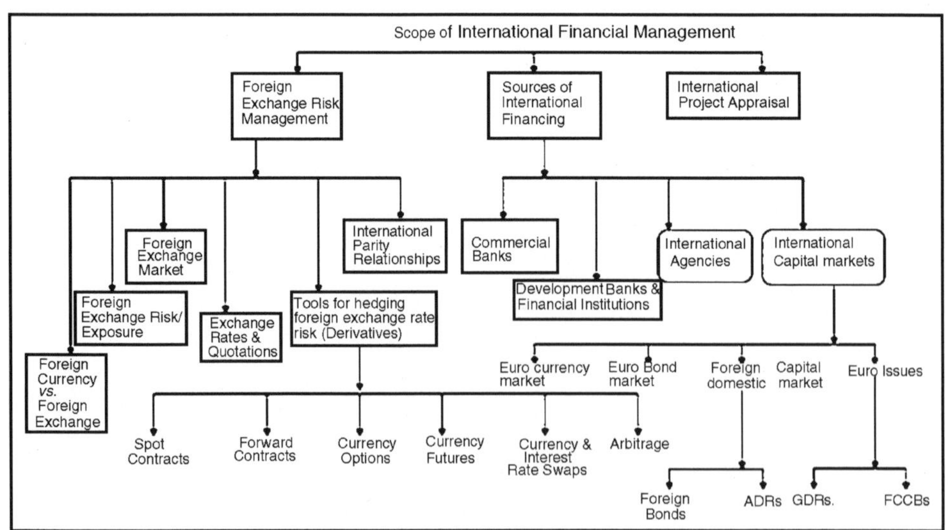

This is because employment is being provided within their village, generating community assets and enhancing their spending capacity. In each of the four survey districts, most of the women felt that the Act is "important" or "very important" for them. In Rajnandgaon and Cuddalore, the proportion who felt that NREGA is "very important" was as high as 70 per cent and 61 per cent, respectively.

When asked about their decision to work under the NREGA, most respondents said that the decision to work at NREGA worksites was their own. Rajnandgaon was exceptional in this regard: 93 per cent of the women said that they had taken their own work decision. In the other three districts as well, this figure was remarkably high: 81 per cent in Mayurbhanj, 68 per cent in Cuddalore, and 67 per cent in Jhabua. Evidently, NREGA employment has encouraged women to take the decision to enter the sphere of the cash economy.

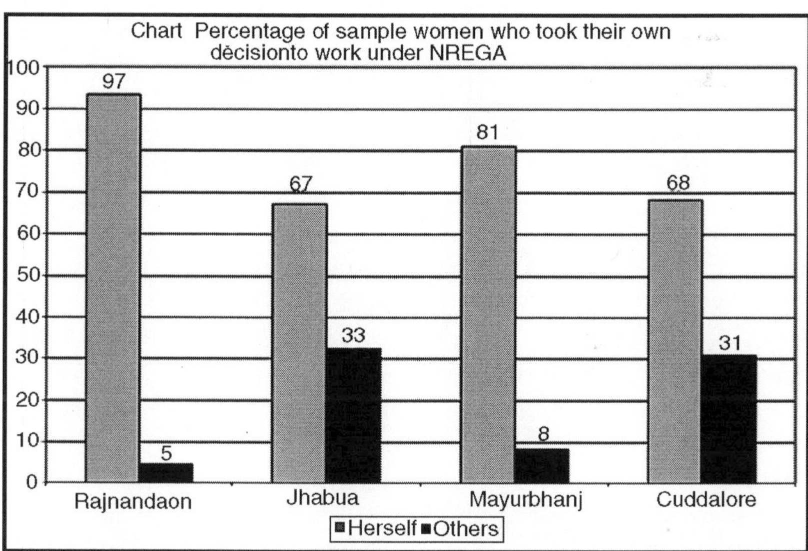

Another important point that emerged from the survey is that women workers were, by and large, receiving their wages in person, rather than through husbands or other proxies. In Rajnandgaon and Cuddalore, over 91 per cent of the women collected their own wages. In Jhabua and Mayurbhanj this figure stood at 60 per cent. Despite the substantial proportion of women not receiving their wages in person in these last two, this is also an encouraging finding.

Inevitably, women's NREGA earnings are increasing their contribution to household income. A large majority (72 per cent) of the respondents said that they spent wages earned at NREGA works on regular food and consumer goods. The increased income locally available through NREGA work, they felt, was helping ensure at least two regular meals a day. For the most part, the amounts earned through NREGA are insufficient to repay debts. Nevertheless, 28 per cent of the respondents said that they had spent their wages on repaying small debts.

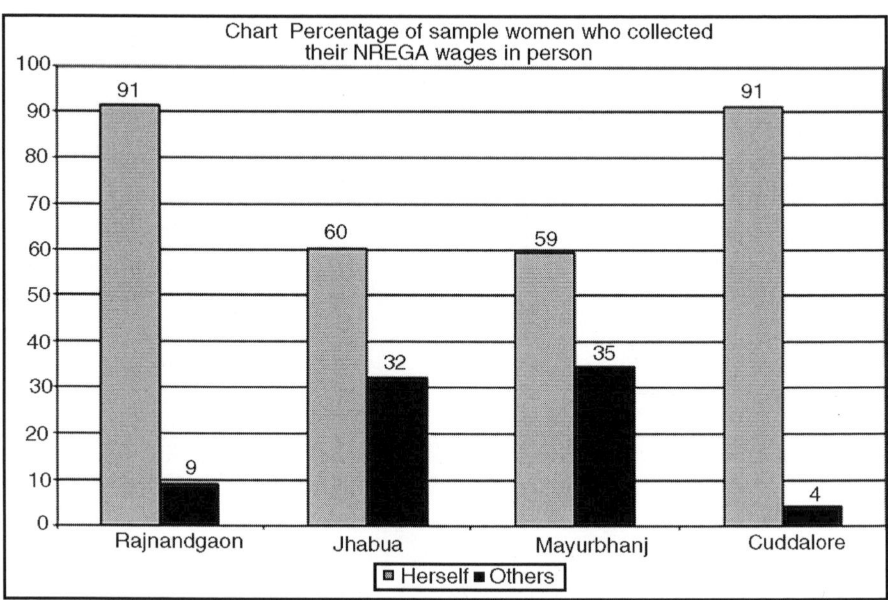

Further, it helps them to keep themselves away from the clutches of local moneylenders. A significant percentage of workers – almost 34 per cent - also spent their NREGA wages on their children's education. The other large expenditure regularly met through NREGA wages is health care, with around 40 per cent of the respondents having spent earnings on this. All this taken together seems to sketch out the beginnings of a marked shift from the previous role of women. While women's labour (farm and non-farm) has always been an essential component in the functioning of rural households, it has been made invisible due to the absence of any monetary remuneration. By putting cash earnings in women's hands, NREGA has both increased and diversified the contributions that women are making to household incomes as wage earners.

MIGRATION – CHANGING TRENDS

One of the most positive trends in all the districts studied has been the impact of NREGA on migration patterns. 73 per cent of the respondents said that neither they nor their family members had migrated in 2007. The sole exception to this pattern was Jhabua, where 59 per cent respondents stated that they had migrated last year. That being said, even in Jhabua there is evidence of a shift in the pattern of migration. Respondents stated that where earlier entire families would migrate, now only one or two persons tend to leave for seasonal work in neighbouring states or elsewhere in Madhya Pradesh. NREGA seems to have created reasons and opportunities for people to work and remain in their own villages. The strengthening of this perception in rural areas can have significant impacts on questions of security, health and children's education, all of which are often compromised, in one way or another, during migration.

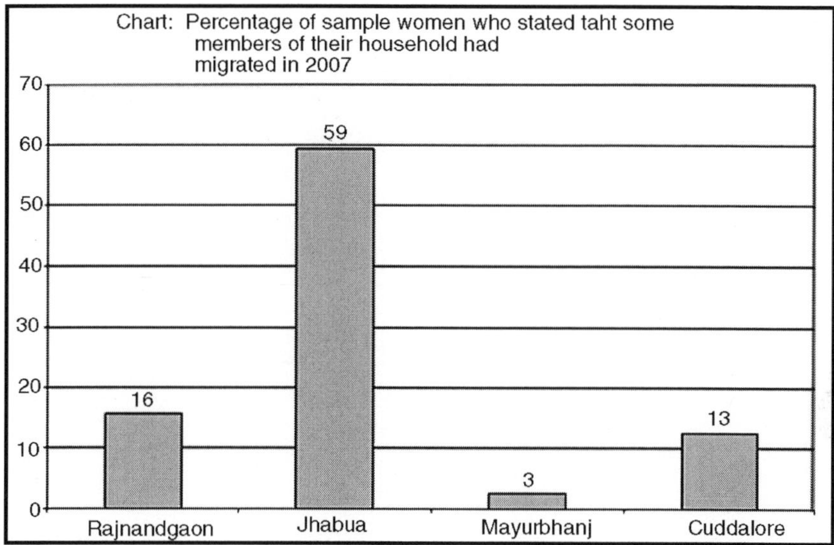

AWARENESS

It is perhaps predictable that awareness about the provision of NREGA will be low among disadvantaged communities. Less than half (48 per cent) of all sample workers were aware of the level of minimum wage in their respective States. Cuddalore is the only survey district in which awareness levels were relatively high (84 per cent were aware of the minimum wage).

Most women were aware that under the Act each household is guaranteed 100 days of work in a year. But awareness regarding operational guidelines, household registration, the job card distribution process, work applications and entitlements such as worksite facilities and unemployment allowance was inadequate. Only 43 per cent of women workers reported having made a formal application for a job card.

In all four districts, most people just applied orally or gave their names when asked whether they wanted a job card. The situation was even worse with respect to applications for work.

Only 18 per cent of the women surveyed were aware of the work application process and had applied for work themselves. The low level of awareness, even in districts where NREGA has been implemented for over two years, are indeed worrying. Generating much higher awareness about NREGA work clearly constitutes one of the key challenges for authorities, NGOs and popular movements.

POOR WORKSITE FACILITIES

The NREGA is committed to ensuring a workplace conducive to productivity and workers' welfare. With this in mind, NREGA funds have been allocated for the provision of safe drinking water, shade for periods of rest, first aid and child care facilities at the worksite.

The last of these, in particular, is significant in order to make NREGA work a viable option for women with young children who cannot be left alone at home. It is disturbing, therefore, to find that most of these facilities are routinely absent from worksites. Only 68 per cent of worksites had drinking water facility. Most striking, however, is the almost complete lack of child care facilities in any of the four districts surveyed.

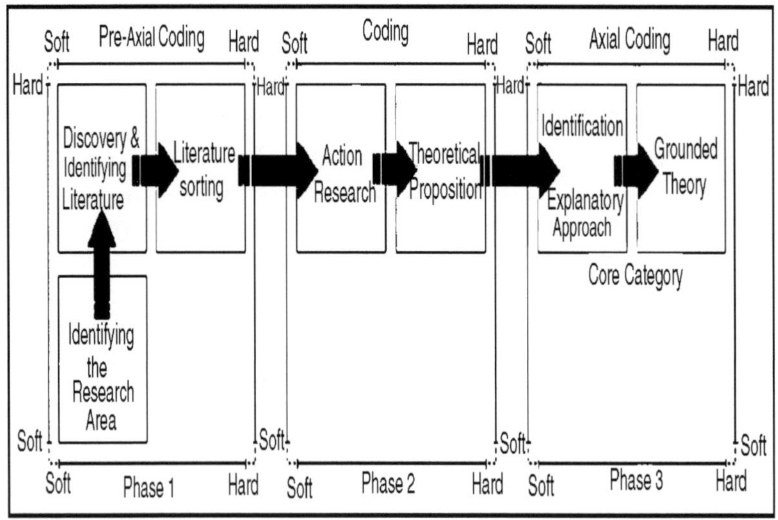

PARTICIPATION IN PANCHAYATI RAJ INSTITUTIONS (PRIS) AND GRAM SABHAS

NREGA is designed to be largely implemented through PRIs – at least 50 per cent of all sanctioned works are to be implemented by the Gram Panchayats. The Gram Sabha too plays a crucial role in the selection of works and the conduct of social audits.

Participation of people at large and women in particular in these institutions and assemblies is, then, critical to realising the participatory potential of the Act. During the survey it was found that women workers did not generally take part in Gram Sabhas.

This is partly due to lack of awareness about the significant role to be played by the Gram Sabhas in making a shelf of projects and conducting social audits of NREGA works. Women's participation in Panchayati Raj Institution (PRIs) was also very low - not even 1 per cent of the respondents in all the districts said they were involved in PRI's activities. This is despite the reservation of one third of all seats in local elected bodies for women (under the 73rd and 74th Constitutional Amendment Acts). Most elected women tend to be "rubber stamp" leaders, the vast majority of them are illiterate and politically untrained.

While women are increasingly visible as part of the NREGA workforce, there is still much scope to increase their involvement in PRIs to tackle issues like water, sanitation, health, education and of course the implementation of NREGA.

WOMEN'S EMPLOYMENT IN THE AGRICULTURAL AND NON-AGRICULTURAL SECTORS

Within rural areas, work may be classified along two dimensions; a) by sector, viz., agriculture or non-agriculture, and b) by employment status, that is whether a person is in regular employment, is self employed or is casually employed. An analysis of women's employment by sector and employment status can tell us a great deal about the outcomes for women and if the work they do promotes their well being or is low-end, low paying and driven by distress. What is the significance of this classification and what does it tell us about the nature and disparities in women's employment? It illustrates vividly the more disadvantaged position of women in the rural labour market. Firstly, wages are higher for men in all categories of employment. The disparity is highest for regular workers in non-agriculture. Second, women are concentrated in agriculture where the wages are lowest. Thus 90 per cent women are in agriculture and only 10 per cent are in non-agriculture among casual labourers. Thirdly, there is a very low proportion of women in regular work where the wage rates are the highest, employment is more secure and working conditions are relatively better. This is the case both in agriculture and in non-agriculture.

How does economic status relate to the nature of work that men and women do? Along expected lines, the percentage of casual labourers among both male and female workers declines sharply with rising household MPCE deciles. The percentage of self-employed among workers shows an increasing trend with MPCE deciles, except for the highest deciles, where it dips. The share of regular workers is low throughout showing the scarcity of regular work; is negligible in the lower consumption deciles but rises in the highest deciles. For rural female workers, the share of the self-employed remains higher for each MPCE decile compared to male workers. On the other hand women remain disadvantaged when it comes to regular work. Although the structure of employment by employment status has been remarkably constant across the years, previous NSS surveys showed some increase in casual labour in the rural male and female workforce and a decline in the share of the selfemployed.

But during 1999/00-2004/05, there was a change in the trend; the share of selfemployed workers increased among both female and male workers, while the share of casual work declined. Why this has happened is difficult to say, but it is likely that the overall stagnation in agriculture and the rural economy may have led to this shift. The growth rate in agriculture and allied sectors was only little more than 2 per cent per annum in this period, registering a negative growth in some years. This may have led to shrinking availability of wage work and compelled workers to eke out subsistence from self employment. The next section discusses women's employment in agriculture, while the subsequent section takes up women's employment in non-agriculture. In each, the three broad status of employment are analysed.

AGRICULTURE

In rural areas, nearly 84 per cent women workers are engaged in agriculture, either as cultivators or labourers as compared to 67 per cent male workers. There has been a kind of'creeping feminisation' of agriculture; male workers have steadily moved out of agriculture while for women workers, this movement has been extremely tardy. Men have entered into more diversified occupations in non-agriculture, while women have largely tended to remain in agriculture that has been largely stagnant.

In 1972-93, 83.2 per cent male workers and 89.7 per cent female workers were engaged in agriculture. By 2004-05, only 66.5 per cent male workers were in agriculture compared to 83.3 per cent female workers. This has to be seen in the context of the fact that returns to labour are, on average, higher in non-agriculture than in agriculture, although the size of assets operated and type of employment, among other factors, are also relevant. One implication of the above slow change is that a significant proportion of the incremental female workforce gets engaged in agriculture. Between 1983 and 2004-05, nearly 72 per cent of the incremental rural female workforce was absorbed in agriculture, compared to 40 per cent for the male workforce.

Agriculture: Casual Workers

Compared to 23.2 per cent male rural workers, 29.2 per cent female rural workers were engaged as casual agricultural labourers in 2004-05. There is a disproportionate concentration of the most deprived social groups in this form of labour. Half of the female casual labourers and 43 per cent of male casual labourers in India belong to SCs and STs, nearly twice their share in population. Women agricultural casual workers form a distinct category: they are disadvantaged in many ways. There is significant gender segmentation of operations in agriculture. While men predominate in activities such as ploughing and harvesting, women predominate in weeding, transplanting and inter-culture. The wages are uniformly lower in all female dominant operations. Overall women's wages are estimated at 69 per cent of male wages in 2004-05. Moreover, women also get fewer days of work. Further, women workers rarely get the minimum wages stipulated by the government: more than 95 per cent of female agricultural wage workers received wages lower than the minimum wage. The deprivation of casual workers is aggravated by the fact that not only are their lower than wages in non-agriculture; they have also grown at a lower rate in the recent period, thereby increasing the gap.

Moreover, as already pointed out, women workers who work as casual labourers are able to get work for only part of the year-their estimated employment days was only 184. Women agricultural labourers are also unemployed for more days a year than their male counterparts. The unemployment rate for agricultural labourers is quite high in rural areas by any standard; 16 per cent for men and 17 per cent for women for 2004-05 by the Current Daily Status criterion and this increased over 1993/94-2004/05.

Agriculture: Self Employed Workers

As noted earlier, women workers are increasingly engaged as self-employed in agriculture. There has been a steady increase in the numbers of both women and men farmers over all years since 1983 except 1999-00. The sharpest increase has taken place in the recent quinquennium when the share of women farmers increased to 41.8 per cent, the highest in 32 years. These results attest to the large role played by women farmers although they do not confirm a systematic trend towards feminization. Such a large presence of women farmers requires systematic public support to them, which is lacking mainly because women are not seen as principal producers in agriculture and because they do not have ownership or control over the assets on which they work.

The poor support to women farmers has been highlighted in several studies and reports, notably Planning Commission and NCEUS. Srivastava *et al.*, 2007, have shown that despite legislative changes few women have control over land. However, the Agricultural Census provides information on operational holdings, that is, agricultural holdings operated and controlled by men and women, whether or not they are owned by them. The Agricultural Census 2000-01, only 11.6 per cent of cultivated agricultural land holdings covering 9.1 per cent area were operated by women.

There is a systematic decline in the percentage of land holdings and area controlled by women as the size of holding increases. In the smallest size class the percentage of land holdings operated by women was 13.4 whereas the area operated by them was 12 per cent. In large holdings, the corresponding percentages declined to 5.7 and 5.6 respectively. These figures could partly be explained by the pattern of outmigration since it is in smaller holdings where male outmigration is also likely to be higher. However, cultural and social factors are also very important in explaining the fact that a miniscule proportion of women have control on this critical resource.

This is brought out by the regional pattern of women's control over land holdings. The percentage of such holdings was much higher in the more progressive Southern states and in some of the North-eastern states. In Kerala women operated 21 per cent of the land holdings and 18 per cent of area. In Andhra Pradesh the corresponding figures were 20 per cent and 17 per cent respectively while in Tamil Nadu they were 18.1 per cent and 15.1 respectively. In the absence of land titles, women farmers have much smaller access to institutional credit compared to male farmers, and receive a much lower degree of institutional support.

NON-AGRICULTURE

Non-Agriculture: Casual Workers

Wages of casual workers estimated from the 2004-05 NSSO Survey show that female wages are lower than male wages across all industry groups. The relative male-female wage gap is larger in non-agriculture where female casual workers earn 65 per cent of male wages. In manufacturing, female wages are only 59 per cent of male wages. The low wages of female workers are principally due to the undervaluation of work and skills in activities in which women predominate. Thus the segmentation of women workers in certain types of activities largely determines the gender gap which exists.

A number of national and international studies have documented the sex-typing of occupations. In India, this has been noted in a number of industries such as knitwear and garments. These jobs provided limited opportunity for upward mobility.

Such segregation can also be found in the services sector. In the health and education sectors, women are concentrated at the lower end as paramedics, teachers in lower grades, or support staff. The hierarchy of jobs within manufacturing or services is then used to value the jobs where women are concentrated as low skilled workers even if it involves exceptional talent and years of informal training.

Non-Agriculture: Self-Employed Workers

As we have noted earlier, the self-employed workers are not a homogeneous group. They fall into three sub-groups. The first are the'employers'. The second are the'own account workers', and the third group is constituted by the'helpers' who assisted the main family workers in an unpaid capacity. A significant percentage of self-employed women workers are classified as helpers *i.e.*, they are recognised only as auxiliary workers and this percentage is much larger than among male self-employed workers in nonagriculture among whom 15.2 per cent are classified as unpaid workers. Further, while one of the stated advantages of self-employment for women is that this work can be done based at home and women can work at their pace and convenience, this results in multiple disadvantages in the form of limited opportunities, seclusion, and lower earnings.

Female Proprietary Enterprises

The NSSO informal enterprises survey, 1999-2000, provides a profile of female and male proprietary enterprises. The survey found that about 12 per cent of proprietary enterprises were operated by women and these were mainly own account enterprises. Approximately 10 per cent of the workers in proprietary enterprises were engaged in the female proprietary enterprises. A distinction is made between Own Account Enterprises employing no hired labour and Establishments which hire one or more labourers. In general, urban enterprises are larger in size, and for the same category, female proprietary enterprises are smaller than male proprietary enterprises.

In rural areas, female proprietary enterprises are very small in size, with an average fixed investment of less than ₹8000, while female establishments had a total fixed asset base of ₹123,786. The gross value added per worker was less than ₹7000 per annum, while in the latter it was slightly more than ₹26,000 per year. Among rural female OAEs, about 34 per cent of them have value of fixed assets of less than ₹1000, while only 7 per cent had value of assets greater than ₹25000.

Not only are few women involved in running non-agricultural enterprises of any kind, the scale of operation of women operated units is distinctly very tiny particularly in rural areas. Compared to the National Minimum Wage, 89 per cent of female OAEs and 42 per cent of male OAEs gave lower imputed daily returns.

Home Workers

Nearly 81 per cent of rural female enterprises and 39.5 per cent of male enterprises operated from home in 1999-00 *i.e.* they were home based enterprises. About 40 per cent of these enterprises in rural areas work on sub-contracted basis *i.e.* their workers were homeworkers as defined by the ILO. Home-workers work at the lowest end of a value chain, usually dealing with petty contractors, on whom they depend for supply of work, raw material and sale of finished goods.

This dependence on the contractor together with the isolation undermines their ability to bargain for higher piece-rates, timely payments or overtime pay. The annual gross value addition of the rural female home-workers is, on average, ₹5270, much lower than even the ₹9000 that accrues in female OAEs.

The average value of fixed assets engaged by them is also very low at ₹3800. About 79 per cent of the women and 63 per cent of the male home workers were paid on a piece-rate basis. This wage has many hidden costs, including use of the house and electricity, delayed payments, and arbitrary cuts in wages on the pretext of poor quality..

Non-Agriculture: Regular Workers

Female regular workers in rural areas form a very small part of the female workforce as also of the total proportion of regular workers in rural areas. Outside of agriculture, they are mainly concentrated in education, manufacturing, private households, health and social work and public administration. Work in private household earns women the lowest wages of ₹39 per day, followed by employment in hotels and restaurants, manufacturing, and agriculture.

While the sectors with the highest daily remuneration, such as electricity gas and water, transport; financial intermediation; and real estate employ very few women on a regular basis, among the sectors where a larger proportion of women take up employment, education and health sectors afford reasonable daily earnings. The daily earnings of women regular/salaried workers are more than twice as high as women casual workers.

However, within regular work, as with casual work, there is a large gap in male-female earnings across most sectors, ranging from a female-male earning ratio of 0.3 in mining to 0.87 in construction. Even in the social sectors, there is a large gap in earnings, with this ratio being as low as 0.59 in education and 0.69 in health and social work. Women workers in these sectors tend to be concentrated in the lower segments-as paramedics, support staff, contract teachers or teachers in low grades.

VULNERABILITY FOR WOMEN WORKERS

We now briefly draw attention to the characteristics of women workers and poverty levels in rural India. We have used the official poverty line as a benchmark, but have categorised the population into six groups following the methodology adopted by NCEUS. Consumption characteristics and social development levels, of households have been divided as follows:

- Extremely Poor: up to 0.75 PL;
- Poor: Between 0.75Pl and PL;
- Marginal Poor: Between PL and 1.25 PL;
- Vulnerable: between 1.25 PL and 2 PL;
- Middle: Between 2 PL and 4PL;
- Higher Income: Above 4 PL.

The four lower categories have together been characterised as"Poor and Vulnerable". The percentage of casual workers declines rapidly with improving economic status, the percentage of regular workers is only high in the last category. The Self-employed have a presence in all economic categories, but are more predominant as economic well being improves.

In terms of industrial composition, it can be seen that while agricultural workers are present in all categories in a large proportion, their weight declines in the highest while that of tertiary sector workers increases. It can also be seen that workers with higher levels of education are almost entirely present in the higher economic categories. One of the major attributes of women engaged in agriculture is their low level of educational attainment.

With the ongoing commercialisation of agriculture, crop diversification, introduction of new technologies and the imperative for better information processing, education has to be reckoned as a key input in any attempt at overall development and modernization of agriculture. However, the grim picture is that about 86 per cent of female agricultural labourers and 74 per cent of female farmers are either illiterate or have education below the primary level. Shocking as it may seem, the average education of a female agricultural labourer was less than one year in 2004-05.

WOMEN'S WORKFORCE PARTICIPATION

In this section the determinants of participation of rural women in employment is analysed by use of regression analysis. In the absence of a single data set containing all the relevant variables, this thesis first does a Logistic Regression based on unit records of the NSS Employment-Unemployment Survey of 2004-05; this is followed by a similar analysis using the unit data records of another large-scale survey, viz. the National Family Health Survey of 2005-06 which also has information on women's autonomy using certain indicators. As both these analyses confirm significant differences across states/regions, an analysis using state level variables is also carried out.

DETERMINANTS OF PARTICIPATION IN EMPLOYMENT USING NSS DATA

The analysis attempts an explanation not only of why women participate in the workforce, but also why they participate in specific types of employment.The independent variables used are: age group, marital status, education status, caste group, religion, presence of children under 5 years, land holding size category, monthly per capita consumption quintile, and region. As mentioned earlier, Logistic Regression is used since the model does not make distributional assumptions on the predictors, which can be both continuous and discrete.

Agriculture: Determinants of Work Participation

As one would expect, possession of land has a very important influence on a woman's participation in employment. Controlling for land, the household's consumption level has a negative influence. Among the individual characteristics, it is seen that compared to women in the age group 15-29, older women have a higher probability of participating in work and women in the age group 30-44 have the highest odds ratio. Compared to never married women, married, divorced and separated women have a higher probability of participating in work, with divorced or separated women having the highest odds ratio. Compared to illiterate women, women with higher levels of education have a lower probability of being in the workforce. The odds ratio declines with rising levels of education, recouping somewhat only for women who are diploma holders or graduates. Compared to scheduled tribes, all other caste groups have lower probability of participating in work, with higher castes having the lowest probability. Muslim women have a much lower probability of being in the workforce compared to Hindu women. Finally women in all other regions have significantly higher probability are being in the workforce compared to those in the eastern region.

Agriculture: Casual Workers

In this case, younger women workers have the highest probability of working as casual agricultural labourers. The marital status variable is not significant. Scheduled caste women workers have a significantly higher odds ratio of being an agricultural labourer and this probability declines steeply with rising levels of education, for Muslims and for women workers with young children. Casual agriculture wage status for workers is much less probable for women workers possessing larger holdings and in higher consumption quintiles.

Agriculture: Self-Employed Workers

The highest proportion of women workers are engaged as self-employed in agriculture. The probability of a woman worker being self-employed in agriculture is highest for the high age group and for currently married women. The odds ratio are lower for divorced or separated women indicating that these women no longer have access to land.

The odds ratio declines with increasing levels for education and is the lowest for women workers who are graduates or diploma holders. SC women workers who have the lowest access to land also have the lowest probability of being self-employed in agriculture. Muslim women workers again are less likely to be engaged in farming. As one may expect the probability of engaging in agriculture increases sharply with bigger landholdings and also with higher levels of household consumption. Women workers n the Northern region have the highest probability of being engaged in agriculture as self-employed, while women workers in the Southern region have the lowest probability of being so engaged.

Non-Agriculture: Determinants of Work Participation

Since female workers have largely remained confined to agriculture, the characteristics of workers who have moved out of agriculture are of great interest. Any type of worker in non-agriculture is taken up first. The probability of being a non-agricultural worker is highest for women in the age group 30-44 than for workers in the youngest age group and is lower for currently married women. It rises sharply with increasing levels of education. Compared to illiterate women workers, those with secondary education have an odds ratio of 4.787 while those with graduate or vocational education have an odds ratio exceeding 30. Compared to ST women workers, all other social groups have significantly higher odds ratios, the highest being for"other" caste women. Muslim workers are more than twice as likely to participate in non-agricultural work. The odds ratio declines with increasing size of land holding and is significantly higher than one for women workers belonging to the highest consumption quintile.

Non-Agriculture: Wage Workers

Non agricultural wage workers are younger and either unmarried or divorced women. The odds ratio is 0.58 for the highest age group and 0.61 for currently married women workers. The odds ratio steadily declines with higher levels of education. While there is no significant difference across social groups, Muslims have a significantly lower than 1 odds ratio. These ratios also decline dramatically with higher land holdings. The consumption level has a smaller influence on this variable but the odds ratio is significantly lower than one for the highest quintile. Compared to the reference region, the West and the North both have significantly lower odds ratios.

Non-Agriculture: Self Employed Workers

The probability of being self-employed is higher among young women workers and those who have never married. The odds ratio is significantly lower among currently married and widowed women workers. Education of the worker increases the probability of taking up self-employment, but the highest odds ratio are for those with secondary or higher secondary level of education. All social groups have higher odds ratio compared to the reference group and for the Muslim women workers, the odds ratio is more than twice as high as Hindu workers. This is principally due to the hereditary involvement of these workers' households in artisanal activities. Odds ratio declines steadily with increasing possession of land and is significantly higher than one only for the second quintile in terms of household MPCE. Women workers in the Eastern region have the highest probability of being so employed.

Non-Agriculture: Regular Workers

This is the smallest segment of workers among rural women. Compared to the reference groups, the odds ratio is higher for higher aged women and for widowed/separated women. It increases dramatically with increasingly levels of education. Among social groups it is significantly lower than 1 for OBC and upper caste women workers. The odds ratio falls with increasing size of holding and is significantly higher than one for the highest quintile. The regressions bring out a number of interesting relationships between individual, household and regional characteristics in rural India.

First, possession of land is naturally a very strong determinant of the participation of women in work and particularly their employment as women farmers. Controlling for land, the household's consumption status raises the possibility of a woman worker being self-employed either in agriculture or nonagriculture, but reduces this possibility in all other cases. It may be noted that these cases would require the worker to be employed outside the home where cultural and social roles begin to play a bigger role. Muslim women not only have a significantly lower than one odds ratio overall, this also holds for all types of employment except non-agricultural selfemployment. As far as social/caste groups are concerned, our reference is the Scheduled Tribes among whom access to land and common property resources is much higher than that for SCs which accounts for their high WPR, the odds ratio for this being the lowest among upper castes. For the same reason, SCs have the highest odds ratio for participating in agricultural wage employment, as one might expect. In non-agriculture, overall STs have the lowest probability of participation, followed by SCs, OBC and upper castes. The surprising result is that among workers, upper castes and OBCs have a lower likelihood of participation in regular work than SC/ST, controlling for all the other factors.

Considering the three demographic variables, the last has the smallest influence of participation in any/all type of work. Currently married women have a lower likelihood of working outside of homes, while single women are likelier to participate in self-employment. Other than this widowed and separated women have a higher likelihood of participating in most types of work. Other than land, education appears to be the most important determinant of employment status. Participation in the workforce as well as participation in wage employment declines with level of education, while the likelihood of participation in non-agricultural work as a whole, as well in self-employment or regular work increases with rising levels of education. From these regressions, it is apparent that while the level of education may not positively influence a woman's participation in work, for women who are in the workforce, education is indicated as the most important determinant of better quality non-agricultural work. It must be emphasised again that we are examining the outcome of social, cultural and economic processes. The potential availability of work is highest in rural areas for women whose households possess a measure of adequate landholdings. But even here, actual participation may be determined by socio-cultural factors as is evident from our results. The absence of education relegates women workers to wage work, whereas having education improves their chances of being in non-agricultural self-employment or regular work, with the latter mainly requiring higher education qualifications. Participation in wage work or non-agriculture also requires a greater measure of autonomy for women, confining the rest principally to self-employment in agriculture.

DETERMINANTS OF PARTICIPATION IN EMPLOYMENT USING NFHS, 2005-06 DATA

The National Family Health Survey has been carried out in India periodically since 1992-93. The latest round of results are available from the third round carried out in 2005-06. The NFHS collects detailed information on socioeconomic, reproductive and health characteristics of women in the age group 15-49, along with certain health and other characteristics of young children and the spouses of the women interviewed. Since the focus of the survey is on women in the reproductive age group, compared to the NSS, which covers the entire population, the NFHS gives the characteristics of a truncated age group of women.

The employment characteristics of these women are captured in the survey but not in the same manner or depth as the NSS. The survey enquires whether women are currently working or have worked in the last year. It also asks whether they work for family production or paid. The women workers are classified as per their occupational categories. Logistic regression is used to estimate the influence of several variables on participation in employment, by status and industry so that the types of employment participation considered are similar to those in the NSS analysis. But it should be noted that the NFHS does not distinguish between paid casual and regular/salaried employment which are clubbed together.

The main distinguishing feature of the NFHS, because of which this data set has been analysed in this thesis, is that it collects information on women's autonomy using a number of indicators. Among these indicators, it used a set of three indicators to capture women's freedom of mobility which in our view is central to their participation in the labour market. The three indicators of women's mobility are if they are allowed to go alone to the market/health facility/ or outside the village or community. The variables are similar to those used in earlier analysis, but with the following significant differences. First, this data has a younger age cohort. Second, as mentioned earlier, employment has been measured differently in this survey. Third, the NSS does not provide information on how many children a woman has, though it does give the number of children in a household.

With NFHS data it is possible to identify the mothers with young children. Fourthly, this thesis uses the synthetic wealth indicator given by NFHS which is built on a factor analytic score based on 33 assets. Finally, the NFHS does not allow us to estimate consumption expenditure as in the case of the NSSO and hence this variable has been dropped from the analysis. These results are similar to the earlier results in many basic ways and are not discussed here. Attention is drawn only to fresh findings.

Three main conclusions emerge sharply from the above analysis. First, the role of education is delineated more sharply among this age cohort of women. Increasing levels of education increases the possibility of women being in non-agricultural vocations. This result holds separately, both for self-employment as well as for paid work. Second, women's autonomy, proxied here by their ability to make mobility decisions autonomously, significantly increases the probability of their participation in all types of employment, except agricultural self-employment.

The reason for this is that whether it is in low paid work as casual labour or better paid work as regular workers, both take women out of the confines of the house and therefore require women to have freedom of mobility. However, where women do not have this freedom and are constrained by social norms to the home, but still need to work, self employment provides the answer. Third, women with young children are most likely to be working as self employed in agriculture and least likely to be employed as paid workers or in non-agriculture. This suggests the urgent need to provide early child care and crèche facilities for rural women.

DETERMINANTS OF STATE LEVEL VARIATIONS IN EMPLOYMENT PARTICIPATION

The large state-wise and regional difference in rural female employment participation in India has been alluded to earlier. The logit regressions confirm these differences but the NSSO data set gives very limited measures of socio-cultural differences. We therefore explore the impact of additional variables, gleaned from other data sources such as the National Family Health Survey, the Agricultural Census, the Central Statistical Organisation, and the National Bank for Rural Development on state-level variations in female employment. The WPRs by employment status and sector are also presented. Total WPRs are high in some of the Southern, Western and Hill states. They are the lowest in the Eastern states. There are important sectoral differences. For example, states such as Kerala, West Bengal and Orissa which have low total WPRs show a high participation of women in non-agriculture and the highest participation rate of women in regular work is in Kerala.

It is anticipated that these differences could be a result of supply related characteristics such as:

- The percentage of SC/ST households in a state;
- Mean years of education of women,
- Variables which could proxy women's autonomy to undertake economic activity;
- Rural wages; or
- Employment demand.

Since our objective is to understand not only total work force participation rates, but also women's participation in specific types of work, especially in non-agriculture, these rates are regressed for 20 states across the variables, selecting only one variable. The'best' fits are presented below. Some of the independent variables that were considered were found to be highly correlated, in particular with Mean Years of Education and were dropped from the analysis. Fewer numbers of variables have therefore been tested and used in the regression analysis. These are briefly discussed below.

- *Total WPR*: The share of SC/ST in the total population is highly significant variable. A one per cent increase in the share of SC/ST in the population would increase total WPR by one per cent. Share of women operated holdings in total is also marginally significant. The Mean Years of education of the population is not significant.
- *WPR in non-agriculture*: The Mean Years of Education of the female population and the density of Self-help Groups are both significant variables. Increase in Mean Years of Education would increase the WPR of women in non-agricultural vocations by 1.35.
- *WPR in non-farm self-employment*: The only variable significant in this case is the state Density of Self-help groups. The Mean Educational attainment of women in a state is not a significant determinant of state level variation of WPR in non-farm self-employment.
- *WPR in non-agricultural wage work*: Mean Years of education and Share of area operated by women are both significant variables. A one level increase in education would increase the WPR in non-agricultural wage work by 0.81. The coefficient of share of area operated by women is 0.21.

- *WPR in non-agricultural regular/salaried work*: Mean Years of education is a highly significant variable; one level increase in education would increase the WPR in regular/salaried work by 0.82. The share of area in holdings operated by women is also significant but only at 10 per cent level of significance. The coefficient of this variable is quite low.
- *Discussion*: The share of SC/ST in the population emerges as the only significant variable in explaining inter-state variation in total rural female WPR. However, interstate variations in WPR in non-agriculture as a whole, as well as participation in non-agricultural wage labour are determined by the average educational level of the female population and by variables which reflect women's economic autonomy and control over resources. However, education is not a significant variable in explaining the inter-state variations in participation by women in nonagricultural self-employment, but here also their autonomous participation in self-help groups is an important determinant. It has already been noted that the above regression analysis has been able to incorporate demand side factors to a very limited extent. This probably accounts for the fact the adjusted Coefficient of Determinations are on the low side.

CONCLUSION AND POLICY IMPLICATIONS

While women workers in general constitute a marginalised category within the class of workers, rural women workers occupy a lower position compared to their urban counterparts, and the lowest layer among them is constituted by those belonging to the bottom strata of the society *i.e.* SCs and STs. Women's time use in economic activities that give them a return is limited but their participation in household activities that indirectly contribute to the economic output of the household far exceeds that of men. But women have lower work participation rates in SNA activities. For rural women these are higher than urban women but also closer to men.

These rates are also higher for women belonging to SCs/STs than the other women. A significant percentage of rural women workers are engaged in subsidiary status work. An important argument in this thesis is that higher work participation rates *per se* do not indicate a higher level of welfare. Only when higher work participation rates are accompanied by higher educational capabilities and/or asset and income, higher work participation rates become meaningful from a welfare and, especially, income point of view. We show that rural women workers are concentrated in agriculture to a much larger extent than men. On the other hand, a much smaller proportion among them work in nonagricultural jobs, particularly the more valued regular/salaried jobs. The conditions of work, especially of women wage worker, are quite dismal. Women workers are also subjected to various forms of discrimination including job-typing which gives them a lower wage compared to men. Among the women wage workers, a proportion of those who report regular employment also work in poor conditions, receiving low wages with long hours of work, no social security and very few holidays. The position of self-employed women in non-agriculture is also poor.

Their capital base is low and consequently their value addition is also low. One third of them operate from their own homes. The overall picture that emerges is one of greater disadvantage for women workers in general and those belonging to rural as well as SCs/STs in particular. Apart from inherited social disadvantages in a patriarchal structure, the other important contributory factors are a limited access to assets and other resources, and low level of education and skills. We show that women with low levels of education and autonomous mobility whose households operate land are concentrated in agriculture as self-employed.

Poorer women who lack land but have some degree of mobility are concentrated in agricultural wage work which pays most poorly. All types of non-agricultural work require, on average, relatively more education and some degree of autonomy. The more valued jobs require a greater quantum of these. We show that these variables also determine the variations in women's participation in the more valued jobs outside agriculture. The poor status of rural women in terms of their autonomy and control over assets, and low level of education and employable skills calls for interventions of a promotional nature from different entry points. In this concluding section we draw attention to some of the major issues which emerge from our analysis;

- A higher level of education and employable skills for women workers is a sine qua nom for improving their levels of productivity and enabling them to move into nonagricultural vocations. The emphasis on universalising elementary education has undoubtedly narrowed the enrolment gap between men and women, but given the low levels of education and employable skills and the gap between men and women workers, initiatives should also focus on the exiting workforce. Further, as the results of this thesis and the evidence from other studies shows, break point occurs when women and men acquire a higher secondary level of education, enabling them to enter higher quality jobs.
- Women's autonomy, measured here in terms of access to land and control over its operation, mobility, and willingness to join self-help groups affects their ability to access resources and improve productivity, and also to move into non-agricultural vocations. Such

autonomy responds to a complex set of social factors. But policy initiatives can move the frontier outwards and can improve women's access to knowledge, technology and resources, empowering them as economic agents. Fostering a group approach, drawing upon some of the existing experiences documented by FAO and Indian experiences can help to overcome many of the existing asymmetries.

- The bulk of women workers remain in agriculture as farmers and the most recent figures indicate an increase in their proportion among farmers. As shown by a Planning Commission Sub-group and by NCEUS, they are regarded as peripheral producers and are marginal recipients of benefits of government programmes and from development and credit institutions. There is a strong need for a gender sensitive agricultural strategy which strengthens the role of women workers in all aspects of agriculture.
- Labour market segmentation and discrimination has kept the returns to women workers low, in most cases well below the legal minimum. The analysis in this thesis supports the creation of a body which can examine the issue of valuation of women's work in those activities in which women predominate in fixing minimum wages in casual wage work as well as home based work. This is in line with a recent proposal made by the National Commission for Enterprises in the Unorganised Sector which has asked for the creation of a Skill Certification Council. The Commission has also recommended a tri-partite dispute settlement framework which can help to enforce non-discriminatory practices in the informal labour market in India.
- Finally, rural women workers, especially agricultural labourers, have high rates of unemployment and underemployment among women workers. These workers also receive abysmally low wages for a variety of reasons. The National Rural Employment Guarantee Programme which has been initiated in 2006 and which has now been extended to all rural areas can play a major role in improving demand for women's labour, increasing reservation wages, and setting labour standards in rural areas. While some impact has already been felt in a number of areas, much more needs to be done to implement this scheme effectively and to increase opportunities for quality and decent work in rural areas. In our view this programme constitutes the axis around which the employment conditions of the poorest women workers can improve in rural India.

4

Women Empowerment and Micro Credit

INTRODUCTION

Alleviation of poverty, the core of all developmental effort, has remained a very complex and critical concern among developing countries. Microfinance programmes are important institutional devices for providing small credit to the rural poor in order to alleviate poverty. Professor Yunus, Managing Director of Grameen Bank, promoted it in 1974 in Jobra, a village in Chittagong of Bangladesh, and it has spread all over the world. The strength of micro credit lies in its ability to organize idle women into a productive workforce with their proven creditworthiness. In India, the emergence of liberalization and globalization in early 1990's aggravated the problem of women workers in unorganized sectors from bad to worse as most of the women who were engaged in various self employment activities have lost their livelihood. Despite tremendous contribution of women to the agriculture sector, their work is considered just an extension of household domain and remains non-monetized. This document puts forward how Micro Credit has received extensive recognition as a strategy for economic, social and personal empowerment of women and seeks to examine the impact of micro credit with respect to poverty alleviation of rural women.

METHODLOGY

For the purpose of this study data were collected from both primary and secondary sources. Secondary sources include journals, plan documents of Government of India and various study reports of NGOs and welfare organizations for women. Primary data was collected by personal interview method using structured schedules. Study was conducted in Palakkad district which is one of the backward districts of Kerala state in India. Most of the women belong to orthodox families and depends on agriculture income. Out of six taluks, three taluks namely, Ottapalam, Palakkad and Alathur taluks were selected for data collection, because the number of educated unemployed women is high in these taluks. Ten Kudumbasree units from each taluk were selected.

Two members from each Kudumbasree units were interviewed using structured questionnaire.

REVIEW OF LITERATURE

"Millions of women in our hamlets know what unemployment means. Give them access to economic activities and they will have access to power and self-confidence to which they hitherto have been strangers"— Mahatma Gandhi

Micro Credit programmes for women are promoted not only as a strategy for poverty alleviation but for women's empowerment as well. Since the early 1980s empowerment has become a key objective of development. Empowerment has been considered both an end and as a means of development. There has taken place a steady accretion of literature on the subject ever since the concept gained wide acceptance among academics and policy makers. Depending on the context concerned, empowerment is defined variously. In the present context, empowerment may be defined ideally as 'a continuous process where the powerless people become conscious of their situation and organize themselves to improve it and access opportunities, as an outcome of which women take control over their lives, set their own agenda, gain skills, solve problems and develop self-reliance.

Three different approaches have been identified by Batliwala:

i. The integrated development approach,

ii. The economic approach,

iii. Consciousness-raising-cum-awareness approach.

They are not mutually exclusive and have the potential to be linked with one another. Where (i) and (ii) address the practical needs or material conditions of women, (iii) addresses the strategic needs or position of women. Consciousness and awareness raising approach has the potential to bring about longlasting changes in the position of women and also other profound implications. The formation of Self-Help Groups is "not ultimately a micro-credit project but an empowerment process". Women's income and assets played a very important role in enhancing women's economic independence and sense of self-confidence.

Micro-credit initiatives have become increasingly popular as a way to mobilise poor communities through the provision of loans through specialised financial institutions. Small groups are formed, and loans are allocated to members, based on group solidarity instead of formal collateral. Micro credit can be a powerful vehicle for enhancing incomes and protecting households from the risk of crisis. Micro-credit schemes have been particularly targeted towards poor women, who are often discriminated against not only by institutions, but also within their own households. The provision of loans to women may then serve the dual goals of increasing household wealth and empowering females. In a country where poverty is prevalent, government can use micro credit as a tool for poverty alleviation. Micro credit serves as a precious tool rather than a panacea in the empowerment of rural women.

The evidence with respect to the impact on women's status and well-being is mixed. Some studies have found positive results, including female empowerment and decreased violence against women. Other studies have cited unintended side effects of micro-credit, including increased violence against women, negative peer-pressure linked to loan repayment, and emotional stress of females due to family-related conflicts. Personal trust between group members and social homogeneity are important to explain repayment. During the past few decades micro credit has enjoyed tremendous growth and women continue to be the major beneficiaries. During 1997-2005, the number of people receiving micro credit increased from 13.5 million to 113.3 million with 84% of them being women. For SHG programmes, the results seem to indicate that the minimalist microfinance approach is not sufficient. Additional services like training, awareness raising workshops and other activities over and above microfinance programmes that merely focus on financial services are also an important determinant of the degree of its impact on the empowerment process of women.

In India the importance of the Self Help Group is expected to grow rapidly. National Bank for Agriculture and Rural Development [NABARD] expects by the year 2009, at least one third of the rural population will be covered by one million SHGs, unlike many poverty alleviation programmes implemented in third world countries,

KUDUMBASREE PROJECTS IN KERALA

Kerala is located on the South Western tip of India. One is first struck by the greenness of the state, full of coconut groves, paddy fields, coffee plantations, and forests. Kerala is home to 32 million people, whose livelihoods depend largely on agriculture. The density of the population is very high, even by Indian standards. It is often difficult to differentiate urban and rural areas. The typical 'urban bias' with greater access to public services in urban areas, seen elsewhere in low-income countries is not present in Kerala. This is attributed both to the dispersal patterns of the population and the directive public policies towards rural development.

Table. Basic Information about Kerala

Capital	Thiruvanathapuram
Language	Malayalam
Land area	39, 000 sq km
Population	31, 838, 619
Density of population	819 per sq km
Literacy rate	90.92

In all developing countries state actions are being reinforced in streamlining poverty alleviation programmes. The Institutional formations of various means are also invigourated for initiating schemes of poverty alleviation successfully. Poverty alleviation schemes based on micro- credit system have been implemented in many of the developing countries in recent years. The Government of Kerala state in India has introduced a novel scheme of poverty alleviation based on micro-credit and self help grouping, Kudumbasree. The scheme aims at improving the living levels of the poor women in rural and urban areas. It seeks to bring the poor women folks together to form the grass root organizations to help to enhance their economic security.

The project aims at removing poverty among rural women households through setting up of micro credit and productive enterprises. The activities such as micro credit and micro-enterprises under the scheme were undertaken by the locally formed Community Development Societies consisting of poor women. The State Poverty Eradication Mission-Kudumbasree launched by the Government of Kerala in India is a massive poverty eradication programme in contemporary history. It has proved without doubt that women empowerment is the best strategy for poverty eradication.

Women, who were regarded as voiceless and powerless started identifying their inner strength, opportunities for growth, and their role in reshaping their own destiny. The process of empowerment becomes the beacon light to their children, their families and the society at large. It opens new vistas in development history. A new paradigm of participatory economics has been found emerging in "God's Own Country". Kudumbasree presents a unique model of participatory development, which can very well, be emulated other developing countries. Kudumbasree is a major initiative in Kerala aiming at women empowerment. It can be counted as a big initiative from government side after Land reformation, Complete literacy, Peoples planning and Curriculum reformation. Its has several unique achievements like:

- First major women empowerment initiative with clear targets.
- The best model for women empowerment initiatives.
- Real Kerala model initiative.

In 1991 the Government of Kerala, along with the United Nations Children‘s Fund, initiated the Community-Based Nutrition Programme in urban Alleppey town in Kerala to improve the health and nutritional status of children and women. CBNP facilitated collective action by forming and developing the capacity of three-tiered CDS, the members of which were exclusively women.

Women from families identified as poor, using a nine-point non-incomebased index, were organized into neighbourhood groups of 20 to 45 families. Each group elected a five-member committee to develop, co ordinate, and facilitate community development and action plans. NHG were federated at the ward level as area development societies [ADS] and these, in turn, were federated at the municipal level as CDS.

By 1994, the CDS approach was extended to the rural areas of Malappuram, one of the 90 most underdeveloped districts in India. Based on the positive experiences in urban Alleppey, and subsequently in rural Malappuram, in 1998 the government of Kerala scaled up the programme to cover the entire state under the name Kudumbasree. Kudumbasree is an interdepartmental initiative with staff deputed from 19 line departments.

Kudumbasree employs four key strategies to promote community development: convergence of various government programmes and resources at the CDS level, participatory antipoverty planning and implementation, formation of thrift and credit societies, and the development and nurture of micro enterprises.

The core structures of Kudumbasree are neighbourhood groups [NHGs], which meet weekly. At the weekly group meetings women deposit savings and the collective savings in turn provide the basis for small loans. The groups also become a venue for other activities. Women who demonstrate exceptional capacity and inclination to seek further economic opportunities beyond thrift may then be invited to join Self-Help or Enterprise Group comprising similarly entrepreneurial women from other NHGs. Members of SHGs receive training, and are advised on how to obtain loans for productive purposes.

ANALYSIS OF KUDUMBASREE PROJECT

For an analysis of the impact of micro credit on women's empowerment it is useful to review the kudumbasree projects in Kerala. 60 members from kudumbasree units were interviewed and data were collected on various aspects and benefits. With the help of these data analysis was done and the results were presented in this part of the document.

GENERAL INFORMATION ABOUT THE RESPONDENTS

General information about the respondents includes age, marital status, family income and occupation.

Table. Age Wise Classification of Respondents

Age	No. of Respondents	
Below 25	3 (5%)	
25-35	24	(40%)
35-45	18	(30%)
Above	45	15 (25%)
Total	60	(100%)

Table shows the age wise classification of the respondents. The age of respondents are classified as below 25 (5%), 25-35 (40%), 35-45 (30%), above 45 (25%).

Table. Classification based on Marital Status of Respondents

Age	Single	Married
Below 25	1 (1.67%)	2 (3.3%)
25-35	3 (5%)	21 (35%)
35-45	1 (1.67%)	17 (28.3%)
Above 45	1 (1.67%)	14 (23.4%)
Total	6 (10%)	54 (90%)

Table shows the marital status of the respondents. Among the total respondents 10% are single and 90% are married.

Table. Classification based on Monthly Family Income of Respondents

Income	No. of Respondents
Less than 1125 ₹	12 (20%)
1125 ₹ – 3375 ₹	33 (55%)
Above 3375 ₹	15 (25%)
Total	60 (100%)

Table shows the monthly income of the respondents.20% of the respondents are having an income less than 1125 ₹, 55% are having income between 1125 ₹ to 3375 ₹ and 25% are above 3375 ₹.

Table. Classification Based on Occupation of Respondents

Occupation	No. of Respondents
Employed	12 (20%)
Self-employed	15 (25%)
Unemployed	33 (55%)
Total	60 (100%)

Table shows the occupation status of the respondents. 20% of the respondents are employed, 25% are self employed and 55% are unemployed.

BENEFITS FROM KUDUMBASREE

The ranking of benefits based on economic, social, and personal. When asked about benefits from the group, the answers were in terms of Income, loans, wealth, savings, mutual benefits, unity, sympathy, mutual cooperation, knowledge sharing, mutual help, group strength, discussion, feeling of togetherness, greater interaction with the society, freedom, recognition, self confidence, communication, dignity, model to others, security, not to be shy, awareness, personality change and so on but when asked to rank the benefits according to importance, the responses revealed an understanding of collective strength.

A group is a resource which enables members to have mutual help, cooperation and unity. Access to this resource results in a capability to communicate, interact with people outside the household, negotiate bank loans, thus expanding their freedom to avail of opportunities for generating incomes and stabilizing household consumption, which gives them greater security.

Table. Rating of the Respondents

Benefits	Rank I	Rank II	Rank III
Economic	28	15	17
Social	15	20	15
Personal	17	20	13

RANKING OF FACTORS RELATED TO BENEFITS FROM KUDUMBASREE

Table. Conversion of Rank Percentage to Score

Rank	Percentage	Score
1	16.67	69
2	50	50
3	2.13	31

Table. Preference of Rank Converted to Score

Rank	1	2	3	Total
Economic	1932	750	527	3209
Social	1035	1000	465	2500
Personal	1173	1000	403	2576

Table. Rank Based on Average

Factors	Total score	Average score	Rank
Economic	3209	53.48	1
Social	2500	41.67	3
Personal	2576	42.93	2

Tables, depict the ranking factors related to benefits from kudumbasree. It is clear from the Table that economic benefits is the factor which influenced women to become member in the Kudumbasree followed by personal and social benefits.

Table. Factors Relating to Benefits

Economic	Social	Personal
Income	Mutual benefits	Freedom
Savings	Unity	Recognition
Loans	Sympathy	Self confidence
Wealth	Mutual cooperation	Communication
	Knowledge sharing	Dignity
	Mutual help	Model to others
	Group strength	Security
	Discussion	Not to be shy

Feeling of togetherness	Awareness
Greater interaction with society	Personality change

Table. Rating of the Respondents Regarding Economic Factors

Economic Factors	1	2	3	4
Income	18	27	11	4
Savings	22	29	6	3
Loans	7	26	12	5
Wealth	13	32	13	2

Table. Conversion of Rank Percentage to Score

Rank	Percentage	Score
1	12.5	72
2	37.5	56
3	62.5	43
4	87.5	27

Table. Preference of Rank Converted to Score

Rank	1	2	3	4	Total
Income	1296	1944	792	72	4104
Savings	1232	1624	336	168	3360
Loans	301	1118	516	215	2150
Wealth	351	864	351	54	1620

Table. Rank Based on Average

Factors	Total Score	Average Score	Rank
Income	4104	68.4	1
Savings	3360	56	2
Loans	2150	35.83	3
Wealth	1620	27	4

Table depict the ranking of the respondents regarding economic factors. It is clear from the Table that income is the most important economic factor which influences women to become members of Kudumbasree followed by savings, loans and wealth.

Table. Rating of the Respondents

Factors	1	2	3	4	5	6	7	8	9	10
Mutual benefits	15	11	8	7	6	5	3	2	2	1
Unity	14	11	10	9	5	4	3	2	1	1
Sympathy	1	1	2	2	3	5	5	10	13	18
Mutual cooperation	9	11	12	8	6	5	3	2	2	2
Knowledge sharing	1	1	1	3	4	8	9	10	11	11
Mutual help	3	8	7	4	3	9	8	10	5	3
Group strength	4	3	6	5	9	11	7	3	4	8
Discussion	1	3	4	2	8	4	16	3	13	6
Feeling of togeth-	7	8	7	11	9	7	2	5	1	1

erness										
Greater interaction with the society	5	3	3	9	4	2	4	13	8	9

Table. Conversion of Rank Percentage to Score

Rank	Percentage	Score
1	5	81
2	15	70
3	25	63
4	35	57
5	45	52
6	55	47
7	65	42
8	75	36
9	85	29
10	95	18

Table. Preference of Rank Converted to Score

Rank	Total
Mutual benefits	3709
Unity	3740
Sympathy	2353
Mutual cooperation	3550
Knowledge sharing	2224
Mutual help	2946
Group strength	2844
Discussion	2526
Feeling of togetherness	3323
Greater interaction with the society	2629

Table. Rank Based on Average

Factors	Total Score	Average Score	Rank
Mutual benefits	3709	61.82	2
Unity	3740	62.33	1
Sympathy	2353	39.22	9
Mutual cooperation	3550	59.17	3
Knowledge sharing	2224	37.07	10
Mutual help	2946	49.1	5
Group strength	2844	47.44	6
Discussion	2526	42.1	8
Feeling of togetherness	3323	55.38	4
Greater interaction with the society	2629	43.82	7

Tables depict the ranking factors regarding social benefits. It is clear from the Table that unity is the most important factor which influence women to become members of Kudumbasree followed by mutual benefits, mutual co-operation, feeling of togetherness, mutual help, group strength, greater interaction with the society, discussion, sympathy and knowledge sharing.

Table. Rating of the Respondents

Factors	1	2	3	4	5	6	7	8	9	10
Freedom	13	12	10	8	6	4	3	2	1	1
R recognition	5	11	12	4	9	3	5	6	2	3
Self confidence	8	14	10	8	7	6	3	2	1	1
Communication	1	4.	6	1	1	7	10	10	8	12
Dignity	1	1	3	5	9	6	8	7	9	11
Model to others	2	1	3	1	3	11	5	8	12	14
Security	10	5	8	9	7	8	4	6	1	2
Not to be shy	2	1	1	6	1	4	6	15	11	13
Awareness	8	4	1	3	5	9	11	3	14	2
Personality change	10	7	6	15	12	2	5	1	1	1

Table. Conversion of Rank Percentage to Score

Rank	Percentage	Score
1	5	81
2	15	70
3	25	63
4	35	57
5	45	52
6	55	47
7	65	42
8	75	36
9	85	29
10	95	18

Table. Reference of Rank Converted to Score

Rank	Total
Freedom	3724
Recognition	3306
Self confidence	3605
Communication	2397
Dignity	2422
Model to others	2108
Security	3366
Not to be shy	2222
Awareness	2497
Personality change	2947

Table. Rank Based on Average

Factors	Total score	Average score	Rank
Freedom	3724	62.06	1
Recognition	3306	55.1	4
Self confidence	3605	60.08	2
Communication	2397	39.95	8
Dignity	2422	40.36	7
Model to others	2108	35.13	10

Security	3366	56.1	3
Not to be shy	2222	37.03	9
Awareness	2497	41.61	6
Personality change	2947	49.11	5

Tables depict the ranking factors regarding personal benefits. It is clear from the Table that freedom is the most important benefit enjoyed by the members of the Kudumbasree followed by self confidence, security, recognition, personality change, awareness, dignity, communication not to be shy and model to others.

BRIEF HISTORY OF MICROFINANCE IN INDIA

The post-nationalization period in the banking sector, circa 1969, witnessed a substantial amount of resources being earmarked towards meeting the credit needs of the poor. There were several objectives for the bank nationalization strategy including expanding the outreach of financial services to neglected sectors.

As a result of this strategy, the banking network underwent an expansion phase without comparables in the world. Credit came to be recognized as a remedy for many of the ills of the poverty. There spawned several pro-poor financial services, support by both the State and Central governments, which included credit packages and programmes customised to the perceived needs of the poor.

While the objectives were laudable and substantial progress was achieved, credit flow to the poor, and especially to poor women, remained low. This led to initiatives that were institution driven that attempted to converge the existing strengths of rural banking infrastructure and leverage this to better serve the poor.

The pioneering efforts at this were made by National Bank for Agriculture and Rural Development (NABARD), which was given the tasks of framing appropriate policy for rural credit, provision of technical assistance backed liquidity support to banks, supervision of rural credit institutions and other development initiatives.

In the early 1980s, the GoI launched the Integrated Rural Development Programme (IRDP), a large poverty alleviation credit programme, which provided government subsidized credit through banks to the poor. It was aimed that the poor would be able to use the inexpensive credit to finance themselves over the poverty line.

Also during this time, NABARD conducted a series of research studies independently and in association with MYRADA, a leading non-governmental organization (NGO) from Southern India, which showed that despite having a wide network of rural bank branches servicing the rural poor, a very large number of the poorest of the poor continued to remain outside the fold of the formal banking system. These studies also showed that the existing banking policies, systems and procedures, and deposit and loan products were perhaps not well suited to meet the most immediate needs of the poor. It also appeared that what the poor really needed was better access to these services and products, rather than cheap subsidized credit.

Against this background, a need was felt for alternative policies, systems and procedures, savings and loan products, other complementary services, and new delivery mechanisms, which would fulfill the requirements of the poorest, especially of the women members of such households.

The emphasis therefore was on improving the access of the poor to microfinance rather than just micro-credit. To answer the need for microfinance from the poor, the past 25 years has seen a variety of microfinance programmes promoted by the government and NGOs.

Some of these programmes have failed and the learning experience from them have been used to develop more effective ways of providing financial services. These programmes vary from regional rural banks with a social mandate to MFIs. In 1999, the GoI merged various credit programmes together, refined them and launched a new programme called Swaranjayanti Gram Swarazagar Yojana (SGSY).

The mandate of SGSY is to continue to provide subsidized credit to the poor through the banking sector to generate self-employment through a self-help group approach and the programme has grown to an enormous size. MFIs have also become popular throughout India as one form of financial intermediary to the poor.

MFIs exist in many forms including co-operatives, Grameen-like initiatives and private sector MFIs. Thrift co-operatives have formed organically and have also been promoted by regional state organizations like the Cooperative Development Foundation (CDF) in Andhra Pradesh. The Grameen-like initiatives following a business model like the Grameen Bank.

Private sector MFIs include NGOs that act as financial services providers for the poor and include other support services but are not technically a bank as they do not take deposits. Recently, microfinance has garnered significant worldwide attention as being a successful tool in poverty reduction. In 2005, the GoI introduced significant measures in the annual budget affecting MFIs.

Specifically, it mentioned that MFIs would be eligible for external commercial borrowings which would allow MFIs and private banks to do business thereby increasing the capacity of MFIs. Also, the budget talked about plans to introduce a microfinance act that would provide some regulations on the sector.

It is clear from the previous that the objectives of the bank sector nationalization strategy have resulted into several offshoots, some of which have succeeded and some have failed. Today, Self-Help Groups and MFIs are the two dominant form of microfinance in India. This report focuses on the aspects of the SHG as an effective means to provide financial services to the poor.

EMERGENCE OF THE SHG MOVEMENT

While no definitive date has been determined for the actual conception and propagation of SHGs, the practice of small groups of rural and urban people banding together to form a savings and credit organization is well established in India. In the early stages, NGOs played a pivotal role in innovating the SHG model and in implementing the model to develop the processfully.

In the 1980s, policy makers took notice and worked with development organizations and bankers to discuss the possibility of promoting these savings and credit groups. Their efforts and the simplicity of SHGs helped to spread the movement across the country. State governments established revolving loan funds which were used to fund SHGs.

By the 1990s, SHGs were viewed by state governments and NGOs to be more than just a financial intermediation but as a common interest group, working on other concerns as well. The agenda of SHGs included social and political issues as well.

The spread of SHGs led also to the formation of SHG Federations which are a more sophisticated form of organization that involve several SHGs forming into Village Organizations (VO)/Cluster Federations and then ultimately into higher level federations (called as Mandal Samakhya (MS) in AP or SHG Federation generally).

SHG Federations are formal institutions while the SHGs are informal. Many of these SHG federations are registered as societies, mutual benefit trusts and mutually aided cooperative societies.

SHG Federations resulted in several key benefits including:

- Stronger political and advocacy capabilities
- Sharing of knowledge and experiences
- Economies of scale
- Access to greater capital

Some states have developed SHGs further than others. This report is based on the experience that APMAS has had in working with SHGs in Andhra Pradesh and limited experiences in other states.

SUPPORTING THE SHG MOVEMENT

The impact of the SHG movement on various aspects of civil society has been varied. The development of SHGs has varied from state to state but, regardless of the phase of evolution, SHGs require external help to continue to grow and have greater outreach and impact to civil society. It is clear from research that some of the obstacles to evolution are beyond the control of the SHGs. The following is a pointed analysis of where government, NGOs, Banks and others, including the private sector, can work together to help answer the needs to SHGs in a measured and effective manner in hopes of not overloading them leading to failure.

Political: Training on Governance

The impact of SHGs on women in the politics is clear; they have helped women enter the political area as they are being elected to various public offices and SHGs themselves are engaged in discussion with governing bodies. SHPIs need to be at least a few steps ahead of the SHGs, in order to be useful to them in their role in politics. Specifically, there is a need to train women on good governance because the history of poor governance has been long established. If there is to be lasting change, women need to occupy the offices of where strategic planning is done.

Social Harmony: Creating a Mixed Caste Model SHG

SHGs do not appear to be managing social tensions well. The reason for this lack of unity is difficult to identify but it could very well be the deep rooted beliefs of the caste system which tends to exclude social disadvantaged groups. These are problems have are ingrained in the ethos of the villages and it will take a very long time to change.

For SHGs to better manage social tensions, there needs to be a perception among members of equity, or ownership, in a enterprise that exists for mutual benefit. Fostering this cohesiveness is very difficult in a given the environment. SHPIs can encourage the formation of mixed groups of SHGs and make these "model" organizations for others to follow.

Social Justice: Awareness of Legal Rights and Entitlements

SHGs have played an important role in the lives of distressed members. Given the years of suppression of women in India, it is to be expected that SHGs take up the cause of their members. However, they are also responding from a desire to see justice done. Therefore, if helped to process the pros and cons of various situations and arriving at just and sustainable situations, women could be chosen by local communities as arbitrators. Arbitration in most villages is currently a male domain, but the experiences of women in negotiating for women's rights could be taken to the next logical step of involvement of women in local justice issues, whether or not a member is involved, and whether or not a member is "right". Similar to the political arena, SHPIs need to be able to provide the technical support to help SHGs equip themselves as arbitrators.

Communities: Provide Strategic Support

SHGs have helped their members and their communities. By taking a leadership role in community development, SHGs are perceived to be a guiding force for the village. Though the instances of SHGs engaging in community development is low, given the capacity, there has been proven results.

SHPIs could help facilitate processes whereby women made long-term plans for their villages as a whole, and worked steadily towards the transformation of their villages into modern and equitable hubs of creative and sustainable actions.

They might choose to focus on some core issues in each set of plans that they make, and work towards the fulfillment of these. Having persons trained to work on a larger canvas can contribute to a new cadre of political activists. Women may choose to engage directly in party politics, or to play a watchdog role from the environs of civil society–either way, they will usher in a new era of more responsible politics and public life.

Livelihoods: Technical Livelihood Support

The support of livelihoods is increasingly being seen as an important area related to microfinance. Indeed, the term of livelihood finance has been coined and is en vogue at leading NGOs. The need for livelihood support is critical to SHGs development as livelihoods are typically financed by the loans that members receive from the SHG.

The needs of SHGs varies from the introduction of new livelihoods to providing support such as market linkages or procurement techniques to refine existing livelihoods.

State government programmes such as Indira Kranthi Patham (IKP) in Andhra Pradesh have successful executed livelihood interventions on various non-timber forest products that have brought about increased cash flows to SHG members as they have been able to bypass middlemen and sell their goods at market and cut costs.

Experience has indicated that these benefits would not have possible without external intervention. Thus, SHPIs can provide the technical livelihood support as needed to help develop SHGs.

Policy Considerations

In addition to actual technical support, government policy can help support the SHG movement. Poverty is invariably characterized by lack of public investment in infrastructure or dysfunctional public systems including education and health care and underdeveloped markets. Large scale investment is required to build infrastructure like roads and bridges so that there can be access to markets.

These sorts of investment will have to be completed by the state government. The payoff such costs though is infinite. An improved infrastructure will help to increase investment and mobility of staff. Further, livelihoods can be enriched through greater access to markets. In some areas, there is a reasonable amount of infrastructure that state-owned rural banks operate.

As some SHGs have grown and matured to a sizeable scale, they need access to more financial services. Governments can address this need through their state-owned banks by introducing flexible and easily accessible products. Specifically, products such as innovative savings products, micro-insurance, larger loans and enterprise financing can be introduced.

Banks lending to SHG federations could also facilitate access to livelihood finance by the women SHG members. Not only will programmes such as these address the service gap but it will also change perceptions among bankers. If the state-owned banks take the lead, other bankers will likely follow and make an investment to work with the poor and expand their services to them.

The other Side of the Coin

This chapter has outlined several areas of working with SHGs to further their impact on civil society. It should be noted though that the sustainability of SHGs to effect such change is directly linked to their financial sustainability. While this latter issue was not the intended focus on the report, any external intervention to SHGs should bear this issue in mind. Research has shown that SHGs financial management is average or weak.

Thus, it is vitally important that both government and NGOs work to bear all the costs in mind of interventions to make them sustainable otherwise the SHGs will be over-burdened and destined to failure. Government regulations could help manage this risk and increase the emphasis on sustainability of SHGs.

There are key areas of SHG financial management that need to be improved such as internal controls, accounting, management stewardship, organizational efficiency and others. If the government were to enact policy that would regulate the quality of SHGs and tied this to their eligibility for SHG Bank Linkage, then this would help bring about a more measured and responsible growth to the movement.

Both for SHGs and SHG federations there is a need to aspire to attain standards following the best practices. As the SHG federations are emerging as community owned microfinance institutions, there is a need for significant invest-ment in providing institution building support.

These SHG federations being bodies like corporations as they are registered under an appropriate legal form, must comply with the prudential and legal norms. There is a need for a well developed third party rating system for SHG federations before they are linked with financial institutions to act as an intermediary as they handle large volume of funds from the bank linkage and also undertake savings from their members.

There is a need for establishing a computerized MIS for SHGs and SHG federations to monitor their performance on a regular basis. SHG Federations must be able to publish their annual reports and share those with all their members. Governance of SHG federations is a major challenge.

For the SHG members to manage their own institutions with professional staff and large volumes of transactions will be difficult. SHPIs must provide the needed support for the SHG federations to develop into sustainable institutions of the poor. Considerable investments would be needed to facilitate and sustain SHG federations across the nation.

EMPOWERING WOMEN THROUGH MICROFINANCE

According to the State of the Microcredit Summit Campaign 2001 Report, 14.2 million of the world's poorest women now have access to financial services through specialized *microfinance institutions* (MFIs), banks, NGOs, and other non-bank financial institutions. These women account for nearly 74 percent of the 19.3 million of the world's poorest people now being served by microfinance institutions. Most of these women have access to credit to invest in businesses that they own and operate themselves. The vast majority of them have excellent repayment records, in spite of the daily hardships they face. Contrary to conventional wisdom, they have shown that it is a very good idea to lend to the poor and to women.

So, given these impressive statistics, can we pat ourselves on the back for our service to poor women and assume that women's empowerment and other gender issues will take care of themselves? Although women's access to financial services has increased substantially in the past 10 years, their ability to benefit from this access is often still limited by the disadvantages they experience because of their gender. Some MFIs are providing a decreasing percentage of loans to women, even as these institutions grow and offer new loan products. Others have found that on average women's loan sizes are smaller than those of men, even when they are in the same credit programme, the same community, and the same lending group. Some differences in loan sizes may be a result of women's greater poverty or the limited capacity of women's businesses to absorb capital. But they can also indicate broader social discrimination against women which limits the opportunities open to them, raising the question of whether microenterprise development programmes should do more to address these issues.

And looking at the leadership of many MFIs, we see very few women. Their contributions—whether setting the vision on a board of directors, designing products and services, or implementing programmes—are missing. Thus, as the industry becomes more sophisticated in developing targeted products and services, it makes sense to look at both targeting women and empowering women. Microfinance programmes have the potential to transform power relations and empower the poor—both men and women. In well-run microfinance programmes, there is a relationship of respect between the provider and the client that is inherently empowering.

This is true regardless of the methodology or approach (whether the institution takes a minimalist approach of delivering financial services only or a more holistic or integrated approach). As a consequence, microfinance has become a central component of many donor agencies' and national governments' gender, poverty alleviation, and community development strategies. Several studies and the experiences of a number of MFIs have shown, however, that simply putting financial resources in the hands of poor women is not enough to bring about empowerment and improved welfare. In this paper we demonstrate that although microfinance does not address all the barriers to women's empowerment, microfinance programmes, when properly designed, can make an important contribution to women's empowerment. We begin by examining some of the theories and assumptions behind the targeting of women for microfinance and the resulting implications for empowerment. Drawing on the studies and experiences of microfinance institutions in Africa, Asia, and Latin America, the paper looks at what evidence is known about impact on women, in terms of both welfare and empowerment. While acknowledging that there is no set of indicators of empowerment that can be applied universally across cultures and regions, we present evidence of several types of changes that are relevant and important for empowerment across a range of cultures. The heart of the paper is an in-depth case study of the impact on women achieved by Sinapi Aba Trust (SAT), Opportunity International's partner in Ghana. Based on that study and the experiences of other MFIs, we identify several programmatic factors and strategies that can make a positive contribution to women's empowerment and holistic transformation, including business training, discussion of social issues, support and advice for balancing family and business responsibilities, experience in decision making and leadership, and ownership and control of the credit institution.

We also look at the role that women's economic contribution to the household and community plays in empowering them. We then look at some strategies used by MFIs for reaching and empowering women and their results, identifying some of the most promising. Our reading, research, and experience have turned up rich examples of empowerment, but have also raised many questions that suggest some important areas for future work. We therefore conclude by issuing a call to action for practitioners and donors, so that the tremendous potential of microfinance to empower women can be fulfilled.

TARGETING WOMEN

International aid donors, governments, scholars, and other development experts have paid much attention to microfinance as a strategy capable of reaching women and involving them in the development process. The microfinance industry has made great strides towards identifying barriers to women's access to financial services and developing ways to overcome those barriers. A 2001 survey by the Special Unit on Microfinance of the United Nations Capital Development Fund (SUM/UNCDF) of 29 microfinance institutions revealed that approximately 60 percent of these institutions' clients were women. Six of the 29 focused entirely on women. Among the remaining 23 mixed-sex programmes, 52 percent of clients were women. The study also showed, however, that those programmes offering only individual loans or relatively high minimum loan amounts tended to have lower percentages of women clients.

These findings affirm the importance of designing appropriate products for women. According to USAID's annual Microenterprise Results Report for 2000, approximately 70 percent of USAID-supported MFIs' clients were women. Considerable variation among the regions was seen, however, with percentages of women clients ranging from 27 percent in the Near East to 87 percent in Asia. In Eastern Europe, where USAID has traditionally supported individual-lending programmes, the percentage of women clients dropped as low as 48 percent in 1999 before rising to 54 percent in 2000, when USAID began to support more group-lending programmes offering smaller loans.

Although the UNCDF study found that larger programmes tended to have lower percentages of women clients, data collected by the Microcredit Summit Campaign found no statistically significant correlation between the number of very poor clients served by each institution and the percentage of those clients who were women. Microfinance institutions around the world have been quite creative in developing products and services that avoid barriers that have traditionally kept women from accessing formal financial services such as collateral requirements, male or salaried guarantor requirements, documentation requirements, cultural barriers, limited mobility, and literacy.

Nevertheless, in a number of countries and areas few or no institutions offer financial services under terms and conditions that are favourable to women. Together, these findings confirm that the type of products offered, their conditions of access, and the distribution of an institution's portfolio among different products and services affect women's access to financial services. They also suggest that much more can be done to serve poor women in certain cultural and economic contexts.

WHY TARGET WOMEN? THEORIES, ASSUMPTIONS, AND REALITY

Many different rationales can be offered for placing a priority on increasing women's access to microfinance services.

Gender and Development

Research done by UNDP, UNIFEM, and the World Bank, among others, indicates that gender inequalities in developing societies inhibit economic growth and development. For example, a recent World Bank report confirms that societies that discriminate on the basis of gender pay the cost of greater poverty, slower economic growth, weaker governance, and a lower living standard of their people. The UNDP found a very strong correlation between its gender empowerment measure and gender-related development indices and its Human Development Index. Overall, evidence is mounting that improved gender equality is a critical component of any development strategy.

Microfinance has come to play a major role in many of these donors' gender and development strategies because of its direct relationship to both poverty alleviation and women. As CIDA recognizes in its gender policy, "Attention to gender equality is essential to sound development practice and at the heart of economic and social progress. Development results cannot be maximized and sustained without explicit attention to the different needs and interests of women and men." As part of its poverty reduction priority, CIDA supports programmes that provide "increased access to productive assets (especially land, capital, and credit), processing, and marketing for women." By giving women access to working capital and training, microfinance helps mobilize women's productive capacity to alleviate poverty and maximize economic output. In this case, women's entitlement to financial services, development aid, and equal rights rests primarily on their potential contribution to society rather than on their intrinsic rights as human beings and members of that society.

Women Are the Poorest of the Poor

It is generally accepted that women are disproportionately represented among the world's poorest people. In its 1995 Human Development Report, the UNDP reported that 70 percent of the 1.3 billion people living on less than $1 per day are women. According to the World Bank's gender statistics database, women have a higher unemployment rate than men in virtually every country. In general, women also make up the majority of the lower paid, unorganized informal sector of most economies. These statistics are used to justify giving priority to increasing women's access to financial services on the grounds that women are relatively more disadvantaged than men.

Although many scholars and development agencies have noted an apparent trend towards the "feminization of poverty," measuring the extent to which this is occurring presents many challenges. Because most methods of measuring poverty assess the level of poverty of the household as a whole, it is likely that poverty experienced by women as a result of discrimination against them within their households is underreported to a great extent. In addition, Baden and Milward note that "Although women are not always poorer than men, because of the weaker basis of their entitlements, they are generally more vulnerable and, once poor, may have less options in terms of escape." By providing access to financing for income-generating activities, microfinance institutions can significantly reduce women's vulnerability to poverty. A reduction in women's vulnerability can sometimes also translate into empowerment if greater financial security allows the women to become more assertive in household and community affairs.

Women Spend More of Their Income on Their Families

Women have been shown to spend more of their income on their households; therefore, when women are helped to increase their incomes, the welfare of the whole family is improved. In its report on its survey findings the Special Unit on Microfinance of the UNCDF explains, "Women's success benefits more than one person. Several institutions confirmed the well-documented fact that women are more likely than men to spend their profits on household and family needs. Assisting women therefore generates a multiplier effect that enlarges the impact of the institutions' activities." Women's Entrepreneurship Development Trust Fund (WEDTF) in Zanzibar, Tanzania, also reports that "women's increased income benefits their children, particularly in education, diet, health care, and clothing."

According to a WEDTF report, 55 percent of women's increased income is used to purchase household items,18 percent goes for school, and 15 percent is spent on clothing. In her research on the poverty level of female-headed households, Sylvia Chant, a researcher at the London School of Economics, cites a number of studies on Latin America that lend credibility to the commonly held belief that women spend a greater percentage of their income on their households than do men. She writes, "In Guadalajara, Mexico, for example, Gonzalez de la Rocha notes that men usually only contribute 50 percent of their salaries to the collective household fund. In Honduras, this averages 68 percent, and from my own survey data in the Mexican cities of Puerto Vallarta, Leon and Queretaro in 1986, the equivalent allocation is 67.5 per cent. Women, on the other hand, tend to keep nothing back for themselves, with the result that more money is usually available in women-headed households for collective household expenditure."

And Naila Kabeer writes, "there are sound reasons why women's interests are likely to be better served by investing effort and resources in the collective welfare of the household rather than in their own personal welfare." But Kabeer also cautions that it is important to recognize that those incentives may change when women become empowered and have new options. Women who are empowered will have the power to make the life choices that are best for them, and although many empowered women will choose to invest in their families, development organizations must be prepared for the possibility that some will not.

Efficiency and Sustainability

Arguments have been made for and against targeting women on the grounds of efficiency and sustainability. Proponents of targeting women on the grounds of sustainability cite women's repayment records and cooperativeness. A collective wisdom has emerged that women's repayment rates are typically far superior to those of men. Lower arrears and loan loss rates have an important effect on the efficiency and sustainability of the institution. Many programmes have also found women to be more cooperative and prefer to work with them for that reason as well.

The experience of Sinapi Aba Trust, Opportunity International's partner in Ghana, demonstrates a clear difference in men and women's repayment records in its Trust Bank programme, a group-lending methodology similar to village banking. In spite of the large number of institutions serving exclusively or predominantly women while maintaining high levels of financial sustainability, some people argue that institutions that place a priority on serving women also have a tendency to place social goals ahead of efficiency, leading to poorer financial performance. Based on his experience at MicroRate, Damian von Stauffenberg offers one hypothesis along these lines: "In our experience, on average 60–70 per cent of borrowers of MFIs are female.

We sometimes see higher percentages of women borrowers but in those cases portfolio quality tends to suffer. Why this is so is not entirely clear, but one hypothesis is that MFIs which concentrate exclusively on women may place ideological goals ahead of technical competence. Whether this is true remains to be proven." Although it is true that some socially driven institutions may choose to offer additional social services to their clients which may make them less profitable than those institutions focusing solely on profitable financial service delivery, there appears to be no reason that portfolio quality should have to suffer or that social objectives and technical competence cannot go hand in hand.

In fact, a deeper understanding of the social context and forces in which microfinance operates can allow for more effective risk management and more appropriate product and process design that may improve portfolio quality in the long run. In its survey, however, SUM/UNCDF did not find any clear correlation between outreach to women and financial self-sufficiency. The report states, "If anything, in this very limited pool, the institutions with higher levels of self-sufficiency served proportionally more women than institutions less self-sufficient." A related belief is that group-lending programmes that reach women and poorer clients are less sustainable than institutions reaching higher-level clients with individual loans, yet this concern has been thoroughly addressed by Gary Woller in his comparative analysis of village banking institutions and individual lending institutions for the MicroBanking Bulletin. His conclusion is that the answer to the question "'Can village banking institutions become self-sufficient?' is 'Yes!'

Not only that, [VBIs] *village banking institutions* can reach levels of self-sufficiency achieved by solidarity group and individual lenders." Programmes that serve a significant number of men are more likely to use methodologies that require collateral and more extensive monitoring procedures to help reduce the risk of default, while programmes designed to serve primarily women tend to replace formal monitoring procedures with social guarantees. Generally, MFIs are able to balance more costly procedures with larger loans, while many institutions targeting women have relied on client capacity for self-monitoring and cooperation to reach out to women who otherwise might have been excluded because of the small amount of capital they require.

Women's Rights Perspective

Women's equal access to financial resources is a human rights issue. Because access to credit is an important mechanism for reducing women's poverty it has been an explicit focus of a variety of human rights instruments. Both the Convention on the Elimination of Discrimination Against Women (CEDAW) and the Beijing Platform for Action (BPFA) address women's access to financial resources. For example, the BPFA includes 35 references to enabling poor women to gain access to credit. International and national instruments that establish women's rights to credit promote government responsibility and accountability in meeting commitments to women's rights.

Empowering Women

Last, but not least, one of the often articulated rationales for supporting microfinance and the targeting of women by microfinance programmes is that microfinance is an effective means or entry point for empowering women. By putting financial resources in the hands of women, microfinance institutions help level the playing field and promote gender equality.

WHAT DO WE MEAN WHEN WE TALK ABOUT EMPOWERMENT?

Most of us, when asked, have a great deal of difficulty defining empowerment. The word does not even translate literally into many languages. Yet most of us know empowerment when we see it. One loan officer at Sinapi

Aba Trust in Ghana defined empowerment as "enabling each person to reach his or her God-given potential." Some clients have used the terms self-reliance and self-respect to define it. According to UNIFEM, "gaining the ability to generate choices and exercise bargaining power," "developing a sense of self-worth, a belief in one's ability to secure desired changes, and the right to control one's life" are important elements of women's empowerment.

Empowerment is an implicit, if not explicit, goal of a great number of microfinance institutions around the world. Empowerment is about change, choice, and power. It is a process of change by which individuals or groups with little or no power gain the power and ability to make choices that affect their lives. The structures of power—who has it, what its sources are, and how it is exercised—directly affect the choices that women are able to make in their lives. Microfinance programmes can have tremendous impact on the empowerment process if their products and services take these structures into account. In order for a woman to be empowered, she needs access to the material, human, and social resources necessary to make strategic choices in her life. Not only have women been historically disadvantaged in access to material resources like credit, property, and money, but they have also been excluded from social resources like education or insider knowledge of some businesses. Access to resources alone does not automatically translate into empowerment or equality, however, because women must also have the ability to use the resources to meet their goals. In order for resources to empower women, they must be able to use them for a purpose that they choose. Naila Kabeer uses the term agency to describe the processes of decision making, negotiation, and manipulation required for women to use resources effectively. Women who have been excluded from decision making for most of their lives often lack this sense of agency that allows them to define goals and act effectively to achieve them.

However, these goals also can be heavily influenced by the values of the society in which women live and so may sometimes replicate rather than challenge the structures of injustice. The weight of socialization is eloquently expressed by one woman activist from Prishtina, Kosovo: "There is education in the family: first you shouldn't speak because you are a girl, then later you shouldn't speak because no one will marry you, then later you shouldn't speak because you are a new bride. Finally, you might have the chance to speak but you don't speak because you have forgotten how to." The influence of society over the range and exercise of choice also means that if we seek to promote empowerment, we must also consider factors affecting women's status and rights as a group. Although many microfinance programmes promote social solidarity at some level, most microfinance organizations tend to focus their attention on promoting changes at an individual level—a woman who, for instance, is now able to send her children to school, negotiate lower prices for her raw materials, or even dream bigger dreams for herself, her family, and her business. The achievements of individual women can have a powerful impact on the way women are perceived and treated within their communities, but the levels of empowerment individual women may achieve are usually limited if women as a group are generally disempowered. For that reason many organizations also include elements designed to uplift women and communities as a collective rather than just as individuals. Some examples:

- A women's Trust Bank in Colombia organizing to bring electricity to their barrio,
- Women fighting against domestic violence after learning about their rights in their lending centers in Nepal, and
- Working Women's Forum in India organizing women weavers to break the monopoly access to raw materials that the all-male government-sponsored weavers' cooperatives enjoyed.

At Opportunity International empowerment is a critical part of our vision for holistic transformation. Seeking to enable the poor to become agents of change in their communities, our approach encompasses social, economic, political, and spiritual empowerment within the individual, household, business, and community. In most cases, we have found that these processes are mutually reinforcing. The empowerment of women at the individual level helps build a base for social change. Movements to empower women as a group increase opportunities available to individual women, and economic empowerment can increase women's status in their families and societies. Practically speaking, the interrelatedness of different aspects of empowerment and between empowerment and development makes it very difficult to move far ahead in any one area without corresponding changes in other areas. Sooner or later, lack of empowerment will slow down economic and political development, just as a lack of progress in meeting people's basic needs will limit empowerment because poverty itself is disempowering.

WHY SHOULD MFIS CARE ABOUT WOMEN'S EMPOWERMENT?

"Empowerment of women and gender equality are prerequisites for achieving political, social, economic, cultural, and environmental security among all peoples." As this statement from the Fourth United Nations World Conference on Women and much of the evidence presented thus far in this paper have shown, women's empowerment is a critical part of sustainable development. Yet microfinance's great potential to empower poor women to a large extent often goes unrealized. Although studies show that microfinance can and does empower women, it has the potential to empower many more, even more greatly.

OBJECTIONS TO A FOCUS ON EMPOWERING WOMEN

Given the enthusiasm that many donors and practitioners have shown for the empowering potential of microfinance, why are many MFIs reluctant to focus on women's empowerment when designing their systems and programmes? Their rationales range from the belief that empowerment will happen naturally as a result of a good microfinance programme to the concern that paying attention to empowerment will distract MFIs and their managers from running their institutions sustainably. In this section we explore a few of these concerns.

DOES ACCESS TO CREDIT AUTOMATICALLY LEADS TO EMPOWERMENT?

The basic theory is that microfinance empowers women by putting capital in their hands and allowing them to earn an independent income and contribute financially to their households and communities. This economic empowerment is expected to generate increased self-esteem, respect, and other forms of empowerment for women beneficiaries. Involvement in successful income-generating activities should translate into greater control and empowerment. Closer examination shows us, however, that this equation may not always hold true and that complacency in these assumptions can lead MFIs to overlook both opportunities to empower women more profoundly and failures in empowerment. The ability of a woman to transform her life through access to financial services depends on many factors—some of them linked to her individual situation and abilities, and others dependent upon her environment and the status of women as a group. Control of capital is only one dimension of the complex and ever-changing process by which the cycles of poverty and powerlessness replicate themselves. Women also face disadvantages in accessing information, social networks, and other resources they need to succeed in business and in life. Only by evaluating the needs of women will an MFI be able to maximize its empowerment potential.

Programmes Seeking to Become Financially Sustainable Cannot Afford to Focus on Women's Empowerment

Some practitioners are reluctant to adopt women's empowerment as a central focus of their programmes because they fear that it will interfere with the efficiency and professionalism of their financial operations. They fear that an intentional focus on women's empowerment may lead them to additional activities that could draw resources and energy away from the core business of providing financial services to the poor in a sustainable way. We do find, however, that there are "empowering approaches" to delivery of traditional microfinance services that are often compatible with and no more costly than other ways of achieving organizational efficiencies. An empowering approach is often found among organizations that are committed to excellence and particularly excellent customer service.

For instance, FORA in Russia places a high priority on short turn-around times between loan approval and disbursement, as a means of respecting the client's time and business, and a 1997 study of Sinapi Aba Trust in Ghana found that the most empowering aspect of its various programmes was the respect with which clients were treated by people at all levels of the organization. These practices are empowering without being costly. Knowing and understanding your clients and potential clients is an important part of ensuring that products and services are empowering for them. Maria Otero, President and CEO of ACCION International, reminds us of the basics of designing products for women that were groundbreaking just 20-30 years ago. She writes: "a sustainable institution that empowers women can do so by first paying attention to the following:

- understand the characteristics of women's economic activity: (for example, smaller businesses than men, smaller cash flow, more likely reaches a smaller market);
- know the skill and time constraints of women (less literacy, fewer marketable skills, domestic and child care responsibilities)."

This kind of client awareness helps MFIs offer loans and other products that are appropriate and empowering. Sofol-Compartamos, an ACCION affiliate in Mexico, has successfully created this client feedback loop by bringing together the general manager, loan officers, and some clients to discuss the characteristics of current products as well as products that clients would like to access in the future. It does not have to be expensive to incorporate client input into programme design. Sofol-Compartamos-a fully financially sustainable, regulated finance company-has grown to serve more than 100,000 clients while continuing to be responsive to clients' needs.

CETZAM, an Opportunity partner in Zambia, estimates that just a one percent drop in arrears resulting from programme improvements would pay for the cost of its impact and client satisfaction monitoring. "Soft" services like health education, literacy training, business training, or discussion and support groups on issues like domestic violence or divorce rights are often assumed to be costly and to lack clear, easily measurable outputs and outcomes. Yet, as Christopher Dunford so eloquently argues in his paper "Building Better Lives," there can be powerful synergies between the provision of financial services and some non-financial services like education. Programmes with development objectives can achieve "economies of scope" by "packaging two or more services together to minimize delivery and management support costs and to maximize the variety of benefits for people's multiple needs and wants." And, in an innovative example of incorporating non-financial services in a cost-effective way, village banking programmes invest in client leadership development in return for cost savings as clients take on some of the responsibilities for managing loan repayments and other transactions of their lending groups. Another reason for the lack of attention to women's empowerment in mainstream microfinance is that MFIs fear that building empowering elements into their programmes will threaten their financial sustainability ratios and limit their access to funds from major bilateral and multilateral donor agencies.

Many donors agencies' funding criteria focus primarily on outreach and institutional sustainability criteria and do not "reward" programmes that are able to demonstrate greater and more sustainable impact on their clients. The incentive structures lead many MFIs to consider including programme elements intentionally empowering for women as "extras" or "luxuries" rather than as an integral part of their programme design and goals. But many MFIs with a strong focus on empowerment maintain very high levels of operational and financial sustainability, suggesting that a great deal can be done to enhance women's empowerment even within the constraints of financial sustainability.

Working Women's Forum (WWF) in India, for example, is fully financially sustainable and offers a range of non-financial services, including organizing women in the informal sector to achieve better wages and working conditions. WWF also empowers poor women through its institutional structure by training them to act as health promoters and credit officers in their neighbourhoods. Several Women's World Banking affiliates also manage to maintain a balance between strong financial performance standards and empowerment. For example, ADOPEM, in the Dominican Republic, has more than 28,000 borrowers and a financial sustainability ratio of 127 percent and is in the process of becoming a regulated financial institution. Yet ADOPEM, whose mission is to incorporate women and their families into the economic and financial system through the provision of credit and training, and to strengthen the position of women entrepreneurs with micro-, small-, and medium-sized businesses, provides more than just loans to its clients. ADOPEM not only provides business training for its clients but offers training in a range of areas including democratic processes and civil society participation designed to encourage women's empowerment and leadership. In addition, ADOPEM supports the Association of Women in Small and Microenterprise (ANAMUMPE), which provides access to information on training events and legislative issues and has given women an opportunity to participate in working groups organized by the government on issues affecting microenterprise. Women's Empowerment Is a "Western"

Concept

The question has been raised, not only in microfinance but also in the broader field of international development, whether it is ethical and appropriate for development institutions to promote women's empowerment. The empowerment or disempowerment of women and other groups in each society is closely linked to the culture of that society. The promotion of women's empowerment implies advocacy for cultural and social change, which some fear is an inappropriate imposition of "Western" values on non-Western societies. Yet, even if we set aside culturally relative values for a moment and look objectively at human welfare, we can see that gender inequalities and discrimination against women contribute directly to the perpetuation of poverty in many nations.

Many independent, indigenous women's organizations around the world have contributed to their countries' development by leading long and successful struggles for women's empowerment. Organizations like SEWA and Working Women's Forum in India have organized and mobilized hundreds of thousands of Indian women to work for women's empowerment and rights with little or no "outside" assistance or influence. For example, in areas where women beedi-rollers' poverty was exploited by contractors, and often led to permanent indebtedness and child mortgage or bondage, WWF successfully organized women to demand higher wages and the release of children from bondage. Moreover, in some cases poor countries have surpassed developed countries in terms of women's representation, existence of women's machineries and ratification of instruments and conventions. This illustrates government awareness of the need to address women's empowerment. Although desired outcomes and goals of empowerment are culturally relative, empowerment itself is not a Western concept.

IMPACT ON SELF-CONFIDENCE

Self-confidence is one of the most crucial areas of change for empowerment, yet it is also one of the most difficult to measure or assess. Self-confidence is a complex concept relating to both women's perception of their capabilities and their actual level of skills and capabilities. It is related to Kabeer's concept of agency that allows women to define and achieve goals as well as the sense of power women have within themselves.

Jeffrey Ashe and Lisa Parrott's study of the Women's Empowerment Project in Nepal showed that an increase in self-confidence and enlarged spheres of influence were the top two changes reported by 200 sampled groups. URWEGO in Rwanda found that the greatest impact of its programme on empowerment had been on self-esteem, with 69 percent of clients reporting increased self-esteem. Self-esteem and self-confidence are closely linked with knowledge as well. Fifty-four percent of URWEGO clients reported an increase in their level of knowledge about issues that affect themselves and their families, and 38 percent of clients reported an increase in business knowledge.

IMPACT ON WOMEN'S STATUS AND GENDER RELATIONS IN THE HOME

Access to credit and participation in income-generating activities is assumed to strengthen women's bargaining position within the household, thereby allowing her to influence a greater number of strategic decisions. Particularly in poor communities, men's domination of women is strongest within the household.

As Naila Kabeer points out, "Many feminists recognize that poor men are almost as powerless as poor women in access to material resources in the public domain, but remain privileged within the patriarchal structure of the family." In some societies, being seen by neighbours as in control of his family and wife is a key element of men's social prestige—particularly in impoverished communities where men may be able to boast of few other status symbols. In Costa Rica, for example, none of ADAPTE's women clients who were surveyed reported feeling that their gender limited their occupational choices.

One woman even commented that she thought that she could do better at business because she was a woman. Such responses seem to indicate that these Costa Rican women enjoyed a great deal of freedom of choice in their occupations. Yet many of the responses of the husbands of ADAPTE clients reflected a deep ambivalence and struggle with their wives' new economic independence. One husband commented that he appreciated his wife's ability to earn her own income so that she could pay for things she wanted without asking him for money.

He liked his wife's independence because "although she doesn't give me anything, neither does she ask for anything from me." He considers the growth of her business to be generally positive but then adds that it has not been easy for him to become accustomed to it. When asked how he felt about his wife's increasing independence and growing tendency to make decisions alone, he explained, "Because of my machismo I see [the changes] as negative, but deep down, I know that they are positive for her." In spite of the difficulty that some men have in accustoming themselves to their wives' new role, most women report improved relationships with their husbands and families. Evidence of changes in gender roles within the household, however, is limited. World Education reported that although husbands, in-laws, and children help out at home while the women attend programme meetings, women's workload increases as they start utilizing their loans more. Also working in Nepal, CSD found that the economic role of women remained restricted to managing the loans and supplementing household income to meet household expenses but did not lead to a substantial change in gender relations in the home in the majority of households.

IMPACT ON FAMILY RELATIONSHIPS AND DOMESTIC VIOLENCE

Although there have been a few studies that have asserted that women's participation in microfinance leads to an increase in domestic violence, most practitioners have reported the opposite experience. The concerns arise over a "backlash effect" that may occur as a result of women challenging gender norms and asserting their rights. Microfinance programmes can strengthen women's economic autonomy and give them the means to pursue non-traditional activities. In some cases, women who begin to assert themselves and their opinions in their households incur the wrath of angry husbands who feel their authority and sometimes their reputations are being threatened by their wives' behaviour. Although there are many good reasons for MFIs to be watchful for potential rises in domestic violence, the bulk of the evidence and experience thus far seems to point to the conclusion that participation in microfinance strengthens and improves family relationships rather than destroying them.

Poverty, scarcity, and feelings of helplessness take an undeniable toll on personal relationships. Many practitioners have found that family relationships can be strengthened when the home becomes a more comfortable place to be, and when each member of the family feels secure in his or her ability to contribute productively to the family. Women at Sinapi Aba Trust in Ghana, for example, clearly attributed the increase in respect from their husband and the reduction in arguments to their economic contribution and a reduction in scarcity. Naila Kabeer's study of SEDP shows women making a direct causal link between their contribution to the household and a reduction in abuse. For example, one client of SEDP quoted by Kabeer states:

- He gives me more value since the loan. I know, because now he hands all his earnings to me. If I had not gone to the meeting, not taken a loan, not learnt the work, I would not get the value I have, I would have to continue to ask my husband for every taka I needed.... Before, my husband used to beat me when I asked him for money, now, even if he doesn't earn enough every day, I can work, we don't have to suffer.

Balbina, a client of ASPIRE, Opportunity's partner in the Dominican Republic, described the frustration that she and her husband felt about their poverty and their inability to work productively to change their situation. That changed when she used her first loan to invest in a business making and selling chicharrones (pork rind snacks) together with her husband. She talked about the difference within their home as a result of having productive work and greater assets: "We were fighting tooth and nail because my husband was unemployed and we had nothing to do.

Now we work together, and each of us has something productive to do and a way to direct our energies." Hashemi et al. found fewer incidences of violence against women among women who were members of credit organizations than they found among the general population. Although fear of public exposure clearly played a role in the reduction of violence, there is considerable anecdotal evidence of women attributing the reduction of abuse directly to their access to credit and their economic contribution to the household. Another study by Schuler et al. suggests that the level of women's economic contribution to the family may also be significant. Evidence suggests that participation in microfinance programmes may give women the means to escape from abusive relationships or limit abuse in their relationships. Working Women's Forum found that 40.9 percent of its members who had experienced domestic violence stopped it because of their personal empowerment, while 28.7 percent were able to stop it through group action. CSD in Nepal also noticed a greater resistance to wife beatings and alcoholism among its clients. And in Bangladesh, where social pressure to remain married is high, Kabeer found that several women in abusive relationships were able to establish spheres of autonomy for themselves within their marriage so that they would have to depend on their husbands as little as possible.

There is anecdotal evidence of reducing domestic violence against children as well. For example, Sabina Cutiba, a client of ADEMCOL, Opportunity's partner in Bogotá, Colombia, had experienced a lifetime of abusive relationships but learned a new way to interact with her children as a result of her Trust Bank programme. "I used to fight, complain a lot, be negative. I would complain to friends of mine and cry out with my frustrations.... This lady who has been giving these conferences and talking with me has really strengthened me. I've had a total change.... Before I used to beat my children. I hit them a lot. But not anymore—now I'm a different person." In spite of fears by some that giving loans to women could disrupt social order and destroy families, there is little evidence of this occurring. In her study of both male and female clients of SEDP, Naila Kabeer found that women were much more likely to seek the strengthening of their relative position within an interdependent relationship with their husbands than they were to seek independence and autonomy.

IMPACT ON WOMEN'S INVOLVEMENT AND STATUS IN THE COMMUNITY

Several microfinance and microenterprise support programmes have observed improvements in women's status in their communities. Contributing financial resources to the family or community confers greater legitimacy and value to women's views and gives them more entitlements than they would otherwise have. Studies of microfinance clients from various institutions around the world show that the women themselves very often perceive that they receive more respect from their families and their communities— particularly from the male members—than they did before joining a microfinance programme. Where women have the freedom to move about publicly, their success in business is often highly visible in the community. Their success can pave the way for them to become respected and valued members of society. For example, in Zanzibar, Tanzania, women from one of WEDTF's credit groups enjoyed considerable prestige and empowerment as a result of their successful joint business selling kerosene:

- Before the credit support we never even went to the market. We were solely dependent on our husbands. Now group activities and the intensive training from the scheme have opened our eyes. We now know that we are better in business than men. We were the only women selling kerosene in the village. The whole community admired our determination. We have urged our fellow women to put their veils down. Some have started their own income generating activities.—Halima Juma Hamadi

Most studies have been based on women's perceptions of how others treat and perceive them, so it is possible that their responses were affected by their own increasing self-esteem and self-confidence as much as by actual changes in the way they were perceived in the community. Some women, however, do cite specific examples of how their interactions in the community have changed and how the improvement in their status is manifested. One woman in Ghana commented that men no longer spoke to her disrespectfully but spoke to her rather more as an equal.

Other women noted that they have been invited to participate in and speak at community meetings, whereas before they would have been ignored or excluded. Similarly, a study done by Freedom From Hunger on its programme in Ghana noted that significantly more participants than non-participants were giving advice in their communities—particularly on topics they had studied in their credit groups. Eighty-seven percent of Credit With Education clients had given business advice in the last six months at the time of the study, compared with 35 percent of non-participants and 50 percent of members of control communities. The Freedom From Hunger study also showed that substantially fewer (44 percent) of these women had given business advice in the six months before joining the programme three years earlier. In the CSD programme, women members own their center houses that provide them with a social space for gatherings. These houses are a symbol of their unity, strength, and positive contribution to the community and are a source of pride for the women.

In CSD communities, the perception of women's economic role is slowly changing. Women are gaining respect for their work, which has traditionally been undervalued. Women's increased economic role is improving their position in society by allowing them to prove their economic capabilities. The awareness of the importance of their economic roles has given some women the confidence to detach themselves from the conservative practices of purdah that used to confine their activities to their homes. As we have shown in this section, women are gaining respect. CSD, however, found no noticeable change in traditional gender relations and socially prescribed roles and norms—particularly at the level of the household.

Women's mobility has increased, but only as related to income-generating activities. Although CSD's centers have succeeded in creating a space for women to gain experience in making decisions and acting upon them, a social stigma is still attached to women's mobility that has not changed significantly since CSD began its operations. CSD concluded that these limitations were due in part to the program's central focus on creating income-generating opportunities for women who had never had them before and that "women's empowerment takes much more than access options. The programme needs to consider some strategic or structural changes and incorporate gender mainstreaming actions in order to inch towards the overall empowerment of women." Many programmes, however, do encourage women from village banks, self-help groups, lending centers, and Trust Banks to organize to bring about social change or solve community problems as a group. Trust Bank members from Opportunity's partner AGAPE in Barranquilla, Colombia, organized to bring electricity to their community. Trust Banks from ADEMCOL, Opportunity's partner in Bogotà, often organize health fairs for their families and communities, bringing the services of doctors, dentists, and psychologists within easy access of poor communities that lack their own health services. They also organize day care and community social events. Organizing such events has proven to be an important learning experience in and of itself because for many women it is their first contact with local authorities. In order to gain permission and support to hold the events, women must learn to navigate through the bureaucracies that affect their daily lives.

KEY PROGRAMMATIC FACTORS THAT CAN CONTRIBUTE TO EMPOWERMENT

Developing a programme that strikes a balance to maximize empowerment, wellbeing, economic development, and sustainability can be very challenging. No single programme fits all environments and populations, and no programme strategy will have identical results for all potential clients. Naila Kabeer sums up the challenge well, explaining, "Different aspects of women's disempowerment, and hence empowerment, are closely related so that initiatives in relation to one aspect are likely to set off changes in other aspects, although not in easily predictable ways."

The most effective programme strategies will be devised when staff at microfinance institutions listen to clients and carefully evaluate their resource bases, strengths, and vulnerabilities so that they develop products and services that build on strengths and existing resources. As Noni S. Ayo, managing director of ARDCI, in the Philippines, expresses it, "All efforts at improving an MFI's impact on women boil down to really understanding a woman's needs, her predicament and what she dreams of. Even before all the questions can be answered, the basic question that must first be answered is who she is." At the outset of our research, we hoped to find evidence of the impacts of different programme strategies that were intentionally designed to empower women. We hoped to be able to determine not only which programme elements made the greatest difference in empowering women but also which were the most cost-effective. However, we found objective data hard to come by. Nevertheless, drawing on our own experience within Opportunity and the experiences of many other MFIs, in this section we present some promising programme practices that have achieved good results in their particular context or across a range of countries—many of which have a low incremental cost, and many of which are equally applicable to minimalist and holistic programmes.

BUSINESS TRAINING

Business training can benefit poor women entrepreneurs when the training is carefully designed to complement their existing skills and address their most pressing needs. With the help of market research and other tools to ensure relevance for clients, business training can be a valuable component of microlending programmes. At Sinapi Aba Trust, most of the women interviewed commented that their ability to plan, calculate and project profit, and manage money had improved considerably as a result of the training they received from their orientation and Trust Bank meetings. Several of these women especially appreciated the training in "customer care" they had received from their Trust Banks because they believe that it has helped them sell their goods faster, retain customers, and work less. In Costa Rica, the majority of the spouses of ADAPTE's clients indicated that the training their wives received from ADAPTE was the most important aspect of the programme.

Interviews with ADAPTE clients revealed that they value both the training and the credit they received, and in a recent round of focus-group discussions on client satisfaction SAT clients indicated that they would be willing to pay even more for more extensive training. Opportunity's experience in integrating business training into its Trust Bank lending groups is discussed in the paper "Bundling Microfinance and Business Development Services: A Case Study from ADEMCOL in Colombia." The paper notes that "ADEMCOL's loan officers also have found that those clients who have received business training services and have remained with ADEMCOL are often the bestperforming clients." Seamstress Diana Rojas, an ADEMCOL Trust Bank member in her fifth loan cycle, attributes her increased ability to retain and satisfy her clients to her participation in business training offered by ADEMCOL. Ana Moreno Ruiz, a saleswoman who has been a client of ADEMCOL for three years, has participated in several training modules, including those on human relations, costs, marketing, and bookkeeping, and says that "With the training I have received, I have learned to work better with people, and this has permitted me to increase my sales. I have retained my clients." Since the introduction of more advanced business training, ADEMCOL's client retention rate has increased substantially, meaning that more women are staying in the programme longer—and presumably enjoying benefits from their participation.

At SAT, too, 66.5 percent of exiting clients liked training on business topics best. 85 percent of current clients interviewed with the empowerment tool said that they now have a better relationship with their customers and suppliers as a result of the training on customer care and retention, planning and good pricing, and up-front payment of suppliers. Several of the women interviewed even mentioned that they now have the confidence to share business skills and ideas with their friends and other competitors because they are not afraid of competition. This is in comparison with 24 percent of the clients who said that before they joined SAT they felt too shy to associate with other traders and competitors in the market because they thought their businesses were unimpressive and would be mocked by what they called the well-to-do in the market.

ACCION International's Diálogo de Gestiones (loosely translated as "A Dialogue about Work") is a programme of training with over 40 modules on topics including assertiveness training, negotiating skills, confidence-building, leadership skills, business training, and learning new trades—as well as a gender module designed specifically to address women's needs. After a three-year development process, the programme is being carried out in 11 countries with 31 institutions and has trained 158,000 clients. ACCION has found the programme to be so essential that it is also offered independently of its credit programmes: a recent study found that 51 per cent of the trainees also receive credit, but 49 per cent have no credit at the time of training.

WOMEN'S GENERAL EDUCATION AND LITERACY

"As it is often said, knowledge to the poor is power to the poor. It is this that empowers the rural poor in VAWA projects." Women's general education and literacy are important if they are to reach their full potential and become empowered. Illiteracy creates a situation of dependency on others that can limit an individual's prospects for empowerment. Many MFIs have found illiteracy to be a major stumbling block for their clients. Some, like WEDTF, try to adapt by making sure that there is at least one literate member in every group or that at least one member has a literate child who can assist the group.

Many MFIs use participatory training techniques that do not require literacy to educate clients, but very few are able to offer literacy training since most methods for providing it are relatively expensive and time-intensive for both staff and clients. Although many illiterate entrepreneurs are able to keep accounts in their heads, their ability to interact with the formal sector will always be limited. Some NGOs such as World Education and Women's Empowerment Project in Nepal have come up with innovative and low-cost methods of training women in literacy that have significantly enhanced the empowerment benefits of the savings and credit groups to which the women belong.

By using existing lending groups and providing materials for women to train themselves, the literacy programmes have grown rapidly for a relatively low cost in contrast to many literacy initiatives. These programmes have shown that literacy and education contribute powerfully to empowerment and complement the financial independence that microfinance provides. In the case of WEP, the literacy rate among its members rose from 21 percent to 85 percent during the first 30 months of the programme. Helen Sherpa of World Education writes, "In new groups these women start as 'nobodies' leading groups that have no money and no respect. These groups' funds grow and they become increasingly self-reliant breaking the hold of male money lenders and male family members over economic decisions. This suddenly elevates the status of the groups as well as the individual members and leaders. Leaders in the groups become role models because these are 'women like them'—poorer women, women who have become literate later in life."

In addition, educating women has additional benefits for their children. World Education has documented that women who attend education programmes dramatically increase their commitment to educating their children and to educating their daughters in particular. Because lack of money for school fees is the major cause of school dropouts in Nepal as well as in many other countries, the income generated from microenterprises plays an important role in helping women realize their dreams for their children. Kashf in Pakistan found a similar linkage. An independent study found that 35 percent of Kashf members see their educated loan officers as role models for their daughters. More than 50 percent of the women wanted to educate their daughters, and more than 40 percent wanted to pursue a different future for them.

BALANCING FAMILY AND WORK RESPONSIBILITIES

In addition to educational disadvantages, one of the most difficult challenges that many women face as they start or expand businesses is the balancing of their increasing business responsibilities with their household responsibilities. Although the ultimate goal may be for household responsibilities to be shared between the men and women in the household, this sharing never happens overnight.

In many cases, women's businesses remain small and concentrated in less profitable sectors in large part because of the time constraints that women's domestic responsibilities create. Not only do women have limited time to spend on their business activities, but often they also must be able to abandon them altogether for periods to deal with family crises or children's illnesses. As a result, many women's employment opportunities are limited to those that can be done on a part-time and often irregular basis. The experiences of Opportunity International's partners have demonstrated that women often need help to develop strategies for managing and meeting the expectations of family and community members while still having the time and energy to run their businesses well. Women also need support in negotiating the complex changes in gender roles that must ultimately take place in order for them to succeed as microentrepreneurs.

Many of Sinapi Aba Trust's clients as well as clients of Opportunity International's other partners in Africa have highly valued the advice on time management and "managing your husband" that they have received. Some Opportunity partners and other MFIs are also recognizing that more outreach efforts are necessary to secure husbands' cooperation and support. It comes as no surprise that the most successful clients of many MFIs are the ones who have the most supportive husbands and that those with more problems often have problems with their husbands as well. Because most MFIs deal primarily with women, however, husbands are often not directly included. Some MFIs are experimenting with ways to influence husbands through including them in selected orientation sessions, having special events for spouses, and inviting them to group meetings occasionally.

DIALOGUE ON SOCIAL AND POLITICAL ISSUES

Discussion of social issues affecting women's lives and communities can lead to greater awareness of the causes of the problems they face and allow them to take more effective action to address the problems that are holding them back. Discussion of women's rights, community problems, politics, and common family problems can foster a sense of solidarity that can empower women both as individuals and as a group to address their problems. With some support, groups of economically empowered women can take steps to address the cultural and legal barriers that limit their social and political empowerment. CSD, for example, found that as a result of the discussions of social and legal issues held in lending centers, women have greater knowledge of their civil and legal rights and are more aware of their position and the choices they can make. They have increased knowledge of how relevant institutions can help them when they need legal assistance, and this knowledge has allowed more women to resist domestic violence and alcoholism and demand fair minimum wages. Several studies point to the importance of social and cultural structures in determining an individual's level of empowerment or social value. For example, a study by Dreze and Sen shows us that "structural variables making up gender relations in different parts of India are far more important in determining the extent to which the girl child is valued within the family than the individual characteristics of their parents."

Other studies show that structural characteristics are more important in determining the social value or empowerment of an individual than any of the individual's actions or circumstances are—including participation in microenterprise programmes. These findings underscore the importance of at least attempting to address some of the wider social structures that are contributing to the disempowerment of women as well as helping women tackle some of the personal problems that are limiting their potential. More formal training programmes on topics such as women's rights, domestic violence prevention, and family planning could substantially improve women's ability to face these challenges. Such education efforts, however, will likely be most successful when they are developed in cooperation with the clients themselves. At SAT, Trust Banks develop their own education and training programmes in each loan cycle in cooperation with their loan officers. This ensures that the training provided and the topics discussed are those most relevant and useful to the clients. In many Grameen replications, the women control their own programme through their centers. Such training and discussion does not have to be expensive to provide, and the potential benefits of empowerment far outweigh the costs. Involving the women themselves in planning and even preparing training can help keep costs low while at the same time giving women the power to control their programme.

EXPERIENCE IN DECISION MAKING AND LEADERSHIP

One of the positive contributions that group-based lending methodologies make to women's empowerment is the opportunity for women to gain experience in making decisions and leading and influencing others. As Essma Ben Hamida of ENDA Interarabe in Tunisia puts it, "Participation in the micro-credit programme constitutes an apprenticeship of democracy through the self-managed solidarity groups which elect their president and treasurer: in many mixed groups, a woman has been elected as president, an astounding development in a still male-dominated society." When they join microfinance programmes, many women have had little opportunity to voice their opinions or participate in decision making. Some will have had little experience even formulating an opinion that can be expressed since they have had little opportunity to do so.

A synthesis study done by Jennefer Sebstad and Monique Cohen found that "[lending] groups provide a means for women to know and be known by other women; a forum for learning leadership and public speaking skills; and a basis for development of trust, friendship, and financial assistance." Although actual levels of control vary according to methodology, in most cases, women are called upon to develop and use skills in group dynamics and persuasion, to exercise authority, and to command the respect of others—some for the first time in their lives. Opportunities for leadership are affected not only by the structure of the programme but also by the group's internal policy. Groups that set policies to rotate their leadership frequently give more women a chance to develop leadership skills than ones that do not, although groups without a rotation policy can allow a few women to develop even stronger and more lasting leadership skills. In addition, if the rotation of leadership is coupled with specific training on leadership and organizational skills, it can help foster a sense of equality among the women and break down other social barriers such as caste as well as gender. Programmes like SAT's deliberately try to break down traditional notions of leaders being chosen from an elite in order to instill the idea that everyone is capable of being a leader. Mixed-sex and mixed-caste lending groups have the potential to empower, but if such groups do not make a deliberate effort to stimulate the meaningful participation of all members, they may end up replicating existing patterns of social inequality.

Much depends on the policies established, however, and some trade-offs in empowerment may apply, because allowing groups complete freedom to establish their own policies incurs a greater risk of replicating existing social structures and putting the same people in power inside the lending group as outside. In contrast, setting guidelines for internal policies can help promote healthy leadership experiences but constrains the autonomy of the groups. MFIs can help maximize the empowerment potential of lending groups by providing training and coaching to client leaders, developing cost-effective methods for clients to manage their own loans and savings, ensuring that women have a chance to lead in mixed lending groups, and encouraging the active participation of all group members.

OWNERSHIP, CONTROL, AND PARTICIPATORY GOVERNANCE

One contribution to empowerment that self-help groups and other savings-based community groups offer to members is the pride of ownership and autonomy. Even though some self-help groups are given training and support from NGOs, the majority of even these externally supported groups rely primarily on member savings for their capital instead of on external capital as most village banks or solidarity groups do. Savings-based approaches that rely on minimal external support have several advantages. Women are proud to own their capital and have savings they can rely on. The capital stays in the community, and the women manage it themselves according to their own needs and interests. Because the external support costs are minimal, women are able to charge a lower rate of interest, and a large percentage of that interest goes back to the women in the form of interest on their savings and community projects. The empowerment benefits derived from independence and autonomy are often partially offset, however, by weaker economic empowerment benefits. By depending on the savings of very poor community members, capital is more limited than it would be with external support, which in turn limits the growth potential of women's enterprises and income.

Although independent savings-based self-help groups are viable alternatives for reaching remote and impoverished rural areas, the very poverty of these areas may make it difficult to amass the savings necessary to extend credit in the amounts necessary to stimulate the development of a vibrant microenterprise sector. Microfinance institutions should continue to experiment with models that combine women's control of programmes and resources with access to greater amounts of capital.

BUILDING INSTITUTIONS RESPONSIVE TO WOMEN'S NEEDS

WOMEN IN LEADERSHIP

Does it matter whether men or women are at the helm of microfinance institutions? Women have been important as policy-setters and influential donors—through USAID, CGAP, and DFID, for example. They have also been innovators, as seen at SEWA, ProMujer, Women's World Banking, Working Women's Forum, and other organizations. A glance at microfinance trainings and conferences shows plenty of women in attendance. Yet men predominate on boards of directors of MFIs, in senior management, in programme design, and sometimes as loan officers. That means that women and men are not equally involved in critical areas of decision making including setting the vision, defining the client target population, and designing products and services. Within Opportunity International, 85 percent of clients are women. An August 2000 survey on gender issues reported that "the majority of staff (57 per cent) are women, but that women tend not to serve in key leadership roles, especially as senior managers and board members.... However, the largest area of gender inequity is at the board level."

Interestingly, the survey showed that the inequity was just as present among the OI fundraising partners in North America, Europe, and Australia as it was for OI partner MFIs in developing countries. Florence Abena Dolphyne, a Ghanaian scholar, feels strongly that women have a key role to play in good governance. She writes, "In the search for ways of promoting women's emancipation in Africa, the importance of competent women in policy-making positions at all levels cannot be overemphasized. Such women can help initiate and ensure the implementation of programmes and activities that would promote the welfare of women, and encourage women's greater participation in national development.

They can also provide the necessary insights into women's concerns that would ensure that government policies, projects and programmes have the desired impact and achieve the desired goals precisely because due account has been taken of the concerns and views of the different groups in the society." Recognizing the importance of increasing women's representation in governance, Interaction, the association of U.S.-based PVOs in international relief and development, has launched a Campaign for Gender Equity on Boards for their members. In Opportunity International the creation of a women-led subsidiary, the Women's Opportunity Fund, transformed the vision and mission of the entire organization, resulting in new products and services for women and dramatically increasing the number and percentage of women clients served.

Women as Field Officers

Even more interesting than the issue of women in governance is the question of whether it is more desirable to have women as loan officers when most of the clients are women. Grameen Bank is noteworthy for championing women's rights to credit in groundbreaking ways, and about 95 percent of its clients are women. It also reaches beyond most MFIs in that the Bank, which is "owned" by borrowers, includes women clients on its board. According to Alex Counts, executive director of Grameen Foundation USA, as of January 2002, "all 9 borrower-elected Directors of Grameen are women.... Despite there being about 100,000 male borrowers, there has never been more than one of the nine elected members who have been men." This governance structure includes not only women's perspectives but, more important, client perspectives.

Yet, according to Counts, for many years the percentage of female loan officers (called center managers) has remained between 5 percent and 10 percent, with new efforts to recruit female staff balanced by retirements and resignations. "Grameen Bank is certainly not the only agency in Bangladesh where the nature of the work is rural and field-based that struggles with this issue." In the Opportunity International Network approximately 50 percent of all loan officers are women. Anecdotal evidence suggests that the experience of having male loan officers treating women clients with respect and dignity is empowering in and of itself. Yet other women clients say that they can relate more easily to a female loan officer and that female loan officers provide a role model of achievement. Our research at Sinapi Aba Trust in Ghana suggests that female loan officers are especially valued by women clients as role models for their daughters, showing an unplanned secondary impact of the programme. In our experience, a key factor is gender sensitivity—of both female and male loan officers—in ensuring that women are empowered through microfinance. We have found it helpful to screen for gender sensitivity during the hiring process and to provide gender sensitivity training to all staff to ensure that both male and female loan officers are giving the same message about gender and empowerment. In addition, organizations can take a number of steps to help loan officers become more empowering in their work.

Many loan officers interviewed in our research felt that the time they were able to spend with clients was too limited. By minimizing loan officers' paperwork, MFIs can help loan officers spend more time in the field with clients. Also, loan officers could be given performance incentives based on client empowerment as well as portfolio size and quality to reward them for the extra effort they put in to make sure clients are succeeding. Loan officers also should be an MFI's early warning system against negative impacts. Creating an internal feedback loop so that loan officers' knowledge of client empowerment and struggles is fed into product design and implementation can be one of the most cost-effective means of ensuring that programmes are responsive to women's needs. It is important for MFIs to review policies that discriminate against women, whether intentionally or not. An MFI in Zimbabwe did not hire women as loan officers because it was considered culturally inappropriate for women to ride motorcycles, and this was a requirement for reaching remote clients.

CETZAM in Zambia, however, was able to challenge this norm and now has motorcycle-riding women on its staff. An MFI in Colombia found that it was unintentionally paying a higher wage to male programme staff for similar work. An MFI in the Philippines with a client base that is 99 percent women included "preferably male" among the qualifications for a post being advertised, explaining that it was not safe for women to travel alone into their target communities. An MFI in El Salvador had a similar informal policy until a male loan officer was shot while on his rounds; it then realized that the issues of security for women were also issues for men, and implemented changes to protect both men and women on its staff. Around the world, microfinance field staff often face physical discomfort and unsafe conditions along with a cultural bias against women. Some MFIs have been able to challenge these cultural biases and accommodate for the discomfort and lack of safety; others have simply let women select themselves out of the running; and others have intentionally expressed a bias for male field workers. Developing organizational policies to promote gender equity and sensitivity at all levels of the organization is one way to guard against discrimination and build an institutional culture that is supportive of women. These choices are part of the message that MFIs send their clients about women's potential and capacity.

Managing the Challenges of Rapid Growth

As the industry grows and matures, women may be adversely affected by institutional changes resulting from rapid expansion, consolidation, and commercialization. Opportunity's experience is that several partners have provided a lower percentage of loans to women as they have grown. This is, of course, not all bad news: in the context of aggressive growth, the absolute number of women receiving services grows, even if the percentage of women clients decreases. Yet there are some trends that should be monitored, such as the tendency to drop group loans in favour of individual loans. Again, this is not all bad—as long as the individual loan product is thoughtfully designed with women's needs in mind, and as long as the poorest and most marginalized women are not left behind.

The consolidation issue likewise has pro's and con's. Opportunity's recent experience with a few consolidations shows that, as with any consolidation, it is a delicate matter to bring together different systems, policies and products. The blended organizational culture may be stronger in gender sensitivity and gender equity—or it may be weaker. And, as MFIs transform into regulated financial institutions, they must meet the demands of the supervising authority, creditors, and investors.

Pressure to select the most financially profitable products and delivery systems may reduce the accessibility and benefits for women. Part of the pressure is to increase loan sizes—and women, who are disproportionately among the poorest, have a greater need for smaller entry level loans. Therefore, in the midst of this growth, it is important to develop client-centered products that acknowledge not only women's economic needs but their potential for empowerment as well.

DESIGNING PRODUCTS TO MEET WOMEN'S NEEDS

Through impact assessments, monitoring, market research, and client feedback, many MFIs have begun to develop and adapt new products to address the shortcomings of their traditional products and keep pace with clients' changing needs. For example, some MFIs in Africa are beginning to explore giving family business loans to encourage cooperation between the husband and wife, in particular, but also to increase the number of income earners in the family and extended family. ADEMCOL in Colombia is piloting a Senior Trust Bank programme to meet the needs of women whose businesses are maturing and need larger loans and more advanced business training, yet do not want to leave the group-lending programme. Another example of client research leading to the development of more empowering products is research by the Council for Economic Empowerment for Women of Africa – Uganda (CEEWA-U).

Research with several MFIs in Uganda found that very few women are able to acquire assets through group-loan programmes. One negative consequence of this for the women and their businesses was that the productivity of women's businesses was not improving dramatically, nor were women able to access larger individual loans, which often require assets as collateral or a guarantor. In some cases, this hindrance was due to policies requiring loans to be used for working capital only, but in others, it was due to loan terms, amounts, and repayment schedules that did not allow for the purchase of a long-term asset. CEEWA-U developed a capital asset loan product called Kikalu to meet this need, combining a longer repayment period, group guarantee, and flexible disbursement schedule.

5

Rural Women and Development in India

RURAL DEVELOPMENT IN INDIA

Literally and from the social, economic and political perspectives the statement is valid even today. Around 65% of the State's population is living in rural areas. People in rural areas should have the same quality of life as is enjoyed by people living in sub urban and urban areas. Further there are cascading effects of poverty, unemployment, poor and inadequate infrastructure in rural areas on urban centres causing slums and consequential social and economic tensions manifesting in economic deprivation and urban poverty. Hence Rural Development which is concerned with economic growth and social justice, improvement in the living standard of the rural people by providing adequate and quality social services and minimum basic needs becomes essential.

The present strategy of rural development mainly focuses on poverty alleviation, better livelihood opportunities, provision of basic amenities and infrastructure facilities through innovative programmes of wage and self-employment. The goals will be achieved by various programme support being implemented creating partnership with communities, non-governmental organizations, community based organizations, institutions, PRIs and industrial establishments, while the Department of Rural Development will provide logistic support both on technical and administrative side for programme implementation.

Other aspects that will ultimately lead to transformation of rural life are also being emphasized simultaneously. Though the percentage of persons below poverty level in Tamil Nadu has come down significantly between 1993-94 (35.03%) and 1999-2000 (21.12%) as a result of the implementation of various Central and State sponsored schemes, the level of poverty both in absolute numbers (130.40 lakh persons) and percentage of population below poverty line (21.12%) in Tamil Nadu is highest among the four southern States. In spite of huge investments on wage and self -employment programmes, the level of unemployment as per the NSSO 55th round (1999-2000) for Tamil Nadu compared to All India is the second highest among major States in 1987-88 and 1993-94 and third highest in 1999-2000.

The Government's policy and programmes have laid emphasis on poverty alleviation, generation of employment and income opportunities and provision of infrastructure and basic facilities to meet the needs of rural poor. For realising these objectives, self-employment and wage employment programmes continued to pervade in one form or other. As a measure to strengthen the grass root level democracy, the Government is constantly endeavouring to empower Panchayat Raj Institutions in terms of functions, powers and finance. Grama sabha, NGOs, Self-Help Groups and PRIs have been accorded adequate role to make participatory democracy meaningful and effective.

REVIEW OF NINTH PLAN PERFORMANCE

An outlay of Rs. 2000 crores was provided for Rural Development sector during Ninth Plan period. The budgetary support and allocation from 1997-98 to 2001-02 for various schemes/programmes was Rs. 2498.30 crores. The year-wise outlay and expenditure are indicated below:

Year	Financial Performance Budget Provision	(Rs. in crores) Expenditure
1997-98	330.68	440.76
1998-99	490.51	526.45
1999-2000	498.27	484.27
2000-01	423.31	543.50
2001-02	755.53	725.14
Total	2498.30	2720.12

Physical Performance

Year	I.R.D.P No. of Families Benefited	TRYSEM No.of Persons Trained	DWCRA No.of Groups Formed	No.of SHGs Formed	SGSY Economic Assistance Provided	Families Benefited	Individual Assisted
1997-98	180696	16479	2041	–	–	–	–
1998-99	142813	12381	2917	–	–	–	–
1999-2000	New scheme - SGSY introduced			18661	3198	47264	18163
2000-01				25324	4712	71503	11890
2001-02				12132	2158	34098	1259
Total	323509	28860	4958	56117	10068	152865	31312

During the Ninth Five Year Plan, under IRDP, income generating assets were provided to 3.235 lakh families through subsidy and credit.

Under TRYSEM 28,860 rural youths in the age group of 18 to 35 from the families of below poverty line were provided with training enabling them to take up income generating activities.

Under DWCRA 4,958 women groups covering 12.40 lakh beneficiaries were formed and they were provided with revolving fund, credit and subsidy so as to enable them to participate in social developmental activities towards achieving economic self-reliance.

During 1999-2000 the IRDP, TRYSEM, DWCRA were merged to form a new self-employment programme called Swarna Jayanthi Gram Swarojgar Yojana (SGSY) with effect from 1-4-99.

Under SGSY 56,117 Women Self Help Groups (SHGs) were formed from the families of below poverty line. Out of this, 10,068 SHGs have been provided with economic assistance under various trades enabling them to take up income generating activities.

Under SGSY 31,312 individual beneficiaries have also been provided with economic assistance. Mandays generated and Community assets created under Centrally Sponsored Schemes during Ninth Five Year Plan

Sl. No	Name of the scheme	Unit generated/ created	Mandays Assets
1.	JRY/JGSY	Lakh mandays	1048.95
2.	EAS		1344.38
	IAY		
3.	New houses	Nos.	2,08,441
4.	IAY Kutcha houses	Nos.	41,239
5.	PMGY Rural shelter	Nos.	6880
6.	Credit cum subsidy	Nos.	5577
7.	Million Wells Scheme *	Nos.	9588

Note: * Scheme dispensed during 1999-2000 onwards and merged with SGSY.

The total man-days generated under Employment Oriented Schemes like JRY/JGSY and EAS works out to 2393.33 lakhs. These schemes in addition to the creation of infrastructural facilities such as roads, school buildings, improvement of tanks etc. provided employment and income opportunities to the rural poor. Regarding provision of housing facilities, 2.08 lakh new houses were constructed and 41,239 kutcha houses upgraded under IAY, 6880 new houses were constructed under PMGY- Rural Shelter for benefit of rural poor living below poverty line.

Under Credit cum subsidy scheme, 5,577 houses were constructed for the benefit the people above poverty line. Access to pucca dwelling provides basic housing as well as better environment for the beneficiaries and raises the social status of the members of the household. Under Jeevandhara Irrigation Wells Scheme (Million Wells Scheme), totally 9588 beneficiaries were assisted to dig irrigation wells during 1997-98 and 1998-99. During the Ninth Five Year Plan, the State Government introduced new schemes such as Member of Legislative Assembly Constituency Development Schemes (MLACDS), Annamarumalrchi Thittam (AMT) and Namakku Naame Thittam. Under

MLACDS, 42,954 works were taken up at a total cost of Rs. 580.46 crores, 1,05,605 works were taken up a total cost of Rs. 301.86 under AMT and 28,421 works were taken up at a total cost of Rs. 157.11 crores under Namakku Naame Thittam.

GOALS, OBJECTIVES AND STRATEGY

The prime goal of rural development is to improve the quality of life of the rural people by alleviating poverty through the instrument of selfemployment and wage employment programmes, by providing community infrastructure facilities such as drinking water, electricity, road connectivity, health facilities, rural housing and education and promoting decentralization of powers to strengthen the Panchayat raj institutions. The Chief Minister's 15 Point Programme is a visionary programme which seeks to make Tamil Nadu the best State in the country by way of creating growth opportunities in rural areas and eradicating rural poverty. To achieve the above objectives, the following priorities and thrust areas have been identified during the Tenth Five Year Plan period:

- The goal is reduction of poverty from 21.12% in 1999- 2000 to 10% by 2006-07 and near elimination by 2012. Poverty reduction will be attempted
  - By organizing the rural masses into self-help groups and the establishment of micro-enterprises, training, credit linkages, market support, etc.
  - By substantial flow of investment in physical infrastructure like roads, water supply and social infrastructure like health, education and nutrition.
- Special efforts for generation of adequate employment and creation of durable community assets to improve the rural people especially the small farmers, marginal farmers, rural artisans etc., through programmes like Sampoorna Grameen Rozgar Yojana (SGRY).
- Decentralization of the process of planning by entrusting major role to the Panchayat raj bodies in the preparation of local level planning.
- Improving the efficiency and capacity of the officials and elected local body representatives.
- Providing all weather roads to all rural habitations having a population above 500 by 2004.
- Strengthening of Grama Sabha the governing body of village assembly as an agency of social audit and to review the implementation of programmes.
- Special efforts will be made to converge various schemes and

programmes for accelerating the development process through special schemes like Village Self-sufficiency scheme etc.

- Emphasis will be given for the maintenance of the assets created under various schemes.

INTEGRATED SANITARY COMPLEX FOR WOMEN

Tamil Nadu's coverage in rural sanitation is presently at 11% which is lower than national average of 15%. To protect dignity and privacy of the women the Government have launched a new scheme called the Integrated Sanitary Complex for women to provide toilets and facilities for bathing and washing for women under one roof. Each sanitary complex will be spread over approximately 750 sq.ft. with 10 toilets and 3 cubicles for bathing. Each complex has an independent water connection to ensure that the users have a steady and continued supply of water. A pump room and water tank will also form part of the sanitary complex. The operation and maintenance of these sanitary complexes will be the responsibility of the village panchayats and self-help groups. Monitoring committees will also be formed for proper maintenance of these sanitary complexes. An outlay of Rs. 284 crores has been proposed under this scheme during the Tenth Plan period.

OTHER PROGRAMMES/SCHEMES

The outlay proposed in respect of other Rural Development programmes during Tenth Plan is as follows:

Sl. No.	Name of scheme/programme (Rs. in crores)	Proposed outlay
1.	Capital programme of Infrastructure Development by rural local bodies	100.00
2.	DRDA Administration cost	20.08
3.	Other Rural Development Programmes	113.14
	Total	233.22

AREA DEVELOPMENT PROGRAMME

Western Ghats Development Programme

Provision of infrastructure facilities like drinking water, street lights, formation of link roads, construction of school buildings and health subcentres have been proposed to be taken up in the Western Ghats taluks under WGDP. These works will be planned and executed by the concerned local bodies. The outlay proposed under the above head during the Tenth Plan period is Rs. 1.90 crores.

Drought Prone Area Programme

The Drought Prone Area Programme (DPAP) is an integrated watershed development programme with the prime objective of promoting the over all economic development of watershed community by optimally utilizing natural resources so as to mitigate the adverse effects of drought, prevent further ecological degradation and create employment through non-farm activities.

This programme is being implemented in 16 districts viz:

1. Dharmapuri (14),
2. Thoothukudi (18)
3. Sivagangai (7),
4. Ramanathapuram (7),
5. Virudhunagar (7),
6. Pudukottai (4),
7. Tirunelveli (1),
8. Salem (5),
9. Namakkal (3),
10. Coimbatore (5),
11. Thiruvannamalai (1),
12. Dindigul (3),
13. Vellore (6),
14. Tiruchirappali (1).
15. Perambalur (6),
16. Karur (2)

(No.of blocks in brackets). This programme is sponsored by the Government of India and the expenditure is shared in the ratio of 75:25 between and Central and State Governments. The DPAP is implemented on watershed approach. Each watershed covers an area of approximately 500 ha. The allocation per hectare is Rs. 6,000.

This programme consists of 5 major components, namely:

1. Entry point activity
2. Community organization,
3. Training,
4. Developmental activities
5. Project administration.

The Developmental works carried out under DPAP are as follows:

- Land Development including land levelling, summer ploughing, institutional and moisture conservation measures like contour and graded bunds fortified by vegetation, bench terracing in hilly terrain.

- Drainage line treatment with a combination of vegetative and engineering structures.
- Development of small water harvesting structures such as low cost farm ponds, nulla bunds, check dam and percolation ponds.
- Nursery raising for fodder, timber, fuelwood and horticultural species.
- Afforestation activities including block plantations, avenue plantation, shelter belts, sand dune stabilization etc.,
- Agro-forestry and horticultural development.
- Pasture development either by itself or in conjunction with plantations.
- Repair, restoration and upgradation of existing common property assets and structures in watershed to obtain optimum and substained benefits from previous public investments.
- Crop demonstration for popularizing new crops/varieties or innovative management practices.

Proposals - Development works in 297 watersheds sanctioned in the first batch during 1995-96 to 1999-2000 have already been successfully completed with a total outlay of Rs. 53.57 crores covering 42,090 hec. Watersheds sanctioned during 1999-2000 and 2001-02 will be continued during Tenth Plan period. In addition it is expected that 700 more watershed projects will be taken up during Tenth plan period. The outlay proposed under DPAP would be Rs. 210 crores during Tenth plan out of which the State's share will be Rs. 52.50 crores. The total outlay towards Special Programme for Rural Development is Rs. 3500 crores.

Table.Proposed outlay for Special Programmes for Rural Development(Rs. in crores)

No	Name of the scheme/Programme Plan (State share)	Outlay for Tenth
1.	Member of Legislative Assembly Constituency Development scheme (MLACD)	1059.85
2.	Village Self-sufficiency scheme	120.00
3.	Capital Programme of Infrastructure Development by Rural Local bodies	100.00
4.	Rural Sanitary Complex for Women	284.00
5.	Construction of building for VAO's Office	19.80
6.	Villlage Fair Development scheme	5.00
7.	SGSY	131.45
8.	SGRY	303.79
9.	IAY under Special Component Programme	292.89
10.	Special Component Plan for rural shelter	111.14

11.	District Reform facility	225.00
12.	Finance Commission Grants to Local bodies	659.47
13.	DRDA Administration cost	20.07
	Area Development Programme	
14.	Other Rural Development Programme	113.14
15.	Western Ghats Development Programme	1.90
16.	Drought Prone Area Programme	52.50
	Total	3500.00

DEVELOPMENT OF RURAL SECTOR IN INDIA

In the rural areas of India, the statistics regarding who has access to a toilet differ drastically from the urban sector. The numbers are not about how many people use one toilet seat, as we saw in Mumbai, because in many cases not even one toilet seat can be found. Instead, ninety per cent of the rural villages have no access to a toilet. Given the population of these rural areas, this means that over seven hundred million people defecate in the open. In a typical rural area where a census was taken of 1,017 women, only five had a toilet at home; the others used fields and open spaces for defecation. Traditional cultural customs and mores have determined women's control over the domain of the technology of the toilet. For this reason, the statistics associated with the rural sector also often focus on tasks that are considered part of a woman's traditional domain and show how women in these areas are defined by these traditional gender roles most often to their disadvantage. The customs dictate that women are primarily the caretakers of water and sanitation.

This means that they are responsible for all tasks associated with water, from the collection to the management of this precious resource. It is their duty to draw, store, utilise, and manage water as per the daily requirements of their family; they are also responsible for the proper disposal of the family's excreta and other domestic wastes. These daily tasks consume most of a rural woman's day. Seventy-eight per cent of women spend an average of four hours a day in fetching water. The women of these rural villages must walk on average a minimum of six kilometres to transport water from the local water sources. Fifty-three per cent of women polled in the census above complained that they were not able to transport enough water for personal hygiene use, especially during menstrual periods.

What is striking about the case of the women of the rural sector is how this absence of toilets has shaped their communities and how the inception of the toilet that our story will chronicle is defined by a combination of traditional gender roles, current legal reforms, and future economic and environmental endeavors. The traditional gender roles and social attitudes that define women and their daily tasks and chores perpetuate a relatively low status for women in these areas. The main status indicators of the villages are education, ownership of property and resources, and control of new technologies. It is very difficult for women of the villages to have access to any of these resources. Because so much of a woman's life is spent in collection of water, girls are usually engaged in household activities from a very early age rather than being sent to school for an education. Long-standing family properties are rarely ever transferred to a woman's name; she is unable to gain landholdings through marriage or to buy her own piece of property if she remains single. Because they have no land as collateral, women are unable to have credit extended to them for any sort of economic endeavors. Also, new technologies are usually considered to be the domain of the men of the village; as such, technological initiatives are not taught to women or girls within the village communities, which, in turn, deprives these women of technological developments that could enhance their status and daily quality of life.

These customs also dictate the day to day interactions that take place within the village community on several levels, such as between men and women, and also between women of differing castes. Due to the traditional, cultural taboo against menstrual blood, women and men are not allowed to defecate at the same place. Because defecation is done is the open, in fields usually outside of the villages perimetres, and not contained in sanitary containers, there is the possibility that menstruating women could taint others with their menstrual blood. There is also an extreme cultural sensitivity to the possibility that women will be exposed to the eyes of men, thus tainting the women's chastity, while they are in the compromising position of defecating in exposed fields. Both of these examples mean that women are deprived of basic services that are provided during the day in public areas.

In addition, women of the "untouchable" caste are not allowed to use public sources of water and sanitation neither during the day nor at night for fear that they will pollute the rest of the village. They must travel even farther distances than women of higher castes to transport their water and perform their daily ablutions. Because of the lack of women-only public sanitation facilities, all women, regardless of caste, must wait until after dark to relieve themselves and defecate in the open. This has led to many health-related concerns such as bladder and urinary tract infections directly caused by prolonged periods of not being able to urinate and dispense with other bodily wastes. To reduce their need to excrete during the day, women drink and eat less. Not only do they not receive proper nutrition because of this, but they often suffer from dehydration because of the lack of fluids consumed. Being forced to travel long distances away from their village after dark, unaccompanied by men, also poses a personal threat to their safety. Assault and molestation are not rampant in the villages, but the odds of it occurring are increased when women must travel alone at night to isolated areas where they are exposing themselves in order to wash and go to the bathroom. Often their treks to these remote areas take them across train tracks that are notorious "hangouts for unsavory characters prone to drinking".

These train tracks are also hazardous to travel at night as the train conductors cannot see the women in their paths. While the above cultures, customs, and traditions of the village directly affect the health and safety of the women of rural villages, the simple fact of scarcity of safe and adequate water affect the state of the entire village: men, women, and children. Because there are not wells, pumps, irrigation pits, or any other infrastructure to bring clean water to the villages, women are forced to rely upon unsanitary sources for their water supply. This water is used to do the cooking, cleaning, and laundry, and is a main source for basic consumption. These sources of water are so unclean and infected that jaundice, viral and gastro-enteric diseases, and cholera outbreaks occur frequently in the rural villages of India. Diseases that are less common and easily treated in the United States, such as diarrhea and dehydration, result in the death of over 500,000 children every year.

Basic productivity, which is the only resource that a village can offer for its subsistence, is highly compromised due to sanitation-related diseases. Each year, 180 million work-days per year are lost due to illnesses caused by unclean water. This is equivalent to 12 billion rupees per year. These harsh conditions not only exemplify the challenges that women face as the main caretakers of their village water supply, but they also serve as indicators of the important role that these rural women play in controlling the environmental hygiene of their communities. This ability to control and choose water resources, limited as it may be, is a source of autonomy and authority for these village women. This autonomy did arise because water-related issues are not viewed by the village councils as critical to the villages' needs. Men are not concerned with how the laundry got done, how the dishes are washed, food is cooked, or where the water for their bathing comes from as long as it is always accessible to them when they come home from the fields in the evenings. And the women are sure that it always is accessible because it is their place within the community to ensure that it is.

The choices these women have for gathering water may not seem ideal to western standards, but at least the choice is theirs. Women control what water sources are used in their daily routines, whether it is the murky water hole used for doing laundry that is located 6 kilometres away, or whether is the less murky rain-water hole to be used only for precious consumption located 8 kilometres away. Women use their traditionally defined dharma, or duty, to influence the sanitation practices of the village. Part of their water duties entail teaching proper hygiene habits to the children of their community. As teachers, these women influence their family's sanitation habits and are consulted on the design of facilities to improve the cleanliness of the village.

Even though women do have control of the sanitation facilities within their village, their power remains quite limited in scope when it comes to initiating new technological improvements, such as toilets and sanitation systems. This is because women have never been given a forum in their local village meetings and governments to voice their concerns and their interests in bringing new water technologies to their communities. Traditionally, only men were allowed to participate in these local government meetings and to address the needs of the community. Toilets were rarely an issue under these male-dominated village meetings because sanitation, including toilets, was not considered vital to the village's needs.

This is because it falls within the women's dominion; only those technologies that concerned men directly were considered issues worthy of discussion within the village gram sabhas. These primarily focused on bringing new farming technologies to the area in the form of machines and fertilizers. So women's drudgery in obtaining water continued and the village's sanitation and environmental health remained stagnant because women did not have a voice to propose new ideas for technological improvements in the water supply that would be beneficial to their villages. To repeat, this may not exemplify an ideal autonomy over a technology. But it is this symbiotic relationship to water that women have been able to use as an impetus for change through a new Indian law giving women a chance to discuss their issues within the local village governments. This law is helping women to prove that not only are toilets a valid technology, but also a technology that can improve the health, efficiency and productivity of the entire village. The women are seizing the opportunity that this new law gives them to completely control the toilet technology and to retain autonomy over all realms of its creation.

The autonomy that before was quite limiting in scope is now giving these rural women the opportunity to show their village how important sanitation is to overall productivity and, as a result, to bolster their status as women in society-all through the technology of the toilet. In fact, what was previously considered a hindrance, the lack of any sort of infrastructure for sewage and sanitation, is ironically proving to give the women even more freedom. Unlike the urban sector where the women had to work with the infrastructure that was already in place, be it improving dilapidated toilet blocks or using the sidewalls and facades of the buildings where they chose to build their sidewalk communities, the women of the rural sector are given the freedom to choose a technology that will be the most beneficial to their village.

This new law being instituted throughout the rural states is a mandate from the national government that women participate in the local village and state governments through a reservation of elected seats. It is these village meetings that prioritize projects for the entire community. Even though, historically, these village gram sabhas were always present to discuss the needs of the village, they functioned mainly as informal, village council meetings among the men of the community. As part of the independence movement, Gandhi envisioned making these meetings part of a recognized local and state government. He often spoke of Gram Swaraj in which adult villagers would annually elect the government and which would have authority and jurisdiction in the fields of legislation, jurisdiction and executive decision-making without interference from the state government.

Thus, by 1948, twenty native states had enacted Panchayati acts. However, even these covered few villages, were extremely limited in their functions, and did not include women participation. In the period between of 1959-1964 the Panchayat Raj Institutions became the institutionalised three-tier model that it is today and were conceived as local bodies meant to ensure peoples' participation in development. This trend continued through the 60's and 70's. The three tier model was accepted by all states but neither sufficient powers nor sufficient finances were given to, thereby leaving the panchayats to languish to their fate. In such a scenario the importance of ensuring the participation of women took a backseat to having the PRIs institutionalised and recognized. The function of the PRIs was nowhere defined in the constitution and its meaning and scope were never authoritatively interpreted by the judicial guardians of the Constitution, the High courts and the Supreme Courts.

Therefore, there was a growing realization that it was the lack of constitutional support that kept the PRIs from reaching their full potential. As a result, the government of India wrote the three-tier panchayati raj institutions into the constitution of India with the enactment of the 73rd Constitutional Amendment passed in 1992. It was at this time that the 73rd Amendment also incorporated the political participation of women into state and national law. Previous gram sabhas and panchayati initiatives did propose women representation in the forums; however, participation was not mandated and, therefore, never fully accepted by the states.

Because participation was voluntary, most women did not participate in the local governments; they feared speaking out in the village forum because they were regarded as illiterate and unimportant simply because of the fact that they are women. The men of the village certainly did not force the women to take part in the councils because they were happy to keep that distinction for themselves.

In those states where the provision for women to be able to optionally participate in the village gram sabhas was proposed, the panchayati raj system of government was accepted, but the provision for including women was rejected. Without this provision in the previous government, less than 7 per cent of parliamentary seats were won by women. Therefore, a mandate reserving seats for the "poor, marginalised, and the oppressed," was needed to ensure their representation in local governments. The state of India realised that if development initiatives and poverty alleviation programmes were to succeed at the rural level, they needed the local involvement and participation of women. To ensure an effective presence of women in these institutions, the amendment stated that 33 per cent of the local government seats are now to be reserved specifically for women of the rural districts. This Amendment that was passed in 1992 was enacted for the first time in the 1993-1994 state elections.

WOMEN TEACHERS EMPOWERED IN INDIA

A NEW VISION IN EDUCATION

In 1990, international agencies, governments, NGOs, professional bodies and the private sector convened at two major world events to give the highest priority to Universal Primary Education (UPE). The World Conference on Education for All, held in Jomtien, Thailand and the World Summit for Children, in New York crystallized a world movement that had been growing over the past several decades. They provided a new impetus to the universally acknowledged central role of education in development and a better understanding of its frustratingly slow pace in many countries. At Jomtien, in particular, the call from many earlier conferences, research literature and reports culminated in a new commitment to increase the access, retention, and achievement of girls who were clearly lagging behind boys in most developing countries.

For UNICEF, which played a central role in both meetings, 1990 became the start of a decade in which education would become not only a high programming priority but also a call signal for evolving direction and policies. This included increased intersectoral work and a broadened definition of education that expanded its scope from traditional academic study to life skills, peace and conflict resolution, rights and empowerment. In addition, UNICEF incorporated into its new programming efforts a broadening of the focus on children of primary school age to include both very young children and adolescents. In the years following Jomtien, the implications of the shift in vision widened with a growing acceptance of the legal and ethical right of all children to have access to school and to the opportunity for quality educatio n.

At the same time, the arguments about the economic and social benefits of education began to receive greater attention and entered into common political parlance. However, it became clear that achieving UPE by the year 2000 or even in the next decade would not happen merely by redoubling or tripling efforts to increase enrolment. The traditional methods were just not working. The rise in enrolment was not matched by a rise in learning, retention or completion of school, especially among girls. What was needed to reach UPE was a major reform of educational goals, methods, and power relations. Such reform would reflect an expanded vision and new model of education that included improved and more relevant curricula and textbooks, teaching methods, and better trained teachers and administrators.

Reform would require whole systems that were sensitive and relevant to gender and to powerless excluded populations of children, including the poor, ethnic and racial minorities and working children. Still, no commitment to new methods, schedules and curricula would succeed if education systems only resulted in perpetuating the status quo and replicating the western model of education installed and instilled in the psyches of most developing countries. An educational system that goes hand in hand with social transformation was and is still needed. Such a system moves students and teachers from passive recipients and donors of knowledge to active participants in their own learning.

It results in a full understanding and acceptance that a major shift in power structures at all levels is required to bring real change and the possibility of achieving EFA. The international community met again in Dakar in 2000 when new commitments to learners were made. These commitments, as laid out in the Dakar Framework for Action, not only reflect the expanded vision of education as first articulated in Jomtien, but also address some of the new challenges that have exploded since 1990, such as the HIV/AIDS pandemic. The broadened vision of education has called for new and revitalized partnerships, and that is as true post Dakar as it was a decade ago.

There is now a plethora of stakeholders involved in basic education efforts at the global level. They include multilateral and bilateral international development organizations central and local governments, NGOs, teachers, parents and communities. The best partnerships recognize independence, entitlements, and indigenous knowledge; express mutual respect and trust; and work within the framework of national development and educational priorities.

In theory, at least, serious attempts have been made to move away from the practices of earlier decades when grants for education projects usually restricted the receiving country's equipment, experts, and other needs to choices preselected by the donor country or agency. Although the Dakar Framework for Action obligates national governments to fulfil their obligations to learners, a long way must still be traveled to ensure that countries and communities, especially poor and excluded populations, play an active role in identifying their needs and determining what kinds of projects will meet those needs.

THE ROLE OF TEACHERS

To be involved in the dialogue about education systems around the world today is to understand and articulate the key role played by teachers.

Through teachers can flow the ideology, values, and culture of a nation, state, and its people. Misinformation and constricted learning behaviours that students internalize can also be filtered through teachers' lack of knowledge, misjudgements, or biases. Calls for educational reform must therefore emphasize the education and empowerment of teachers that includes the real opportunity for them to share perspectives, power and decision-making. One critical area in which all teachers must be educated is gender equity. Among international agencies and donors, EFA reform efforts have heavily targeted girls and women calling for the elimination of gender gaps in access, learning and retention. Numerous programmes have also been initiated that either focus entirely on females or make a special effort to ensure their inclusion.

Education for girls, however, in strongly patriarchal countries will not result in empowered women who will participate in critical decision making -- unless their teachers are empowered supporters of gender equity. This is especially true of women teachers who must serve as positive role models. Although they are the front- line participants and critical to successful quality schooling, teachers often form a silent majority; they are excluded not only from policy-making, governance and management, but also from day-to-day instructional strategies and decision making.

Teachers as a whole, especially in less developed countries, have held minimal power in educational systems that are organized in hierarchical ways. Women teachers in particular are even less able to participate in decision-making and have even less voice in creating the institutional structures and policies that affect their lives - in and out of school - and the success of their students. Education researchers point out that the structural and institutional aspects of schools, rather than teachers, perpetuate the barriers to empowerment and equity. Structural obstacles encourage the reproduction of current power relations rather than stimulate changes. Even in many educational reform efforts, for example, teachers are often the forgotten or taken- for-granted vehic les used to implement but not to create or initiate reforms.

Pre-service and in-service training are often not planned or integrated into reform efforts; in many developing countries, teachers have no formal pre-service education at all. Yet, in spite of these arguments, it is also true that in many countries teachers are becoming increasingly accepted as essential partners in a dynamic education system. But if efforts to increase student access, learning and retention in primary education are to succeed, relevant and empowering teacher education is crucial. Teachers must become active, fulfilled and empowered professionals themselves. If an educational system is to engender normative change, the entire system mus t be restructured to allow all actors to participate more democratically.

THE STRUGGLE BETWEEN CONTINUITY AND CHANGE, TRADITION AND INNOVATION

The education system in India remains at a critical juncture. The world's second most populous country, with current estimates of over one billion people, India has a literacy rate of approximately 51 per cent. The history of India's educational system is complex, marked by deep debate and many contradictions between policy and practices and between laws and their enforcement. Elements of continuity and tradition have battled those of change and innovation. The power of cultural and historic barriers to change, including nearly two centuries of colonialism and many more centuries of a rigid caste system, have maintained a stubborn barrier to meaningful social transformation.

However, well before the past decade and even the past century, a populist movement continued to challenge very powerful traditional educational values and practices. A brief look at the diverse historical trends and currents can help to illuminate both the deep cultural roots of tradition and the strong reform elements that are critical to the current situation. This history reveals that progress is slow and uneven, and that the future is embedded in the past. Necessary changes must be perceived within the larger historical perspective.

HISTORICAL LINKS BETWEEN WOMEN'S TEACHER TRAINING AND GIRLS' EDUCATION

Viewed through a gender lens, India's history of educational reform reveals more than a century of policies that seemed to anticipate and support the needed links between women's teacher education and education for girls. As early as 1882, the Indian Education Commission supported teacher-training institutes for women. In 1913, the government of India (GOI) passed a resolution that both established teaching universities and emphasized the education of girls. Primary school teachers were required to pass a vernacular middle examination, receive one year of training and take refresher courses. They would receive a salary of not less than 12 rupees, and teach classes with no more than 30 to 40 students. During the struggle for independence in 1947, and in the years following, a growing number of women activists struggled with the ideas of gender and social change, internally, with each other and with society.

These women demanded a revision of the norms perpetuating inequities that would include the right to vote and equal rights to education. In 1944, the women's literacy rate had grown only to 3.4 per cent from 0.9 per cent in 1901. Their demands went far beyond the goals of national leaders and male reformers who promoted a limited view of female education that left the basic patriarchal social structure unchanged. Male leaders aimed to "use education to make women more capable of fulfilling their traditional roles as wives and mothers and not to make them more efficient and active units in the process of socio-economic or political development". Gandhi himself advocated culturally suitable education for women: "There is need for similar distinction between the education of males and females as has been made between them by Mother Nature herself".

POLICY REFORM FOLLOWS INDEPENDENCE

After independence, official GOI policies reflected the development of democratic ideology and institutions. The 1950 Constitution of independent India promised "universal, free, and compulsory education to all children up to the age of fourteen". Within this educational commitment, women were specifically named among "weaker others" to be given special protection and the opportunity to advance. To further these goals, the GOI established committees to reform the system including the Women's Education Committee, which addressed the training and employment of women teachers. Almost twenty years later, in 1968, India's first National Policy on Education recommended that "the education of girls should require emphasis, not only on grounds of social justice, but also because it accelerates social transformation." This document also proposed raising the status and increasing the benefits and training of teachers.

The 1985 "Challenge of Education," a Ministry of Education policy perspective review, cited many shortcomings of the education system and criticized the government's failure to carry out reform. It drew attention to the continuing authoritarian, centralized and monolithic management approach that impeded decentralization and local participation. The system, it said, also created an environment of anonymity and widespread apathy of teachers and the community in regard to primary school. The role of teachers reflected the many, often opposing, currents of tradition, caste, colonialism and reform. On the one hand, teachers held the status of guru deriving from the Brahman ideal of moral authority and sacred knowledge, subduing the curiosity and questioning of students. Yet teachers received poor quality teacher training, low pay and had little decision-making power in regard to substantive or administrative issues.

The Challenge of Education, also declared that: " . . . something will have to be done to change the orientation, work-ethic, knowledge and skills of the teachers, who will have to function much more creatively in a learning rather than a teaching environment, in which they will have to struggle continuously with new ideas as well as new technologies." The document also paid close attention to the quality of education, with a special focus on implementing child-centred and activity-based learning. Looking to education as an agent of basic change, the policy strengthened India's focus on girls' education and its link to women's empowerment. The education system would play an interventionist role in promoting women's studies and empowering women to become actively involved as decision makers and administrators. "The elimination of women's illiteracy and the removal of obstacles inhibiting their access to, and retention in, elementary education will receive overriding priority, through provision of special support services, setting of time targets, and effective monitoring". In 1992, further policy change continued to promote the end of gender discrimination and the empowerment of women to full participation.

The NPE and Programme of Action (POA) viewed education as an instrument of social transformation that would eliminate curriculum biases and enable professionals such as teachers, decision makers, administrators and planners to "play a positive interventionist role for gender equality" To achieve this would require a large-scale overhaul of policies and practices. Such measures included: training all teachers and instructors as agents of women's empowerment; developing gender and poverty sensitization programmes for teacher educators and administrators; developing gender-sensitive curriculum; removal of sex bias from textbooks. They also included giving preference to female teacher recruitment to motivate parents to send girls to school. The NPE set explicit goals for women teachers' recruitment at a minimum of 50 per cent and urged that training facilities ensure an adequate, though unspecified, number of qualified women teachers in subjects that included mathematics and science.

THE STRUGGLE TO NARROW THE GAP BETWEEN POLICY AND PRACTICE

Yet a stark contradiction has remained between policy commitments to women's equality and actual reform. Little real change has occurred despite the clear articulation by Indian educational policy and planning of what is necessary to create democratically structured programmes that will facilitate gender sensitivity and equity. Changing the ideology of a country steeped in cultural, social and economic inequities requires constant struggle. Over the years, the absence of political initiative and funding accompanied by changes in political control has hindered steady progress towards these goals. Women's national literacy rates remain at 42 per cent compared to the rate of 69 per cent for men.

Acknowledging these discouraging statistics, the Indian POA argues that the will to implement institutional mechanisms to ensure the reflection of gender sensitivity in educational programmes is still strongly needed. The limited scope of women's roles must be replaced with a 21st century ideology that makes them full participants in socio-economic and political development. Programmes that attempt to incorporate gender equitable policies, including those for teachers, have been increasing. Because they play a pivotal role in transmitting equality to their students, women teachers must be high on the list of women who participate in more gender equitable programmes.

A PROMISE OF JOYFUL LEARNING

Within this context and expressed need, the Teacher Empowerment Programme emerged as one important programme that focused increasingly on gender equity for teachers. This in-service programme began in the Dhar district of Madhya Pradesh in 1992 as a grassroots effort designed to meet the immediate needs of teachers for new content and skills that would increase their influence on the process of education.

Focused on interactive participation and decision-making of teachers, the TEP aimed to place power in their hands and facilitate its responsible use. Innovative and imaginative, the TEP did not reject official education policy; its general objectives and processes are consistent with the guidelines of the National Policy on Education and its Programme of Action.

TEP'S BEGINNINGS

The TEP began as a UNICEF initiative yet was enabled through a long standing relationship with the Government of India, familiarity with government policies and practices, and a deep understanding of the needs and conditions of teachers.

Through combined goals and efforts, the partnership of UNICEF, the GOI, and the teachers' union capitalized on an increasingly conducive environment and was able to put stated policy goals into practice. For teachers, this meant improved status, teaching skills and materials, greater participation and decision-making in governance and programme development and more joyful training in pedagogy.

The empowerment of teachers would also have a direct and positive bearing on achieving the goals for students that included increased attendance, retention through class five - especially for girls - and higher levels of achievement. Jude Henriques, the UNICEF education officer at the forefront of the TEP's initial development, most education reforms begin with the curriculum, textbooks, and testing procedures. For him, reform begins with the teacher. Henriques was aware that trust and commitment are powerful concepts that are necessary for the programme to succeed.

He worked to make sure that he and the teachers believed in each other and that the seeds of ownership and sustainability spread among them. Together they built strong teacher teams that helped to develop the training module and manual and then served as trainers of other educators at state, district, and school levels. The TEP ties educational developmental theory to practice as teachers learn a child-responsive approach that is joyful and experiential. They learn that teachers must be nurturing and caring and offer concrete contexts so children can learn through play and various hands-on activities. They learn to provide opportunities for children to express themselves verbally and artistically through singing, dancing, and drama and to allow ample time to tell and listen to stories that make sense of their environment and their lives.

JOYFUL LEARNING IN PRACTICE

Unlike most previous in-service trainings, the TEP addresses the lack of joy in teaching, the overburdened curriculum and the unmotivated teachers - all criticisms in various GOI and other education reports. The unshakeable foundation of the Joyful Learning approach is that teachers participate and collaborate through an interactive, hands-on approach. The choice of districts in which to implement the TEP was linked to indicators showing the poorest literacy rates. UP is India's most populous state and one of the five lowest literacy states where the rate stands at about only 41 per cent--55 per cent for males and only 25 per cent for females.

When the TEP expanded to the State of UP, teachers themselves chose the name Ruchipurna Shikshan or Joyful Learning (JL) for their training, reflecting both their ownership of the programme and a new attitude it motivated. Just one month before the training began in UP, on the day annually celebrated as Teachers' Day, over 12,000 teachers pledged and committed themselves to work towards UPE, to avoid absenteeism and drunkenness, and to become better teachers. Since that day, many teachers have pledged or re-pledged their commitment as part of the Joyful Learning Programme. Among the ways in which Henriques promoted the effectiveness of the TEP was to make sure that teachers could participate at low cost and to emphasize activities that were concrete and relevant to the local environment.

Teachers made their own teaching aids such as the cloth pocket board sewn to create rows and pockets. They used colour-coded cards for activities such as matching, categorizing, and sequencing, or word cards that enabled language arts skills such as vocabulary, syntax, or story telling. These activities have remained a part of the training throughout the history of the programme, and flourish today. Low-cost, low-tech and inclusive processes represent activities that teachers can initiate with the children themselves. The portable, pocket board teaching aid has proven particularly effective in environments where there is no classroom. Mamta, one woman teacher, was clearly inspired by the expressive, child-responsive teaching and the opportunity she was given to be creative. She believes that Joyful Learning focuses on the whole development of the child's mental, physical, cultural, and moral being.

- Joyful Learning is good for the students. It is good for the teachers also. The teachers are thinking that we only have to lecture in the class. There is no need to understand the child's mind. But now, they are thinking it is also our duty to see what the children are grasping from us . . . and taking interest in. . . . They were teaching us like the students of Class Two because this was the training for Class Two. . . . We have to know the mind of the students of Class Two. . . . We sing so many songs, we play so many games, and we were doing work in groups. The training was exciting.

Yet just as important as providing teachers with new skills and content, the training in UP went beyond teachers and administrators. It included space for dialogue among teachers, trainers and government officials for reflection, sharing and discussion of concerns. In one training session, for example, teachers expressed concern about outdated syllabi and curricula in the pre-service Basic Teacher Training (BTT) programme. They expressed the need for better communication among department officials, monitors, and the DIET (District Institute of Education and Training) instructors to increase their understanding and ownership of the TEP. The intangible aspects and principles upon which the programme was based are evident during these dialogues respect, trust, commitment, and equity.

The in-service manual for Class One expresses these empowering foundations:

- Teachers are all creative, talented people and respond remarkably when they are respected and included in the decision-making integral to their work in the classroom. They gain a sense of ownership over their work and their classrooms, when they are involved in development of the curriculum, designing of the syllabus, making and selecting of teaching materials and in designing training programmes leading to their own intellectual and professional development.

Placing teachers in a central role, encouraging hands-on interactive activities and the making of teaching aids have garnered strong and wide teacher support in the districts in which the programme has operated. Although implementation is challenging, partners have learned to work together and make the best use of each others' diverse expertise, resources and knowledge. Furthermore, the TEP has begun to converge with other government-sponsored teacher training programmes to spread more widely the joyful learning that ultimately will benefit both the teachers and the students. The discussion of teacher involvement in education reform, Indian policy history and the general goals and processes of the TEP, sets the stage to view the TEP through a ge nder lens.

The training itself may empower to some extent all the teachers who participate. The following part posits that further empowerment - of men as well as women teachers - requires explicit attention to gender and the limitations imposed by institutional and social structures. The following part addresses these issues and highlights specific aspects of the TEP that have been particularly effective in empowering women teachers.

THE TEP AND THE GENDER LENS

One of the key questions emerging from the research was whether and to what extent a genderneutral or gender-blind approach to teacher empowerment would actually result in gender equality and specifically the empowerment of women teachers. Through a closer examination of the TEP in practice, this part links the practical day-to-day realities of the TEP at work to broader feminist principles.

Through the eyes and voice of several participants, it demonstrates the flexibility of the programme, to create and respond to a demand for more gender explicit attention. There is an exploration of the philosophy that a gender neutral approach can bring about equally the empowerment of women as well as men teachers. And finally, this part links particular and individual efforts to prevailing feminist research and the socially constructed and constricted gender roles played by women in India and in many other cultures.

THE GENDER LENS: FEMINIST PRINCIPLES DEMONSTRATE CRITICAL AND CONTINUING REALITIES

Over the past three decades as feminist research has taken on an abstract and theoretical quality, its origins are often forgotten - origins based in the 'lifeblood and 'lived realities' of women's experience. As women's lives keep changing, this earthbound educational reform programme in India is a reminder that change is slow and uneven and that to become empowered women themselves must keep reliving, reviewing and revising their experience. The following precepts bring together feminist principles with the TEP experience.

Numbers Count: Hiring More Women Teachers is a Key Strategy to Increasing Girls' School Participation

Worldwide, and for several decades, the critical role of female teachers in reducing the gender gap in primary and secondary education has been well established. Numerous studies indicate that girls in developing countries "learn better and stay in school longer when their teachers are women". The general assumption had been that the presence of female teachers would provide an automatic incentive for girls to enrol in school; they would create a safe atmosphere that would encourage families to send their daughters to school, and would provide positive role models.

Simply because they were women, female teachers would be gender sensitive in their attitudes and behaviours, fight for more gender sensitive curriculum and provide a safe environment free from sexual harassment. An increase in the numbers of women teachers would accelerate, if not ensure, sustainable gender equality in education. The 1950 Indian Constitution guaranteed free, universal, compulsory education for all children to the age of

14 with female education as a key element of planned development. Yet today, girls in India still conspicuously trail their male counterparts. India has the largest number of out of school girls in the world - over 19.5 million. Current figures suggest that there are over 11 million fewer girls than boys enrolled at the primary level. Literacy rates are 69% for men and only 42% for women. Many approaches have been put in place to reduce this gap--awareness campaigns, child-care centres, more schools closer to home, direct incentives. Experience has proven repeatedly that there is strength in numbers. When a country's teacher education programmes graduate enough female teachers, the likelihood of expanding female education improves. In fact, the Education for Women's Equality chapter of India's 1992 POA notes the direct relationship between dropout rates of girls and the small proportion of women teachers.

In the state of UP, which has one of the lowest literacy rates in India, female teachers number only 21 and 23 per cent in rural primary and middle level schools. In urban areas, these percentages are 56 and 57 per cent. Achieving a critical mass can give groups of excluded members of society mutual support and the motivation to speak out, assert themselves and express in the public sphere what has been for protection only private attitudes and behaviours. Continued exposure of men to large numbers of women on an equal footing will help them to stop seeing women as subordinate and to accept change. As UNESCO, the World Bank, UNICEF and many other agencies have claimed, more female teachers must be hired.

But 'More' isn't Enough: Women Teachers Must also be Empowered

Experience has also shown that hiring more women teachers will not by itself promote gender equity and social change. As long as societal gender discrimination persists, access alone will neither keep girls in school nor produce empowered women capable of significant decisionmaking. Women themselves internalize and replicate the sessions of culture. They carry with them and pass on to girls under their tutelage the societal behaviours and attitudes imposed on them from early childhood. They do this, often unintentionally or unknowingly, through their own culturally determined behaviours and attitudes. As role models, women teachers may communicate to girls the dictates to be obedient or submissive, not to stand up for themselves or take risks. In the classroom, research has shown repeatedly that women teachers may also perpetuate these behaviours and pass on traditional messages by calling on boys first and allowing, even encouraging, interruption, argumentativeness and other traditionally male behaviours while discouraging girls from the same behaviours.

Educators themselves need to be empowered supporters of gender equity and of women teachers who will serve as positive role models. These possibilities imply social transformation and, thus, threaten the existing power structure. If women are to achieve equality in Indian society, women teachers must be in the forefront of those who encourage social transformation for girls. They must themselves be, and help young females to be, critically aware of their society's norms that include an understanding of patriarchy and how and why females have been traditionally subordinated in society. They must help female students to challenge accepted gender roles. "Activism should not ignore the interplay between the empowering and the oppressive in the form and content of our work".

Empowerment has become an important concept in the work of many agencies. It is consistent with the shift in approach from Women in Development - a gender neutral demand for women's equal integration into the development process - to Gender in Development (GID--also often called Gender and Development, GAD) which demands a change in structural relations to create greater power and autonomy. When women both participate and express their views, and have the power to make decisions that affect their public and personal lives, they are empowered. Teacher empowerment programmes that incorporate GID theory promote these goals. It is argued that empowered women teachers lead to greater retention and learning achievement for girls. More critically conscious, educated women can contribute to a more just and equitable social order that includes transformation as a goal of educational reform.

The Personal is Political: Research Through "Lived Realities"

Feminist scholarship has shown repeatedly how the patriarchal construction of knowledge devalues both the intellect and emotions of females. Educational systems are microcosms of societal values and formal education. Their function is to instill appropriate behaviour and cultural norms, which often includes unspoken but clear gender-specific messages.

Schools then, at all levels, are too often vehicles for reproducing stereotyped or limited views of girls and boys, women and men. Examining the issues through women's personal experience, or what is called 'lived realities', helps to better expose and understand the depth of gender messages and how women's private lives and roles are both mirrored in and hidden from the public sphere.

Documenting women's realities and making their lives visible helps to expose and correct the patriarchal bias of social science. Conceptualizing women's private behaviour as an expression of cultural and societal dictates has enabled feminist researchers to bring a persuasive new perspective to the theory of political and social power relations. It also allows women, who understand their own experiences in a new way, to contribute to the creation of a new social order that benefits women, girls and all society. For both men and women, discussion and exploration of experiential forms of expression often result in a better grasp of the strong links between private and public realms.

For example, Kumar rejects theories that define women as totally passive in their responses to restricting and discriminatory structures. Acknowledging the presence of powerful institutional obstacles, she believes that understanding the hidden and subversive ways in which women exercise their independence while outwardly controlled by a repressive normative order is highly relevant to understanding women's experience. "Protest does not have to take only wellrecognized forms, but it can appear in various other permutations of daily life". For example, evasive tactics, genres of song and dance, private correspondence and diary writing may all be forms of data that help feminist researchers to understand other women and their culture and for women to understand themselves.

LOOKING GENDER IN THE EYE - LISTENING TO THE VOICES OF WOMEN TEACHERS

Linking feminist theory to the TEP, this study pays close attention to the voices of women teachers as they strive to make space for themselves as professionals in a patriarchal society. In particular, it depicts two women primary school teachers, Shail and Mamta, both of whom took the TEP training and are now members of the core group of teachers in the RaeBareli District of UP. The study compares their lives, teaching careers, attitudes and relationship to their society and its norms. Listening closely to their life stories, related experiences and private views, brings into sharp focus the link between private and public, between life and education, between the personal and political. It also reveals the complexities, nuances and entrenched attitudes and behaviours behind the theory and the statistics. The voices of these teachers help to reveal how their daily lives, thoughts and feelings fit into the larger public culture and system that helps or hinders women teachers' empowerment.

SHAIL

- Why is a woman always regarded as a 'woman', not as a person? Why are her rights limited only to pieces of thesis and a constitution? A woman gives birth to man and yet is treated as no more than a decorative piece for his bed. He cheats her in the name of love. She has to bear the strain of physical and verbal abuse from him and is forced to face immeasurable humiliation and struggle in society at every step.

The relationship between personal and political, private and public is repeatedly clear in the life of Shail, the author of the above most-private writing - which she shared only after trust had been established.

- "What use," my mother said, "that a girl should be learned! Much good will it do her when she has lusty sons and a husband to look after. Look at me, am I any worse that I cannot spell my name, so long as I know it?"

Shail, whose name means "mountain", was 30 at the time of the study, and a teacher of Class Two in a government school in the RaeBareli district of UP. Her life was like that of many Indian girls. The fictional Indian mother's words quoted above relate to her own experience as a girl struggling to overcome both her family's and village's resistance to continuing her education. This resistance challenged a patriarchal dictate that she follow the traditional path for which females need no more than a Class Five village education.

Today, with a fuller understanding of how the personal is political, she is keenly aware of the structural nature of her own experience. She said, "I very very much struggle in life for girls' education because in the villages are very very many problems." Shail grew up in a small village of about 4,000 in the RaeBareli District with her parents, two older brothers, and a younger sister. Her family owned about ten fields where they grew vegetables and pulses, a form of lentils. When Shail expressed a desire to continue school after Class Five outside the village, community and caste sentiment were aga inst her.

Her friend and neighbour Monica translated for Shail:

- "When Shail was taking her education, the village was against her. They said that she should not have so much education. She is a girl. She should get married and go to her husband's place. If she is going to get so much education, she is going to do something that will destroy our village. But she just said, "No, I'm going to study further."

Where did Shail get her determination? The village fear that she would disturb its pattern of life - - that she would influence other girls to leave the village for education in the city-- nearly swayed her father. Yet her older educated brother was in the military and had seen more of the world. He knew that girls were getting educated, accepted the idea that this was a positive step and helped persuade their father to let Shail leave the village. Monica, "he wanted his sister to be educated and to stand on her feet." Living with an uncle's family in Lucknow, the capital of UP, Shail continued her education through Grade 12. She found a job in a Montessori school near her home village, where she taught and went to school part-time, completing her B.A. in 1986 and her M.A. in political science in 1988. In 1994 Shail earned a Ph.D. in Hindi.

During the period of the study, Shail was living in four small rooms about two kilometres from the centre of RaeBareli. With both of her brothers dead, Shail had become the primary family wage earner.

On her 3,000 per month rupee salary, she provided the main income for herself, her mother, and her three nephews. When she first was interviewed for this study, Shail said that she did not want to get married because she had made a commitment to help provide for her nephews, including a private education. But as she became more trusting, she also became more comfortable in expressing her growing "feminist" views.

Besides the care of her extended family, she acknowledged an additional reason for not getting married: that she did not want a man to control her life. Once Shail overheard me talking with a male administrator who referred proudly to the much lower rate of divorce in India than in the United States. I had responded politely that laws and customs in the U.S. made divorce easier and more acceptable. But from what I had read and seen, many women in India appeared to suffer silently and might be likely to get divorced were it not for the difficulty of the legal process and their fear of social ostracism.

Shail said that she had agreed with my views and believed that the male administrator was downplaying women's problems in India. That, she said, was part of the gender blindness of men and many women. She continued, talking about wife killings and bride burnings, and removed a folder from her bookshelf where she kept her dissertation, her M.Ed., and other important writings.

She explained that she had written much about this struggle, including poems and other writings. These writings were precious to her and she was protective of them, saying that many others, including her family, did not agree with her or even understand. She would not risk publishing such works where she lives for fear of reprisal. Even allowing the use of a short excerpt in this study created some hesitation. Shail has learned to choose her battles wisely.

MAMTA

Mamta has always lived in the centre of the town of RaeBareli. At 25, she was an expressive and upbeat young woman, strong in her Hindu religious beliefs. She usually dressed casually in pyjama-style tunic with loose drawstring pants, rather than in a sari. Unlike Shail, Mamta lived in a large home with groups of small rooms surrounding a centre courtyard. Her mother had died recently and Mamta was living in an extended family of 20, which included her father, three older brothers, their wives and children and her niece. Although Mamta was contributing to her family, they were not dependent on her salary to the same extent as Shail's family. Mamta said that her father always allowed her much choice.

Her brothers were all well educated with engineering and other technical degrees and her sisters- in- law were permitted to work outside the home -- although there were no jobs for them. Mamta spoke English well, and like Shail, was well educated. She went to a public school near her home through Class Five and attended a government school up through Class 12 followed by a two-year B.A. programme from Kanpur University and an M.A. in English where she was the only girl in her class. She also had completed a B. Ed and in 1993 a two-year BTT--Basic Teacher's Training diploma course at the DIET in RaeBareli.

In her own co-educational grade school, Mamta remembered the exact ratio of 13 girls to 27 boys. Why did she remember these numbers so clearly? "Because," she said, "we were less in strength". Although the numbers made little difference in the way she was treated, they did make a difference in the way she felt. Mamta and her female classmates were told that "we are different," she said. "We have certain limitations as 'ladies' and "should not waste much time with the boys." Society would not approve. Despite the fact that Mamta believed her family was freer than many in terms of gender roles, her brothers were still looking for a good husband for her and teased her about this.

A substantial dowry would be required if she were to be matched with any type of professional man. Even though Mamta had a Master's degree and was fluent in English, her status as a primary teacher did not warrant a match with the highest level professional such as a doctor. Primary school teachers are considered public servants, not professionals. While many men in Mamta's class and caste look for educated wives, for many families, especially in rural areas, an educated woman is believed to cause problems and create ripples in the traditional patriarchal structure. Desai quotes Karlekar's discussion with a mother from an untouchable caste who states: "Too much of schooling will only give girls big ideas and then they will be beaten up by their husbands or abused by their in- laws".

For families such as these, girls' education is expected to be tied to functional domestic uses. Mamta's reflection on why she chose to be a teacher mirrored her inherent and socialized "female" character traits and the bringing of private "female" values into the public sphere. "I love children very much," she said without hesitation. "A teacher is the builder of the country and in this way I am helping my country to build a nation -- a good nation". The name, Mamta, meaning "mother love," fits the demeanour of this primary teacher.

She exhibits a particularly caring, nurturing relationship in her teaching--less authoritative than many teachers I observed in UP primary schools. In her former teaching position at a public school, she had more resources to work with in a nicer facility. Mamta knew that the government schools had poorer facilities, yet she received a higher salary than at the public school. She explained that government schools needed furniture, chairs, and a better building and that she did not like sitting in a chair at a desk when the students are sitting on the bare or mat-covered floor; it caused too much separation. Mamta truly had the children's interest at heart and sometimes she felt as though government officials were concerned only about themselves and not about the children.

LOOKING GENDER IN THE EYE - THE TEP IN PRACTICE

Underlying the implementation of the TEP is the philosophy that teachers must be trusted, respected, listened to, and encouraged to nurture their creative abilities. Committed to the empowerment of all teachers, trainers in the earliest sessions in Madhya Pradesh did not include explicit discussion of gender, caste or class issues. No content explicitly targeted excluded populations, structural inequalities and obstacles or patriarchy. The emphasis was on the immediate participation of all teachers through activities that encourage open and equal male and female interaction and break down inhibitions that would obviate the need for specific attention to gender issues.

This mainstreaming, or gender blind, strategy prevalent at the start of the movement for gender equality, acknowledged the need for equal female participation but emphasized that programmes should respond to the needs and concerns of women within the framework of broader human and social development objectives. However, such an approach has also exposed the difficulties of translating mainstreaming goals into visible results and actions and has proven extremely limited in producing significant and speedy improvement in the status of women.

This is true in the most socially progressive societies, but especially in country programmes where the national environment is not conducive to promoting social equity and empowerment of women. Looking at the TEP through a gender lens, what arises as central to the discussion are the relative benefits and drawbacks to mainstreaming gender concerns through gender-neutral practices of equality or to promoting gender-specific analysis and activities. What some call gender neutral or gender-blind approaches to the training do not consciously promote or directly raise awareness of the larger societal, structural inequalities that must be altered.

THE EVOLUTION OF A GENDER EXPLICIT FOCUS

As the programme expanded from MP to UP, the need for specific discussion of gender issues was acknowledged and incorporated into the structure, design and implementation of the programme process. Explicit targeting of gender equity became part of the TEP curricula in UP, opening space for depth of coverage and for additional content. Planners were aware that more time was needed to break down the barriers of women's silence and dispel misconceptions about their acceptance of the status quo. Longer training sessions evolved and the overall training increased in length from one to five days. To achieve equality and empowerment, it would also be necessary to address men's underlying attitudes towards gender. The impetus for this shift came largely from Sahni, a woman trainer, whose own "lived realities" and gender consciousness drove this aspect of the training.

She described this unfolding process:

- We spent about 10 days together around a table trying to develop this package. And we would get up and do things -- perform the package, so to speak. And that's how it developed. We said, "well then the training should take this form too because it was so enjoyable". People liked it and they seemed to gain a lot from it; it seemed to make a lot more sense.

Gender sensitivity was introduced in day one of the training as the group began to learn gendersensitive songs. On the third afternoon, a gender sensitization session focused on the status of women in general and more specifically, on a discussion of discriminatory social and political structures such as patriarchy. These sessions included sharing personal histories and anecdotes; composition and rendition of poems and songs pertaining to the issue of girls' education, and collaborative development of concrete plans for increasing enrolment and retention of girls and for sensitizing the parent community. The State Representative of the UNICEF field office in Lucknow at the time of the study pointed out the new emphasis of gender in both the Class One and Class Two training manuals. She said, "We're getting more and more sensitive about these things this last year and looking at it in a more focused way, rather than in general terms."

CREATING A CRITICAL MASS OF WOMEN TEACHERS

Throughout the research and observations of the TEP, the interdependency of numbers of woman teachers and empowerment surfaced repeatedly. Reasons for restricted women's participation in teaching varied from practical to psychosocial - for example, from competing family obligations to feelings of unworthiness. Both are rooted in gender roles resulting from lifelong discrimination and socialization. Yet attention to lived realities and explicit discussion of gender issues will support woman teachers and gender equity and help to increase the numbers of woman teachers.

The Impact of Being Outnumbered

The study's women respondents referred often to the impact of being outnumbered. As Mamta and others described the gender ratios in their education, they articulated a general sense of discomfort ranging from tension to fear. This discomfort included a quality of being "on gua rd", reluctance to "be themselves," and/or a self-consciousness about what is "appropriate" public behaviour.

Many of the TEP's training procedures and materials were designed by a group of two trainers and ten teachers, a group, however, that included only one woman trainer and one woman teacher. Although two females were better than none, given the special focus on girls' education in the UP programme, more women teachers among this group should have been recruited for the training. Sahni, who was the only woman trainer in the group, said,

- In the first training camp, I was shocked when I saw there were six women in a group of 31 from five districts. That was all. Just six women and all these big burly men. It was a little bit scary. You're on your guard to begin with and you maintain a distance. And you don't know whether they're looking at you or listening to you. So you have to work twice as hard.

As a core teacher, Shail had gone to another Block in her district to help with training only to be turned away by the headmaster because she was a woman. "I don't want you; I don't need you." When Shail returned to her Block, she complained to the district manager and members of the UNICEF team. Nothing happened as a result. Sahni well understood this when she spoke of other "nasty experiences" similar to Shail's; she also reflected on her reluctance to send a woman trainer as one of twelve to supervise for two months in another district.

- I knew it would be too tough going into another district. We selected one [woman]. And she turned it down as I knew she would. [When the department kept saying], "Oh, but there's no woman; we need a woman representative." That made me very angry too. "Why do you need a woman representative when you haven't done anything to make it easier for women to go to these places?"

Uncovering and Overcoming Structural Barriers to Participation

Overt resistance such as that may decrease. Yet other related factors, such as the practical consequences of women's roles or 'lived realities' remain serious impediments to the full participation of women in the training. Domestic duties and family responsibilities, for example, restrict women's time to prepare for teaching, allow for less leisure time and less motivation, or even restrict opportunity to attend the training, especially if it requires travelling to a location away from their home. These structural obstacles are often a form of covert resistance that for two decades has included the arguments: "Women have every opportunity; they just don't take advantage."

"They can't keep up." "They don't pay attention." "They lose interest and drop out." "It interferes with their real work of marriage", etc. Not only is this a self-promoting denial that the obstacles eve n exist, it is also a deliberate transfer of responsibility onto women for the impediments placed in their path by patriarchal social structures and expectations. Exposing these obstacles and understanding their causes help to create alternative solutions. Sometimes bussing it, sometimes on burro, cart, sometimes on foot, and then staying with all sorts of strange men. . . . you're far more vulnerable. But they wanted to fill up, you know, they want to pretend that this whole thing is very gender representative. "So where's the woman?"

I said, "there isn't any". "And why isn't there any?" "Because conditions aren't fit." Sahni was referring to the lack of separate accommodations for women as another gender-based obstacle preventing women who had to travel from attending the training. At one training held in Mirzapur, most of the men who had come from other villages spent the night in the training room. They had stored their bedrolls on top of large supply cabinets in the back of the room and converted the training room to sleeping accommodations. However, this type of accommodation was impossible for women teachers. Because societal proprieties do not allow women to sleep side by side with men, only local women participants there at the school could participate.

At the other two trainings, however, this difficulty did not seem to be present. In Lucknow, for example, the training was held at a pre-service institution that was also the DIET campus. This allowed for comfortable enough dormitory type, separate sleeping rooms for men and women.

It is likely that the situation in Mirzapur was never analysed through a gender lens. When this issue was raised with Henriques, he seemed to imply that it was not a serious problem. His explanation was that most of the women are in urban areas where accommodations are available, or the women can go home at night. He also said that a large number of women teachers were entering the programme from tribal areas.

"They are ve ry powerful teams -- some of them nearly all women. Tribally, women are much more progressive and much more equal." He seemed to accept the truth that women could be as good, even better trainers than men, but he did not take the opportunity to further exp lore this rather pertinent observation. Henriques agreed that men are more likely to become trainers because of required days away from home, and he emphasized the necessity of ensuring the presence of women trainers and role models. At first they tried to schedule the training so that the women trainers would be away from home for only two three days at a time because they had children to care for. They would come back for a few days and then go again.

This would require a team to take a series of threeday trips back and forth. It would require increased expenses, but making the special effort and spending the resources, helped to accept women as part of the team. "They all get sent a clear message that women's participation and girls' education is important". In UP, women were being encouraged to bring their children to the in-service training. That was "part of the package". Henriques explained, "We welcome it; we encourage it to ensure the teacher is there and that she can concentrate".

PARTICIPATION AND PERFORMANCE ACTIVITIES BREAK DOWN GENDER WALLS

Henriques believed that change would happen through a participatory approach to the training where men and women participate equally. In the early MP training, he did not draw attention to gender issues through discussion or analysis of structural or other obstacles. In one series of participatory activities, all participants sat on the floor to reinforce equality.

They engaged in small-group work of mixed genders or in mixed pairs where they created colourful cards for the pocket boards or thought of new ways to use the pocket boards with students. Equality was being modeled implicitly through planning and performing activities together. Henriques argued that "there is no difference between males and females in doing actions."

In fact, he believes that normally woman teachers do much better than male teachers in the participatory activities. "It comes much more naturally to them." Kamaluddin, the UNICEF education officer in UP at the time, also pointed out the improved relations among male and female teachers as a result of greater interaction and modelling by the TEP trainers during the 5-day in-service training. He compared it to the traditional, nonparticipatory, lecture-based "you should do this; you should do that" teacher training method.

- It was so obvious [in the beginning] that the women would not hold the hand of male teachers. After their training they were behaving like brothers and sisters -- part of the same family. I think living together, eating together, thinking together is exceptional. [The traditional teacher training method] is not as effective as if you create an environment and you want me to act in accordance to what you are suggesting. So [within the five days] I find that I'm beginning to remove my blinkers and see world in its right perspective.

Shail confirmed that sitting and working together has had an equalizing impact. Before the Joyful Learning training, the women had no chance to sit with the men. Now, she said, "there's so much work, they have to sit together in order to get it done."

- Before, the lady teachers were not able to talk in front of men; they were very shy and would hide their faces. In our country, if a woman comes in front of a man, she is considered a characterless woman. After the JL in-service, the women thought that teaching is their job, so they should not hide their face in front of men and others. They have more confidence among themselves and speak and sing songs in front of everyone.

Breaking Down Walls for Women

As gender-sensitive women teachers can be role models for girls, empowered women trainers can help teachers they train to understand and reduce stereotypes and prejudices by drawing on women's experience, or "lived realities." They can turn demeaned and devalued traditional female behaviours into respected assets that benefit themselves, their professions and their societies. All cultures have long recognized that "different" is too often a synonym for "deficient" and seen as a consequence of immutable female "nature." This can confine women to stereotyped and restricted gender roles. Feminism in the 1970's understandably accepted the "gender blind" argument that women's differences were a result of nurture (or lack of) rather than nature and if women were given the same opportunities as men, these differences would disappear.

Since the 1980's a voluminous body of literature has acknowledged and heralded women's ways of doing things in which differences--such as skills in and attention to consultation, cooperation and facilitation; and process and consensus building --are celebrated and esteemed and their capacity to transform society is promoted. Gender neutral participatory activities in the TEP brought to the surface many of the differences between men and women and the need to address them directly.

Over the past two decades, the link between women's private and public lives has been at the heart of the international women's movement and the subject of worldwide media attention. Yet the fact that Shail continued to hide her writings on the top shelf is a powerful reminder of the deep reality gap between what women think and feel and are willing to say and do in private and their public utterances and behaviours. In private, women behave a certain way with a certain kind of freedom. When they are in public or around men, the behaviour change is significant. There is a consistent implication that the presence of men (in a setting outside the home) creates a public domain, even in an informal setting.

Sahni said:

- When there are just women, there isn't this tension. There was this part of our training where we hold hands in a circle. I always made sure that I was holding hands only with Rakesh [a man but her friend/ co-trainer]. And that there was always a woman next to me. I would notice that there were all these smiles and snickers (by the men) that said, "Why are we holding hands? Men and women aren't supposed to hold hands." So I just stopped doing that, which is a pity because we were trying. I said, "No, I don't think it's culturally appropriate." [And during the performance aspects of the training,] there were times when I was a lot more on guard than I would have

> been had the group consisted of more women. Because [the men] are not used to familiarity, they can misinterpret it.

Henriques expressed full awareness about the manifestation and consequences of this gap.

- Women are not assertive or empowered in the public sphere. With dramatics, singing, action, lots of activity, it comes much more spontaneously to them. Except when doing it publicly. If they are outside the classrooms, they will not do it because they will be afraid, what will people think--they are dancing in front of other people.

Yet, performance, Henriques reasoned, is known to be an area where women excel and can bring their skills from the private to the public sphere with comfort and ease. He believed that breaking down this inhibition without drawing attention to the reasons behind it, would enable women to perform/ participate publicly, what they are ordinarily only comfortable doing in a private sphere. In the early MP trainings, participants did not discuss these issues. Rather, there was a matter-offact environment of expectation that supported and trusted women's strengths without looking at the problem or its causes.

The attitude expressed to them in the earlier training was: "We know this is what we need to do. We think that if every teacher does it, it's good. Do you think you can do it?" And then, he said, "We let them decide." Henriques also acknowledged that it does not happen automatically and that it took more coaxing at first to get women to perform publicly. But then, he noted that they were better at it. "Some of them came beautifully on. They didn't waste any time and were very good. They become my trainers." Sahni agreed that the performative nature of the training has helped women to surface more.

- . . . performance is culturally considered part of the female domain. If there's a wedding or a festival, the women will sing, not the men. The men are supposed to be strong and all that sort of macho thing. So this gave the women an opportunity to do something that they were supposed to be better at. They emerged much more, volunteered and took centre stage much more and had more of the limelight--which is why I think it helped them be better participants.

And for Men

For men as well, performing helped to break down gender barriers. A key part of the curricula focuses on males and females teaching and singing songs that they will also teach to the children. The songs encourage girls' attendance and success in school. One song is called "The Dreams of Daughters" which is in the Class One manual. The impact of such songs spread beyond the training, just as to Kamaluddin who described how one of the male district leaders began to sing a song that says, "As women, we're not going to stitch our lips and silently tolerate everything you do." The district leader, said Kamaluddin, is a die-hard kind of male chauvinist, but he's basically a Brahmin, a strong kind of personality.

He started singing this song--I couldn't believe it. I thought, he was the man who was going to stand up and say, 'Shut up'. But he didn't. He was singing the song. Kamaluddin also noted that in the hills he heard boys singing that same song -- even though he suggested they probably had no idea what it meant. Sahni described the positive impact on her co-trainer, Rakesh, of the performance activities and of their working together. She also stressed the need for gender consciousness that accompanied the activities.

PERFORMANCE ACTIVITIES: GENDER CONSCIOUSNESS TO COMBAT STEREOTYPES

At the same time, Sahni pointed out the difficulties raised by the performance and more public aspects of the training. For example, given the entrenched roots of patriarchy in her country, she said that many people still found it difficult to take a woman seriously. She found that without close attention, performance aspects of the training tended to perpetuate stereotyped gender roles. "Hypothetically", she said, "it's like the principal and the teacher, or the director and actor."

- If the principal is a man and the teacher is a woman, when there's any kind of demonstration [or] groundwork to be done, the teacher will do it. And the principal will direct the proceeding. Always when there's a man and a woman together, they assume, even if the man has just arrived, that he is in charge. That used to --and continues to -- make me mad. If I would be doing all the work and then suddenly a man would show up from somewhere, it really makes me furious. So then you have to work twice as hard to make yourself heard, to make people listen.

The research for this study revealed many confirming instances of this experience in which the women would be more involved in working on the pocket board while the men appeared to be structuring the events. Yet there were some situations when a man rather than a woman would come forward to share a small group's activity with the larger group. Sahni pointed out the implied sexual innuendoes that men often misread in women's performances and expressed anger about the more blatant provocative behaviour by men. She also noted the difficulty that women had not to back down after making a complaint.

- [Doing these performances] you're really putting yourself at risk sometimes where these men are concerned. Where maybe they just want to watch you. And you never know what kinds of constructions they are putting on all of this. They're not used to performing with women. So all of that takes some steeling and some strength.

- When we were forming these groups, two women refused to come in. They said, "we don't like the men in that group; they say all kinds of nasty things. "We have this game that says, 'What is round?' And then you respond: 'a wheel,' and the other person says 'be quick,' and someone else says 'bindi'. The other person says 'be quick', and they say 'okay, roti, a plate.' It goes like that. One of those men, while this whole game was being played, says, 'and women's breasts.' I was furious. And [the women] said: "We won't hold hands with any of them." I said, "Well fine. I'm right there with that. Let's not hold hands with any of them." So I was very mad. I said, "Which one said it?" They pointed out the one man. I spoke to the district official and said, "This man has just made an obscene remark. And we want him suspended from the training." But the women got upset and said, "Oh poor chap. He has a family and things. Don't do that." Then I said, "No. He's not to be allowed. He can't go out as a trainer. We're not placing other women at risk."

'IF SHE CAN DO IT, WHY CAN'T I?': EMPOWERED WOMEN TRAINERS SERVE AS ROLE MODELS

For Women Teachers

For the TEP to succeed in empowering women, the influence of a gender-sensitive woman trainer on both men and women teachers cannot be underestimated. Sahni's own "lived realities" helped to make her the best kind of role model. She had been sensitive to gender issues since childhood, because of the oppressive behaviour by her father who demeaned and "shouted down" the women at home. In 1983, Sahni founded a women's organization called "Suraksha," meaning "Security". Striving to help women gain an understanding of patriarchy, she ran "Suraksha" from her home for three years with no funding, later receiving support from UNICEF and USAID for small projects. Her own empowerment and concern for gender issues grew, and in 1989 she completed her doctoral work in the United States. Her conscientization and image as a role model contributed greatly to the growth of empowerment in women teachers such as Shail and Mamta. As an Indian, Sahni is able to relate to the contextual and practical difficulties of women teachers in her country. Mamta and Shail recognize Sahni as a model of possibilities for women. They began to develop, especially Shail, an "if she can do it, then so can I" attitude. She says:

- In Joyful Learning there were many songs, which only a woman can sing clearly. So through songs women come in front. Dr. Sahni also provoked the women. . . . [They] thought that she is a lady doctor, and if she could do such things, why can't I? If there would be a man instead of Mrs. Sahni, they [women] couldn't be so frank. They couldn't so easily do the job. In society there is a distance between a man and a woman they had to keep. Because if they are together, another person would say anything about the man or the woman, that the woman is characterless and all.

Kamaluddin, the UNICEF education officer in UP, addressed the importance of a woman teacher role model.

- The ultimate objective is to increase the competencies of the teacher. For example, when Shail was teaching in that school, she was part of a team of four or five teachers. She had to abide by what the head teacher told her to do and often this head teacher was a man. [Since the training] things have changed. You can see a large number of women trainers among the teachers and because of this programme, they have an equal learning opportunity. Shail is getting exactly the same opportunity that the man teacher is getting. Because of the focus of this training, perhaps she's even getting more attention. The other teachers are listening to and acting in accordance with them [the women trainers].

Sahni herself had a clear realization of her importance as a female trainer.

- I think it is [very important] for many reasons. Especially to reach out to other women. . . for support, for safety, for protection. They begin to see you as a role model. There are many women teachers who wouldn't open up if there weren't any female trainers.

She noted that, like Shail, another female teacher trainee, Umila, had become a strong female role model through the training.

- She's quite a remarkable woman and she has flowered, tremendously, with this training. When we conducted the training, the chief guest there made some remark like, "You know what is so nice is to see the weaker sex emerge. " So she got up and said, "There is something I want to say. I beg your pardon. We're really not, and we resent being called the weaker sex. Just women, that's all." That was quite a remark to make.

AND FOR MEN TEACHERS

For the men as well, Sahni argued, women trainers are important. Male trainers had told her their feelings of being "at a loss" when there were no female trainers in the group. They noticed that it was more difficult to reach out to the women trainees and to "get them on your side," or for them to participate wholeheartedly without the encouragement of women trainers. It is also important, Sahni said, for men to see women in more of a power role. But persuading men to change their behaviour comes only by hard and exhausting example that involves women relinquishing their own gender roles and changing their own relationship to power. Sahni recalled how Umeshwar, a Block Leader, had been one of those males who would shout the female teachers down. A particularly telling example of this behaviour occurred in an incident that started as a discussion about language and grew into an explosive argument.

- We were talking about how language is very biased in terms of gender. In Hindi there's the stem "shikshak" and the stem "shikshaka". Shikshaka is a lady teacher and shikshak is generally a male teacher. If you have only one, shikshak is used. And then Umeshwar says, "I think we should just abolish the damn shikshaka; shikshak is enough." I said, "No, why should we abolish the term shikshaka? Why don't we abolish shikshak?" He says, "No, we still like to have the male teacher." I said, "but teacher is gender neutral." We do not have a feminine counterpart in English...there is no teacheress. There's a teacher; there's a teacher, and there's a teacher. And that's it. Men think that in the name of equality, all you need to do is eliminate women. Or -- you eliminate the differences and then we're all equal. How do you do that so you make women to be more like men? I said, "We would like that you try to include both." And I found myself arguing alone. Even Rakesh said, "Ya, it's such a minor thing." I said, "No, it's not a minor thing. Since we are talking about language and gender, you know this is a major issue."

Sahni added that the other women kept quiet and would not say anything. Then Umeshwar said something in a loud voice and Sahni responded.

- "That's the whole trouble; you just keep shouting. That's the way you think, all you do when you meet women, you shout them down." Then I kept quiet. I refused to say anything. So he says, "You look angry." And I said, "Ya, I'm not angry. I'm just upset." And really, I had memories of this happening to me when I was little and my father would do that. Whenever the women in the house had an opinion, he would shout at them. And then you got shouted down and didn't say anything. So I had that same feeling once again. It got very, very tense the whole thing. But people began to think and so we accepted the role, and we bought the terms [both Shikshak and Shikshaka].

Sahni's awareness of what took place in her family home, her history with assertive and direct - as well as compassionate behaviour, proved extremely valuable in helping her to make the link between private and public interaction.

She took quite a strong position and insisted that attempting to keep the language gender neutral with use of the male term, 'shikshak' was just another example of gender blindness. And Umshewar, just as to Sahni, became an excellent example of a man who has learned about his own gender biases. He told her:

- "I didn't think much of women until my experience in this training." He comes from a very feudal background, the warrior caste and very conservative. He admits to being very, very patriarchal and saying that women just have to be told. He says this training has not only revised his ideas, it has taught him to respect women more, to treat them more as equals, and that they have a lot to offer. And he thinks that in Harchandpur, certainly the women have gained a lot.

Co-trainers

Men and women working together can provide role models for women and allow men to see and experience women in leadership roles as well as to experience their own histories and gender biases. Continued exposure to gender equality can help to break down the hierarchical societal roles and facilitate men's respect for the women's skills, even as something they might emulate. This practice coincides with the essence of GID policies--a reinforcement of the necessity of programmes that target both women and men at the deeper structural level--rather than WID policies that had targeted primarily the integration of women.

Sahni said:

- A lot of teaching is role modeling, and with gender, when you're talking about these things, the best thing you can do is just role model it. In fact when we had the gender session, he [Rakesh] did much more of the talking than I did. Otherwise it becomes us against them. If there is a woman carrying on about gender, the men take pride and just argue against it. They just end up doing that, which is why he would take [the lead] and I would play the supportive role in the gender session.

She explained how Rakesh helped to solve the problem described earlier, when the men were being sexually offensive.

- Rakesh spoke to him, [the man who made the offensive remark] and had him apologize publicly. "Look, we're a mixed group here, and these are all supposed to be your sisters. You're supposed to be helping them and each other. There isn't a safe atmosphere if you can't be open to such remarks. And there have been obscene remarks. We won't say what. But we all know. It's not to happen." And he said, "This is enough that he had to apologize."

- That really helped. It helped the women be stronger, and I think it changed everybody's mind. And we've had to do that once or twice. Just take a very stern stance and I think they are less prone to taking liberties of this variety. That's why whenever I had to do this alone, when Rakesh was not with me, I was always much sterner than when he was around. Feeling first more vulnerable and secondly, just wanting, needing to have a greater distance and height too. And it worked. Because that is what is culturally expected.

6

Globalization and Women's Empowerment

INTRODUCTION

This statement made by Ruggiero, the former director-general of the World Trade Organization (WTO), highlights the complex and contradictory nature of economic globalization at the beginning of the twenty-first century. Recent advances in technology, communications and access to information, and the intensification of international flows of goods, services and capital serve to accelerate, broaden, and deepen the processes of economic growth and poverty, albeit unevenly. These changes are re/constituting the socio-political and economic landscapes of high-, middle- and low-wage countries, as well as relations between women and men, and their relations with institutions.

Mainstream analyses of globalization are embedded in a belief in the "free market", and partially informed by acceptance of the notions of "comparative advantage" and a "level playing field". These analyses foreclose discussions, and erase the role(s) and relevance, of political and social institutions and power relations in partially shaping and facilitating economic activities at the macro, meso and micro levels, as well as the material realities of women and men living in poverty. Further, mainstream discourse discards the proposal that unevenness in levels of development, coupled with asymmetrical power relations both within and outside the national and international economic spheres, constitute situations where countries and individuals do not enter, or participate in, markets on equal terms. Thus, economic globalization is represented as an apolitical universal force, whereby the economic and political institutions through which it is facilitated are and Feldman, 1992; Elson, 1991; and Kabeer and Humphrey, 1991) theories, policies and their applications are informed by asymmetrical power relations and patriarchal values, and infected with specific assumptions about particular regions and countries.

Reproductive or caring work is also critical for the maintenance of the economy. Further, the gendered implications of economic liberalization are partially influenced by women's and men's locations within the processes of production and reproduction, and their country's position within the international economic and political orders.

TOWARDS A FEMINIST ANALYSIS OF GLOBALIZATION

The formation of the multilateral trading regime, the implementation of the Uruguay Round agreements, and the facilitation of economic liberalization more generally, are resulting in a decisive shift in the planning focus of, and role(s) of the state in, developing nations. Developing countries are, to varying degrees, more engaged in economic policy-making and planning, particularly within the framework of bilateral, regional and international trade agreements. Many have opened their markets to international competition at a pace that is faster than that experienced in increased growth and reductions in poverty levels at the national level. Through their facilitation of the Uruguay Round agreements, which are legally binding with strong enforcement capabilities, there is also increasing intervention in domestic policy making.

It can be argued that the new trading instruments, particularly through the *General Agreement of Trade in Services* (GATS) and the *Trade Policy Review Mechanism* (TPRM), are important vehicles for the promotion and implementation of specific domestic economic and (indirectly) social policies, as well as the regulation and disciplining nation-states. Further, and at the micro level, "negotiations in such areas as financial services, telecommunications and maritime transport demonstrate that few people around the world will remain untouched by some aspect of the WTO's activities". The multilateral trading agreements have the potential to, and in some cases are, also re/constituting production and consumption patterns. Within this context, and given both the increasing economic interdependence of nation-states and the widening gap between the rich and poor, it is important to identify the various theories, policies, and actors that inform and influence trade rules and norms.

In addition, there is a critical need to examine the scope of the rules, the ways in which they are facilitated, and their effects on women and men. Such analyses have the potential to reveal the ways in which the contributions of women and men to the economy - through productive and caring labour - is erased, as well as the ways in which specific institutions, including the World Trade Organization and economic and social ministries, reinforce, constrain, or expand women's positions in the market and the larger society. The reality of developing countries membership in the World Trade Organization, coupled with the assumption that trade leads to growth and development, underline a principle development belief and approach of multilateral institutions. They hold the view that development must be partially facilitated through the integration of developing countries into the global economy.

This belief ignores several issues that are critical to the processes of economic growth. For example, it fails to take into consideration the fact that a country's initial condition and position within the world economic and political orders influence both its market structure and trade outcomes; and that the history of colonialization, and patriarchy inform the productive, human resources, infrastructure, and reproductive capacities of member states. In addition, and as recent experiences of many countries in Africa, Asia, the Caribbean, Eastern Europe, and Latin America indicate, there is no necessary relationship between economic liberalization and increased economic growth, development, and reduced poverty levels. As the South-east Asian financial crises have revealed, openness can often exert pressures that can result in deepening poverty and the widening of income and wealth disparities within countries. More importantly, there is no convincing evidence that openness systematically reduces poverty or improves the quality of life for the vast majority of women and men in developing countries. As Rodrick argues, "in practice, the links between openness and economic growth tend to be weak, and contingent on the presence of complementary policies and institutions". For him, the "fundamental determinants of economic growth are the accumulation of physical and human capital and technological development."

CARING FOR THE ECONOMY

A feminist analysis of globalization has to:

- interrogate the gendered dimensions of those theories, such as comparative advantage, that inform it;
- reveal the ways in which economic institutions, processes, and relations are not outside of, or prior to, the political and the social but constitutive of it, and gendered; and
- bring into historical visibility women's and men's participation in economic activities – this entails empirical studies, as well as discussions of their role(s) in, and the links between, reproductive and productive work, and the gendered effects of the public/private divide.

Such analyses can result in more complete understandings of the causes of growth, development and poverty, and result in more effective and gender-aware policies aimed at improving the material realities of women and men living in poverty. The division of the world into the economic and non-economic or public and private spheres has resulted in both the theoretical isolation of the economy from the private or reproductive sphere, and the erasure of the role(s) of the latter in the maintenance of the former. Informed by this omission, classical and neo-classical economists, as well as new trade theorists exclude caring labour from their definitions of productive work. The value of reproductive work is further erased by those economic models that calculate production on the basis of monetarily compensated goods and services, thereby excluding unremunerated caring labour. In turn, this erasure has facilitated the formulations of allocative and distributive policies and actions that are gendered, in that they disproportionately favour men, *e.g.*, calculations of social security benefits that are based on paid work. Thus in order to address issues that pertain to the empowerment of women, analyses of linkages and feedbacks between macro policies, such as those influencing labour markets, and meso level institutions such as firms and social service agencies, and the material realities of women and men are necessary. For example, it is important to recognize that at the macro and meso levels laws, norms and rules that govern markets and public services are not gender neutral, and that men and women, in part because of their differing entitlements, are positioned differently in their interactions with these institutions.

The latter point is critical because feminist models for analyzing the effects of globalization must have the capacity to reveal the ways in which gendered structures of production are linked to gender bias in access to resources, *e.g.*, education. This linkage, depending on the sector in question, may pose opportunities or constraints on the export market at the national level, or result in the marginalisation of specific groups of women and/or men, as a result of job displacement, because of the importation of certain products. Within this context it is also important to understand markets, not in isolation, but within their political and cultural contexts. To this end, an engendering of Polanyi's analysis of the market as a social construct enables a partial analytic framing of the multiple and contradictory ways in which gender relations, as well as roles and norms, are re/constituted as women formally and/or informally participate in the global economy, or are marginalised from it. For example, the promotion of the tourism industry in the Caribbean is leading to an increase in employment, a need for training, the privatization of public spaces, the trafficking of women, as well as a rise in female and male prostitution. It also enables an understanding of the fact that, and as Sen argues, "while market expansion in many instances builds on and reinforces pre-existing gender relations, it may also destabilize such relations, and open up new spaces for feminist action". Consequently, political, cultural, religious and economic institutions, relations, and ideologies, which partially re/constitute and inform market relations, also become critical in analyzing the terms through and on which women, men and nation-states enter and negotiate the global marketplace.

As Smith notes: An individual is structurally positioned within hierarchical social, cultural, political and economic systems by forces and institutions that are prior to her will. These structural positions shape the individual's life chances, for they situate her within the relatively stable networks of power relations that shape the distribution of material resources.

In other words, women's structural positionings vary depending on their race, class, age and their country's structural position in the international economic and political orders, and are partially re/constituted through their relations with economic, political and socio-cultural institutions and processes. In addition, women's choices and 'preferences' are informed by their position in society.

Thus, uneven development and asymmetrical power relations within global and national markets constitute situations where nation-states and women and men do not enter into, or participate in, the market on equal terms. For example, within the neo-liberal framework, labour is assumed to be mobile. However, this assumption erases the facts that skilled labour tends to be more mobile than unskilled labour, and that citizenship matters; nor does it differentiate between the differences in the ability and cultural acceptability of female and male workers to move from one type of job to another, or to move from one spatial location to another in the pursuit of a job. For example, in several countries women are often discouraged or forbidden from working night shifts, principally to "protect them from harm" and because of "the impropriety of women travelling at night". This type of protective labour legislation has the paradoxical result of protecting men's jobs, and reinforcing violence against women, primarily because it forecloses discussions of men using violence, such as sexual assault, to regulate women's lives, and maintain their privilege in an insecure labour market.

Thus, a feminist analysis of globalization has to be framed by the ideas that:

- The market is a gendered, social construction;
- Production and reproduction are intrinsically linked and re/constituted through relations of power;
- Women and men often enter and participate in markets on differential terms; and
- Nation-states have differential levels of development, in addition to being unevenly developed within their national boundaries.

Within this context, the 'non-economic' relations that partially re/constitute markets also become important in considering the terms through and on which women and men enter, remain, move within, and leave the market, and in analyses of market structures. Such analyses will provide understandings of where, and some of the ways in which, different groups of women and men are located in the processes of production and consumption, in the re/organization of market structures, and in reproduction. For example, women's ability to enter markets as employees is often hampered by lower levels of education and skills qualification, often due to structural reasons, and restrictions in mobility due to tradition, religion and/or family responsibilities/demands.

In addition, it highlights the need to interrogate the relationships of women and men living in poverty with those institutions that are primarily responsible for both facilitating globalization, including the World Trade Organization, the private sector, and nation- states, and poverty reduction, such as multilateral, regional and national institutions, and civil society organizations. Policing for Poverty Reduction and Women's Empowerment As I have briefly argued above, to more fully understand the implications of globalization for poverty reduction and women's empowerment, it is important to go beyond an analysis of states and markets to issues that pertain to the macro-meso-micro linkages of economic policies, the roles of reproduction in subsidizing the market economy, and the asymmetrical power relations between nation-states, between the nation-state and women and men, between women and men, and among specific groups of women and men. Women's empowerment has multiple meanings and is associated with a diversity of strategies. For example, within mainstream development discourse of the 1990s, it was often used by organizations focused on enlarging the choices and productivity levels of individual women, for the most part, in isolation from a feminist agenda; and in the context of a withdrawal of state responsibility for broad-based economic and social support.

However, in the 1970s, when the concept was first invoked by women's organizations, it was explicitly used to frame and facilitate the struggle for social justice and women's equality through a transformation of economic, social and political structures at the national and international levels. In addition, it recognized the importance of women's agency and self-transformation. Thus, the initial theoretical framework through which the original concept of women's empowerment was produced acknowledged inequalities between men and women, situated women's subordination in the family, the community, the market and the state, and emphasized that women experienced oppression differently according to their race, class, colonial history and their country's position in the international economic order. In addition, it maintained that women have to challenge oppressive structures and processes simultaneously, and at multiple levels, thereby creating the space for empowerment to occur at both the individual and collective levels. Women's empowerment is assumed to be attainable through different points of departure, including political mobilization, consciousness raising and education. In addition, changes where and when necessary, in laws, civil codes, systems of property rights, and the social and legal institutions that underwrite male control and privilege, are assumed to be essential for the achievement of women's equality. According to Batliwala empowerment is both a process and a goal. She states that:

- ... the goals of women's empowerment are to challenge patriarchal ideology (male domination and women's subordination); transform the structures and institutions that reinforce and perpetuate gender discrimination and social inequality (the family, caste, class, religion, educational processes and institutions, the media, health practices and systems, laws and civil codes, political processes, development models, and government institutions); and enable women to gain access to, and control of, both material and informational resources.

Successful empowerment strategies also require the direct involvement of women in the planning and implementation of projects. The process of empowerment evolves like a spiral, involving changes in consciousness, the identification of target areas for change, and analyses of actions and outcomes, "which leads in turn to higher levels of consciousness and more finely honed and better executed strategies". As a result, empowerment cannot be a "top down or one way process", nor can there be a fixed formula for its achievement. Stromquist, in her article on educational empowerment for women, interprets empowerment as a "socio-political concept that goes beyond formal political participation and consciousness raising". She argues that a "full definition of empowerment must include cognitive, psychological, political and economic components".

She explains that:

- The cognitive dimension refers to women having an understanding of the conditions and causes of their subordination at the micro and macro levels. It involves making choices that may go against cultural expectations and norms;
- The economic component requires that women have access to, and control over, productive resources, thus ensuring some degree of financial autonomy. However, she notes that changes in the economic balance of power do not necessarily alter traditional gender roles or norms;
- the political element entails that women have the capability to analyze, organize and mobilize for social change; and
- The psychological dimension includes the belief that women can act at personal and societal levels to improve their individual realities and the society in which they live.

Stromquist notes that there is general agreement that these components are interrelated. In her essay on non-formal education as a means to empowerment, Monkman, adopts the components listed above and argues for the inclusion of a fifth component. She posits that there is a physical element - having control over one's body and sexuality and the ability to protect oneself against sexual violence - to the empowerment process. However useful for the formulation of empowerment strategies, the sense of discreteness promoted by a compartmentalisation of empowerment into different components has the potential negative effect of encouraging and promoting incomplete understandings of the realities of women's lives. The result can be the implementation of "empowerment strategies" that fail to engage with the complexities of women's subordination. In her study of selected empowerment strategies implemented by specific South Asian non-governmental organizations, Batliwala identifies three approaches to women's empowerment:

- Integrated development;
- Economic development; and
- Consciousness raising and organising among women.

She notes that these are not mutually exclusive categories, but argue that they are useful for distinguishing between the various causes of "women's powerlessness" and among the different interventions thought to lead to empowerment.

- The integrated development approach interprets women's powerlessness to be a result of their "greater poverty and lower access to health care, education, and survival resources". Batliwala states that strategies deployed under this approach aim to enhance women's economic status through the provision of services. This approach improves women's everyday realities by assisting them in meeting their survival and livelihood needs, *i.e.*, their practical needs.
- The economic development approach situates "women's economic vulnerability at the centre of their powerlessness", and assumes that economic empowerment positively impacts various aspects of women's existence. Its strategies are built around strengthening women's position as workers through organising and providing them with access to support services. Though this approach improves women's economic position, she notes that it is unclear that this change necessarily empowers them in other dimensions of their lives.
- Batliwala argues that the consciousness-raising and organising empowerment approach is based on a complex understanding of gender relations and women's status. This method ascribes women's powerlessness to the ideology and practice of patriarchy and socio-economic inequality. Strategies focus on organising women to recognise and challenge gender- and class-based discrimination in all aspects of their lives. However, she posits that though successful in enabling women to address their strategic needs, this approach may not be as effective in assisting them to meet their immediate or practical needs.

Batliwala posits that empowerment strategies must intervene at the level of "women's condition while also transforming their position", thus simultaneously addressing both practical and strategic needs. Such analyses facilitates understandings the empowerment process that goes beyond the distribution of resources. In this context, gender is essential as a category of analysis in discussions of poverty reduction. The presence of poverty is in part linked to the gendered and unequal access to, and distribution of, resources, a lack of control over productive resources, and limited participation in political and economic institutions. Women, in particular, face institutional obstacles to control land and other productive resources. This structural poverty is exacerbated in many countries by the processes of globalization. The gendered dimensions of poverty may be usefully understood in terms of the differential entitlements, capabilities and rights conferred to women and men. Poverty is tied to a lack of access to, and control over, productive resources, physical goods and income, which results in individual and/or group deprivation, vulnerability and powerlessness. It has various manifestations, including hunger and malnutrition, ill-health, and limited or no access to education, health care, safe housing and paid work environments.

It also includes experiences of economic, political and social discrimination. Poverty, then, is not merely a function of material conditions but is also constitutive through the institutions and ideologies that differently constitute, in part, the material realities of women and men and ascribe different meanings to their lives. This concept is an essential component of analyses of poverty and the design of strategic responses. For example, different interpretations of the meaning of the household will lead to different poverty eradication strategies targeted at the household level. Regarding the household as a site of both tension and cooperation, rather than as a harmonious unit, emphasizes the relational aspects of intra-household power and poverty and suggests gender-aware approaches to strengthening women's positions.

The effects of trade liberalisation and expansion for women, men, gender relations, poverty reduction, and development are contradictory and partially dependent on resource endowments, infrastructure, labour market policies, skills and educational levels, socio-cultural norms, and women's and men's positions in the processes of production and reproduction, and the position of the country in question within the global order. Within this context, national and sectoral case studies may illuminate some of the gendered dimensions of international trade. However, these results will be limited as it is very difficult to isolate the many variables involved in reconstituting the material realities of women and men. An agenda for eradicating poverty and, in particular, its gendered effects requires the dismantling of the institutions and ideologies that maintain women's subordination and justify inequality in terms of political, social and economic resources. To this end, multilateral institutions can work with governments, non-governmental organizations, and the private sector to:

- Promote, through appropriate laws, legislation and public awareness programmes, the removal of legal obstacles and cultural constraints to women's access to and control over productive resources, such as land and credit;

- Encourage the formulation, and implementation, of gender-aware and development focussed macroeconomic policies and programmes, by facilitating the use of appropriate data in the design of policies and programmes. This will entail the support for research on the effects of trade liberalization, development and poverty reduction policies and programmes on women and men.
- Encourage, through appropriate economic and social policies, the balanced distribution of the gains from trade. In addition, the "winners" should be mandated to compensate the "losers" through taxes, employment re-training programmes etc.
- Encourage the formulation, and implementation of, poverty reduction policies and programmes that are gender aware.
- Ensure that the costs of the export economy are not externalized to facilitate competitiveness;
- Ensure that the implementation of the new trading agreements do not negatively impact prices of basic goods and services, and women's and men's household survival strategies;
- Ensure that gender inequalities are reduced, and not intensified, as a result of globalization;
- Ensure that any loss in tax revenue resulting from economic liberalization will not adversely affect the provision of social services;
- Ensure that social policies are developed and implemented to address the gendered effects of globalization;
- Assist women's groups in monitoring, analysing, and influencing the implementation of economic liberalisation policies on women and men in both the formal and informal sectors; and
- Promote the use of both quantitative and qualitative research methods to analyse the gendered dimensions of relative and absolute poverty and economic liberalisation. To this end it is important to recognise the contributions of unremunerated labour so that it can be accounted for in economic planning and poverty reduction strategies, and emphasise the links between economic production and social reproduction. Research questions can include:
    - At the national level, which are the areas of current or potential comparative advantages? Where, and how, are women and men located in these sectors? What actions are necessary in order to stimulate balanced growth?

- What types of sectoral restructuring are required to facilitate the new trade agreements? What are the effects on women and men, including in terms of employment, wages, income, and access to services? Are the wages paid to women increasing in absolute terms or relative to men?
- What is the desirable pace of trade liberalisation in different sectors? What are the adjustment costs, regulatory challenges, and the effects on the attainment of certain social objectives? For example, in the context of the General Agreement on Trade in Services, could Article I: 3(c) of the GATS threaten "universal" availability to, and quality of, health and education services? Due to lack of resources, governments are outsourcing public services to the private sector, thus these sectors are open to foreign competition. What are the possible gendered implications?
- What are the effects on women and men involved in those sectors that are being promoted for export, or displaced as a result of imports? For example, is export related investment attracted by referring to feminine characteristics? Do the education levels of women hinder or facilitate their participation in the new services industries?
- Are the existing patterns of gendered production further constrained, reinforced, or are women's and men's employment opportunities expanding and diversifying? For example, the outsourcing of service sector jobs from developed to developing countries, particularly in the area of information technology, has opened up new opportunities for women in, for example, call centres, data entry, and medical transcription work. However, these jobs are typically low skilled. Does economic liberalization facilitate employment in industries previously closed to women? If not, why not? If yes, in what ways?
- Is the autonomy of the member states eroded? In what ways is this loss of autonomy linked with women's powerlessness?

CONTRIBUTIONS TO AND LIMITATIONS OF EMPOWERMENT

On the basis of the experiences shared by the men and women interviewed, the Trust Bank programme of Sinapi Aba Trust has clearly contributed to the empowerment of women in a number of ways. Access to credit and business training have helped women expand and improve their businesses, leading to increased respect and decision-making power in the home and community. Advice and peer support have helped women manage their triple roles as mothers, wives, and businesswomen. Education and experience in leadership have helped women become more confident and capable leaders. It is important to note that these substantial evidences of empowerment have been displayed in the context of a highly sustainable institution that is experiencing rapid growth and is on the path to becoming a regulated savings and loan institution.

The study, however, also revealed some mixed outcomes. Although SAT's message that women should continue to perform their traditional duties and be "respectful and submissive" to their husbands limits backlash and promotes family unity, it may also limit the scope of empowerment for women. In many ways, gender stereotypes and expectations remain unaltered. For example, although women have substantially increased their decision-making power—especially regarding the purchase of household assets—and are consulted more often in the decision-making process, men still tend to have the final word on major decisions. Very few men showed any signs of change in beliefs about gender roles, and all were quite satisfied with their wives' "character" and performance of their traditional duties as a wife and mother. One man even commented that people were now using his wife as an "example" of what wives should do. She is contributing to the household finances, but she has not become arrogant or shown any signs of "bad character." All these were regarded as positive outcomes by the men, but they also show that women are still expected to conform to gender norms even if they are also pursuing non-traditional roles for themselves. The interviewees' responses also show a consensus among men and women that women have an important role to play in organizing other women, but none of the men considered the possibility that the women could organize and lead men, and a couple of the women even said that they would step away from their church or community leadership posts if a man were to become involved. Yet women are gaining experience in leading men in many of SAT's mixed-gender Trust Banks, and this experience may ultimately empower them to lead men in other public spaces.

WOMEN'S EMPOWERMENT IN INDIA

Women's empowerment in India is heavily dependent on many different variables that include geographical location (urban/rural), educational status, social status (caste and class), and age. Policies on women's empowerment exist at the national, state, and local (Panchayat) levels in many sectors, including health, education, economic opportunities, gender-based violence, and political participation.

However, there are significant gaps between policy advancements and actual practice at the community level.

One key factor for the gap in implementation of laws and policies to address discrimination, economic disadvantages, and violence against women at the community level is the largely patriarchal structure that governs the community and households in much of India. As such, women and girls have restricted mobility, access to education, access to health facilities, and lower decision-making power, and experience higher rates of violence. Political participation is also hindered at the Panchayat (local governing bodies) level and at the state and national levels, despite existing reservations for women.

The impact of the patriarchal structure can be seen in rural and urban India, although women's empowerment in rural India is much less visible than in urban areas. This is of particular concern, since much of India is rural despite the high rate of urbanization and expansion of cities. Rural women, as opposed to women in urban settings, face inequality at much higher rates, and in all spheres of life. Urban women and, in particular, urban educated women enjoy relatively higher access to economic opportunities, health and education, and experience less domestic violence. Women (both urban and rural) who have some level of education have higher decisionmaking power in the household and the community. Furthermore, the level of women's education also has a direct implication on maternal mortality rates, and nutrition and health indicators among children.

Among rural women, there are further divisions that hinder women's empowerment. The most notable ones are education levels and caste and class divisions. Women from lower castes (the scheduled castes, other backward castes, and tribal communities) are particularly vulnerable to maternal mortality and infant mortality. They are often unable to access health and educational services, lack decision-making power, and face higher levels of violence. Among women of lower caste and class, some level of education has shown to have a positive impact on women's empowerment indicators.

Social divisions among urban women also have a similar impact on empowerment indicators. Upper class and educated women have better access to health, education, and economic opportunities, whereas lower class, less educated women in urban settings enjoy these rights significantly less. Due to rapid urbanisation and lack of economic opportunities in other parts of the country, cities also house sprawling slum areas. Slums are informal sprawls, and most times lack basic services such as clean water, sanitation, and health facilities. Additionally, slum dwellers mostly work in unorganized and informal sectors, making them vulnerable to raids by the state, abuse by employers, and other forms of insecurity. Women and children in slums are among the most vulnerable to violence and abuse, and are deprived of their basic human rights.

As a result of a vibrant women's movement in the last 50 years, policies to advance human rights for women in India are substantial and forward-thinking, such as the Domestic Violence Act (2005), and the 73rd and 74th Amendments to the Constitution that provide reservations for women to enter politics at the Panchayat level. There are multiple national and state level governmental and non-governmental mechanisms such as the Women's Commission to advance these policies, and the implementation of these policies is decentralized to state and district-level authorities and organizations that include local non-governmental organizations.

The policy/practice gap in India cuts across all sectors and initiatives as a result of rampant corruption and lack of good governance practices. State-level governments claim a lack of resources, and the resources they do receive are highly susceptible to corruption. Financial corruption hinders the government's ability to invest in social capital, including initiatives to advance women's empowerment. Since the 1990's India has put in place processes and legislative acts such as the Right to Information Act (2005) for information disclosure to increase transparency and hold government officials accountable. Mistrust of political institutions and leaders remains high in the society with corruption and graft allegations often covering media headlines.

In addition to corruption and inadequate resources for implementation of initiatives at the community level, women's empowerment in India is negatively impacted by the pervasive discrimination of women in the family and the community. Discrimination against women in most parts of India (particularly the north) emerges from the social and religious construct of women's role and their status. As such, in many parts of India, women are considered to be less than men, occupying a lower status in the family and community, which consequentially restricts equal opportunity in women and girls' access to education, economic possibilities, and mobility.

Discrimination also limits women's choices and freedom. These choices are further dependent on structural factors like caste and class.

Empowerment for women in India requires a crosscutting approach and one which addresses the diversity of social structures that govern women's lives. Identity politics in India is a very critical political instrument, which is both used and abused throughout political and social institutions. There are numerous social movements fighting for the rights of the marginalized, such as the Dalit rights movement, the tribal rights movement, etc. These movements have achieved many gains in assuring representation of the traditionally marginalized communities into mainstream society. Women's rights within these movements are largely unarticulated and thus reinforce inequalities within the very structures from which they are demanding inclusion. Empowerment approaches for women therefore is not only about providing services, but also about recognizing their lived realities of multiple layers of discrimination that hinder their access to services.

Similarly, access to education for girls in some of the northern states like Uttar Pradesh and Punjab does not only rely on proximity of schools. Access to education is part of a larger structural concern, including the practice of son preference, which creates inherent discriminatory practices. Education initiatives therefore cannot rely solely on building educational infrastructure, but also need to address some of the root causes of discrimination against women and girls which affect the decisions made by parents.

Women's security, decision-making power, and mobility are three indicators for women's empowerment. In India, and more so for rural and less educated women, these three indicators are significantly low. Data from the NFHS-3 survey on women's decision-making power shows that only about one third of the women interviewed took decisions on their own regarding household issues and their health. Decision-making power among employed urban women was higher than among rural and less educated women. The survey also found that older married women had more decision-making power than the younger married women. Younger women and girls experience an additional layer of discrimination as a result of their age.

Data on women's mobility in India indicates the lack of choices women have, and that urban and educated women have more mobility choices than rural women. The data shows that about half the women interviewed had the freedom to go to the market or a health facility alone. Seventynine percent of urban women from the highest education brackets and only about 40 percent of rural women without education were allowed to go to the market alone.

Mobility restrictions for women are dependent upon how the family and community view women's rights. They also, however, are intrinsically dependent on the prevailing levels of violence against women in the household and the community. Abuse and violence towards women is predominantly perpetrated within the household, and marital violence is among the most accepted by both men and women. Wife beating, slapping, rape, dowry related deaths, feudal violence towards tribal and lower caste women, trafficking, sexual abuse, and street violence permeate the Indian social fabric, and create one of the most serious obstacles in achieving women's empowerment.

EVIDENCE OF EMPOWERMENT

Although the process of empowerment varies from culture to culture, several types of changes are considered to be relevant in a wide range of cultures. Some of these changes include increased participation in decision making, more equitable status of women in the family and community, increased political power and rights, and increased self-esteem.

Although most microfinance institutions can share anecdotal evidence of empowerment, very few have studied the effects of their programmes on empowerment. The information and evidence that are available give us a mixed picture, showing successes as well as some limitations.

IMPACT ON DECISION MAKING

Women's ability to influence or make decisions that affect their lives and their futures is considered to be one of the principal components of empowerment by most scholars. It is much less clear, however, what types of decisions and what degree of influence should be classified as empowerment in different contexts.

In spite of the difficulties, some microfinance institutions are finding ways to evaluate their impact on women's decision making. The Women's Empowerment Programme in Nepal, for example, conducted a study that showed an average of 89,000 out of 130,000 or 68 per cent of women in its programme experienced an increase in their decision-making roles in the areas of family planning, children's marriage, buying and selling property, and sending their daughters to school—all areas of decision making traditionally dominated by men.

The Centre for Self-Help Development (CSD) also reported that women were able to make small purchases of necessary items like groceries independently. But larger purchases and personal purchases, like jewelry, always required the consent of the husband, representing incomplete progress towards empowerment in this area.

World Education, which provides literacy and other education to existing savings and credit groups, found that the combination of education and credit put women in a stronger position to ensure more equal access for female children to food, schooling, and medical care. TSPI, an Opportunity partner in the Philippines, found that the percentage of women who reported being the primary household fund manager increased dramatically from 33 per cent to 51 per cent after participation in the programme.

In the comparison group only 31 per cent of women were the primary managers of household funds. Similarly, the percentage of women managing their enterprise funds nearly doubled from 44 to 87 per cent. Only 1 per cent of clients control of enterprise fund management after joining the programme, and only 5 per cent relinquished control of house-hold fund management during that period.

Through in-depth interviews with 13 clients, URWEGO, a World Relief partner in Rwanda, found that 54 per cent of the clients experienced an increase in their ability to control or influence business decisions, 38 per cent experienced an increase in decision making in their families, 38 per cent in their communities, and 54 per cent in their churches.

URWEGO's impact on decision making, while far from universal, is significant in that the programme was only about 18 months old at the time of the evaluation. Many microfinance institutions focus their attention on women's use of the loan and ability to make decisions about her business as the most direct impact of their programme. Nirdhan Utthan Bank, Ltd. in Nepal found that most of their women clients were making decisions about business investments jointly with their husband, which represents a step forward because previously these women's husbands would have made such decisions alone.

CSD found that most women do have a say in the utilization and management of their loans although occasionally men pressure CSD to give their wives loans so that the husband can use it. They also found that a fair number of loans are ultimately invested in "male" activities like rickshaws, for which it is difficult to ascertain the level of control and influence the women may have.

In her study of the Small Enterprise Development Programme (SEDP) in Bangladesh, Naila Kabeer found that although empowerment and well-being benefits substantially increased when women controlled their loans and used them for their own income-generating activities, just the act of bringing financial resources to the household in the form of credit was enough to secure at least some benefits for the majority of women in her study.

EMPOWERMENT OF WOMEN FOR IMPROVED QUALITY OF LIFE: BAIF'S APPROACH

A woman is the nucleus of the family, particularly, in rural India. She not only collects water, fuelwood, fodder and food but also plays a significant role in preserving the culture, grooming the children and shaping their destiny. Therefore, our Founder, Late Dr. Manibhai Desai always emphasized that although women represent only 50 per cent of the total population, they contribute 75 per cent to the development of our society while men contribute only 25 per cent. Unfortunately, in spite of their laudable and vulnerable roles, which cannot be substituted by machine or men, women have been neglected since generations.

This is happening inspite of a woman being recognized by our ancient saints and culture as not merely a mother but as a superior scholarly Institution. It is said in Manu Samhita *Upadhyaayan-dasacarya acarryanam satam pita; Sahasram tu pitrnmata gauraveratiricyate*. "A Guru who teaches Veda is 10 times superior to an ordinary teacher and the father is 100 times more than a teacher, but the Mother is 1000 times more superior than the father".

For the rural women, the day starts early in the morning with the responsibilities of fetching water, fodder, fuel and cooking food. She takes care of the children and members of the family, their health, orientation and education and attends to various income generation activities. She manages all the household matters, looks after the family assets and livestock, handles the purchases and finance, works for almost 14-16 hours and is the last to sleep at night. Still, when you ask her children what their mother does? Most of them instantly reply “nothing”. There is no recognition for their hard work, just because her work is not evaluated in terms of money. She often falls sick, but does not complain and this goes unnoticed by others in the family as they continue to work as usual for the sake of the family. She manages the family very efficiently with meagre means, but is still treated as illiterate.

Women are ignored in matters, which are of concern to them as well. As a result, today women are the worst sufferers in the society due to drudgery, ill health, illiteracy, deprivation and humiliation. Backwardness of women is a sign of poverty and women are the worst sufferers during the period of scarcity and calamity. No wonder, India hosts over one-third of the poor in the world, as lack of empowerment of women is a significant cause of poverty.

With this background, BAIF has a mandate to ensure women empowerment in the development programmes and thereby strives to create a conducive atmosphere for their effective participation. This strategy for women empowerment programme is addressed through drudgery reduction, gender sensitization among other sections of the community, capacity building to enhance their efficiency and contribute to economic development and ensure equality and status in the society.

Way back in the early 80’s, we promoted the wastelands development programme in the tribal areas of Vansda, Gujarat through establishment of fruit orchards on degraded lands owned by the poor tribal families. This has now become popular as the *Wadi* programme. During those days, Manibhaiji visited the project areas almost 2-3 times in a month and interacted closely with the families. Initially, it was the men who attended these meetings and accepted all the suggestions given by us for shaping their lands and developing the orchards. Accordingly, a suitable action plan was prepared and the participating families were instructed to dig pits and plant grafted mango plants, which were supplied for establishment of orchards. With great difficulty, mango grafts were transported from Konkan region of Maharashtra and distributed to these participants. Subsequently, during the next few weeks, when Manibhaiji visited these plots for supervision, the women started complaining that they were burdened with additional responsibilities. While attending the meetings, the men had accepted all the suggestions and responsibilities but they had no time to follow-up due to other commitments outside the farm. In such a situation, women who had sense of responsibility and commitment, ensured that the commitment made by their men were fulfilled.

Thus, the major development responsibility fell on them. They were engaged in digging pits, protecting plants, fetching headloads of water from distant places to irrigate the plants, which naturally added more pressure to their over burdened daily routine. Naturally, unable to bear the heavy workload, they were unhappy. This gave us a thorough insight into the drudgery faced by the women, their problems of health and deprivation of training and capacity building. Thus, BAIF identified drudgery reduction, community health care and literacy programmes for both children and adult as the basic necessity to bring women into the forefront of development with dignity and equality.

Promotion of *Wavli* was the entry point for Women Empowerment in Vansda. Traditionally, women have engaged themselves in vegetable cultivation in their backyards and men have never staked their claim over these earnings.

This custom known as *Wavli* ensured exclusive right of women over their earnings. Realising that *Wavli* could be an excellent opportunity to empower women, several new activities such as nurseries of fruit and forestry plants, mushroom production, large scale vegetable production and shared cropping by women groups were introduced. *Wavli* attracted a large number of women and the men also extended their cooperation. The earnings from *Wavli* were used by the women for food, clothing and procurement of utensils and ornaments, which were their priority. Hence, *Wavli* turned out to be a golden opportunity to implement the orchard development programme successfully, while enlightening the men about the role of women in economic development. This incidence motivated BAIF to ensure equal opportunity for women in all the development programmes.

DRUDGERY REDUCTION

The extent of burden and sufferings of the rural women in India vary widely with the social and economic status, local customs, size of family and many other factors. Hence, an intensive study with close interaction with women can help to identify suitable solutions for their problems. Based on the needs, the drudgery reduction measures introduced for women include:

- Creation of safe drinking water sources closer to their houses
- Maternal and child health and family welfare
- Strengthening of traditional health care practices
- Training of midwives and upgrading the skills of local healers
- Awareness on health, hygiene and sanitation
- Training of local youth as health guides for first-aid
- Establishment of community grain banks and promotion of nutrition gardens
- Promotion of energy conservation devices: improved woodstoves, biogas, solar devices and energy plantations
- Establishment of *Anganwadis* and awareness of girl's education

These activities have been very well appreciated and are also being encouraged by the male members of the society.

GENDER EQUALITY

While interacting with the rural women, the major obstacles were the elder male members of the family, who were used to seeing their women subdued and non-interfering and who never stepped outside the house on their own. Hence, a dialogue with women threatened their status and dominance. Therefore, it was helpful to sensitize the men about the benefits of women empowerment, particularly, with respect to development of children and enhancement of skills for income generation. The other aspects which required persuasion were opening of joint bank accounts and registering assets and land titles jointly. Recognition of their services to the family and society could empower them further and provide equal status in the society.

Gender Sensitive Approach to Women Empowerment

- Drudgery reduction to facilitate participation in economic development
- Involvement in decision making process, identification of strategic gender needs and addressing them
- Capacity building in technical skills, information sharing and leadership development
- Formation of Self Help Groups for solidarity, awareness and motivation, addressing common problems and micro-financing.
- Economic development: enhance abilities to contribute to family income, access to credit and assets and reduce economic dependence.
- Staff orientation: to adopt suitable approaches to address the problems and encourage participatory development
- Gender vigilance to ensure women's participation in all fronts and access to benefits in training, entrepreneurship and activities of Panchayati Raj Institutions (PRIs)

Creation of awareness among men could enlist greater support for women participation in the various development programmes. In many regions, the men have taken a path contrary to tradition, to empower the women.

In Rajasthan and Uttar Pradesh where *Purdah* system is in practice, the women covered their faces in veil before their husbands and other elderly members. However, they gradually started opening up after regular interactions with the Extension Officers of BAIF. Nevertheless, they immediately put on the veil whenever any elderly men attended such meetings. Realising this constraint, men in many villages have decided not to come and sit in the front of the women. Instead they prefer to sit at the back to enable the members of women's groups to participate freely.

In Uttar Pradesh, some Village Panchayat Committees comprising of 5 men (Panch) announced that all the women in the village should be treated as daughters and sisters, thereby allowing them to remove their veils in the village. This gave a boost to women's participation in various community development programmes. In Rajasthan, where many SHGs had decided to impose fine on members arriving late for the meetings, many men encouraged their wives to attend the meetings on time by taking the responsibility of cooking for the family on those days. A more pleasant surprise was that these men did not mind sharing this information with their friends in the village. Such a change could come about within a period of 2-3 years.

Capacity Building

Subsequently, building of capabilities to create awareness, improve their skills, develop leadership and link with technologies, trade, financial institutions and local governments can empower them to take active part in socio-economic development at par with others. Such steps have led the community towards a literate and progressive society, directly benefiting every family and helped to bring the rural women as key players, into mainstream development.

With various women empowerment activities and training, there has been a significant increase in the confidence of women. They have developed mutual trust, social security, skills and access to technology and credit through their Self Help Groups and various People's Organisations.

The women groups have motivated the entire community to take up hygiene, sanitation, family planning and health care activities with the community. Several groups have established their grain banks to ensure food security for their members. There has been increased awareness about education for children, particularly, girls. Prevention of child marriage has been an important agenda of many Self Help Groups which has been endorsed by the other sections of the community as well.

LEADERS IN COMMUNITY DEVELOPMENT

The community has recognised the status of the women and their contribution in not only managing their families, but also to the economic and social development of the entire community. Women have shown their capacity to play a major role in community development.

With such significant contribution to the society, most women are participating in Gram Sabhas. Many active leaders of the Self Help Groups have contested and been elected for various PRIs, co-operative bodies and other village level organisations. The leadership of women has been recognised by the society. They are now able to influence the Panchyati Raj Institutions to work for the benefit of the communities. The dark days when they had to struggle for their rights and status in the society, are vanishing.

7

Role of Banks in Agriculture and Rural Development

The banking sector has witnessed a huge growth in the recent years. However, despite such a growth, the credit flow by banks to the rural and agricultural sectors remains dismal, which, more or less, has resulted in financial exclusion of the rural masses. The rural and agricultural sectors have to play a very important role if a target of 8 per cent GDP growth per annum as envisioned in the tenth plan is to be achieved and the banks and have a huge role to play in boosting the rural and agriculture sector through product innovation, broadening the reach, promotion of SHGs/Micro enterprises and providing know-how. This article provides an overview of the concept.

In the last few years, the Indian economy has emerged as one of the fastest growing economies in the world. However, the vulnerability of the Indian economy with respect to the performance of the agricultural sector despite other macroeconomic indicators and sectors gaining in strength is well known. For example, the Indian economy grew at an estimated 3.7 per cent in 2002-03 against 5.6 per cent during 2001-02. This was largely because of the negnegative growth of 4.4 per cent in the agriculture sector. Many economists and policy-makers increasingly believe that the future growth of the domestic economy, to a large extent, will depend on the robust performance of the agricultural and rural sector. The manufacturing and service sectors cannot sustain the economy's growth if the rural sector underperforms. The contribution of the banking and financial sector to the current economic growth of the Indian economy is very significant. This is reflected in the growth in aggregate deposits and advances for scheduled commercial banks, which stood at 15.4 per cent and 27.9 per cent during 2004-2005. However, the access of banking services to the rural, agriculture and the common man in general is not as promising. As Mr. V. Leeladhar (Deputy Governor, RBI, on the occasion of the Commemorative lecture at the Fedbank Hormis Memorial Foundation, Ernakulam) said "Despite making significant improvements in all the areas relating to financial viability, profitability and competitiveness, there are concerns that banks have not been able to include a vast segment of the population, especially the underprivileged sections of the society, into the fold of basic banking services." The focus of Indian banks on financial inclusion *i.e.* delivery of banking services at an affordable cost of the low-income groups has been dismal. In India, the focus of the financial inclusion at present is more or less confined to ensuring a bare minimum access to a savings bank account without frills to all. Having a current account/savings account on its own, cannot be regarded as an accurate indicator of financial inclusion.

BANKING IN RURAL AND AGRICULTURAL AREAS

The rural population in India suffers from a great deal of indebtedness and is subject to exploitation in the credit market due to high interest rates and the lack of convenient access to credit. Rural households need credit for investing in agriculture and smoothening out seasonal fluctuations in earnings. Since cash flows and savings in rural areas for the majority of households are small, rural households typically tend to rely on credit for other consumption needs like education, food, housing, household functions, etc. Rural households need access to financial institutions that can provide them with credit at lower rates and at reasonable terms than the traditional money-lender and thereby help them avoid debt-traps that are common in rural India.

Usage of banking services by Indian households (HHs)

Source: Census of India 2001

	Total	No.	% of	HHs	Rural % of Total	HHs
Total No. of HHs	19.19	100	13.83	72.0	5.36	28.0
No. of HHs which use banking services	6.8	35.5	4.16	30.1	2.65	49.5

Debt profile of rural households (in %)

Source: Ministry of Labour, Rural Labour Enquiry Report

SOURCE OF DEBT	1993.94	1999-2000
Government	8.3	5.4
Co-operative Societies	7.9	13.1
Employees	11.4	6.9
Money Lenders	**27.6**	**31.7**
Shopkeepers	7.3	7.1
Relatives & Friends	12.4	15.1
Others	6.2	3.5
Banks	18.9	17.2

TABLE A			
Changes in farmers reliance on the banking system (RBI)			
Year	Farmer Deposits (Rs Crore)	Farmer Borrowings (Rs Crore)	Total (Rs. crore
1992	26211	17835	273
1993	29825	19493	257
1994	36583	19669	251
1995	43341	21334	198
1996	47433	23813	194
1997	53611	27448	188
1998	57442	29442	173
1999	78881	33094	169
2000	91009	36466	162
2001	99812	43420	195
2002	108233	47430	197

Current Trends: A Pointer To Financial Exclusion

Rural Credit: The 2001census reveals the low level of banking usage among Indian households in general (35.5 per cent) and rural households in particular (30.1 per cent). This reflects on the latent demand for general banking needs in rural as well as urban segments. The debt profile of rural households indicates that the major source of credit to rural households, particularly poor income working households, has been informal sector loans like money-lenders, which are usually at very high rates of interest.

The terms and conditions attached to these loans impact the poor adversely. This reflects the inadequate institutional credit flow to rural areas. As on 31-3-2003, rural and semi-urban centres had a Credit/Deposit (CD) ratio of 42 per cent and 35 per cent respectively as compared to a CD ratio of 69.5 per cent and 59.3 per cent for urban centres and national level. These trends broadly indicate that despite the widespread banking network in place, there is a continued migration of rural/semi-urban savings to urban/metro centres, thereby causing a banking divide between rural and urban areas.

Agricultural Credit: An equally important concern that needs attention is the flow of institutional credit to agriculture. The progress of agricultural credit in India has depended crucially on government intervention over the years, *i.e.* package of incentives and policy measures, which the RBI and the Centre formulate and implement. The growth of commercial banks' lending to agriculture and allied activities witnessed a substantial decline in the 1990s as compared to the 1980s. Credit flow to the agriculture sector of all formal sources amounted to ₹ 70,810 crore in 2002-03 and ₹ 86,981 crore in 2003-04, much below the levels envisaged in the Tenth Plan. Agriculture's share in scheduled commercial banks' total outstanding credit as on 31st March 2005 was only ₹1,12,475 crore.

The total agricultural lending by commercial banks is lower than credit in "personal loans" which stood at ₹ 2,66,988 crore, comprising advances for housing and consumer durables. In recent years, retail advances have increased by 41.2 per cent in 2004-05 as compared to the growth of 27.9 per cent in the overall loans and advances of Scheduled Commercial Banks. As a result, their share in total loans and advances increased significantly during the year ended March 2005. However, according to a recent study, only 15 out of 85 banks registered an increase in return on assets as at the end of 2004-05 over 2003-04. Hence, the argument that rural credit drives down the banks profits and increases NPA is not justified.

NPA in rural credit are far less and the rate of retrieval of rural credit NPAs is faster than other advances. The annual growth rate of farm credit is around 15 per cent and this growth in rural advances essentially comes from advances like gold loans for agriculture and Kisan Cards. About 70 per cent of the present rural credit stock of over ₹ 115243 crore is Kisan Credit Cards spread over 4.8 crore of such card holders. This shows the narrow focus of the banks towards shortterm production loans rather than for term loans. Post reforms, the banking system has mobilised more deposits from farmers and extended less credit to a declining number of farmers.

TABLE B

Deposits received under RIDF as on 31st March 2003

Source: NABARD Report 2002-03

Year	Total (Crore)
1995-96	350
1996-97	1042.30
1997-98	1007.04
1998-99	1337.95
1999-2000	2306.63
2000-01	2653.64
2001-02	3590.72
2002-03	3857.09
Total	16145.37

These are reflected in the figures for farmer borrowings and deposits in the last decade as in Table A. Many scheduled commercial banks are shying away from agriculture and priority sector lending even though the commercial banks have an excess investments portfolio beyond the required limits of 25 per cent. Furthermore, scheduled commercial banks are resorting to the soft window option of investing in the Rural Infrastructure Development Fund (RIDF) of NABARD. Table B illustrates the growing contributions to the corpus of RIDF received by NABARD by way of deposits from Scheduled Commercial Banks against their shortfall in priority sector/ agricultural lending during the preceding year.

Policy Initiatives by Government/RBI

To meet the gap that existed in meeting the credit needs of the rural poor, the Government appointed a working group on rural credit, the Narasimhan Committee in July 1975. Based on its recommendations, Regional Rural Banks (RRB) emerged in 1975. These banks were meant to take banking to the rural masses, particularly in areas without banking facilities, make available cheaper institutional credit to the weaker sections of society, mobilise rural savings and channelize them for other productive activities in rural areas and bring down the cost of providing credit in rural areas. The number of RRBs increased dramatically over a period of time. At the end of the fiscal year of 2002-03, there were 196 RRBs spread by a network of 14,350 branches, accounting for 44.5 per cent of the total rural network of all scheduled commercial banks (including RRBs). The bulk of the loans from RRBs have been given to priority sectors, which accounted for over 70 per cent of the total. Agriculture alone took up 46 per cent of the priority sector advances. RRBs have also taken a lead role in the financing of Self Help Groups (SHG's) mostly comprising women leading to their economic and social empowerment. Cooperative banks were formed to promote the rural credit. Cooperative banks and RRBs differ in their ownership and management. Cooperative banks are state-government run banks while RRBs are managed by the sponsor bank with an equity stake of 35 per cent.

The Central Government and State Government hold 50 per cent and 15 per cent equity stake in RRBs. Since independence, the RBI has taken a number of measures to augment the flow of rural credit. It has a unique system of extending General Line of Credit-I for seasonal agricultural operations and General Line of Credit-II for the handloom sector out of the created money. The RBI has also been issuing directives for a long time now regarding 'social and development banking' like imposing a cap on the interest rates and sectoral allocation of credit and expansion of rural branches.

The RBI has also made it mandatory for commercial banks to lend 40 per cent of their advances to the 'priority sector'. The Service Area Approach was introduced by the Government in 1989, which imparted development orientation to agricultural lending. Other major innovations in the field of rural credit delivery in the 1990s were the successful introduction and implementation of Kisan Credit Cards (KCCs) and the extension of micro-finance in the form of Self-Help Group (SHG).

CHALLENGES FOR RURAL AND AGRICULTURAL CREDIT

Agriculture is a matter of livelihood and food security, with nearly 60 per cent of the population depending on it. At the same time, to withstand the global competition, enhanced productivity and sustainability of the agriculture sector has become imperative. In addition, the majority of the country's population, more so marginal and disadvantaged sections of society, stay in villages. Hence, the role of banks in the enhancement of agriculture productivity, expansion of rural credit and poverty eradication assumes high priority.

Despite decades of efforts and experimentation in banking, the organised financial sector is still not able to meet the credit gap in the rural sector. The lower levels of per capita income, lack of infrastructure in the rural areas, focus in the urban sector and lack of proper connectivity were the main hindrances for banks to venture into rural areas. Directed lending, cumbersome procedures, delay in sanctioning loans and lack of statutory backing for recoveries were other major impediments to the growth of banking in the rural sector. The focus in the past has always been to make available cheaper credit. When banks are forced to lend cheap, there has been a tendency for a scramble for credit by the non-target group of beneficiaries.

While interest rates of scheduled banks for advances over ₹ 2 lakh is completely deregulated, loans up to ₹ 2 lakh are subject to maximum of prime lending rate (PLR). In the process of recovering the opportunity lost on income, the banks used to charge a high rate of interest for loans above 2 lakhs. This led to acceleration in the process of willful defaulting. This has really damaged the credit culture and structure in the rural sector resulting in shutting down of non-viable outlets of rural branches of commercial banks, co-operative banks and RRBs in last few years.

ROLE OF GOVERNMENT/RBI IN MEETING THE CHALLENGES

The number of reports on the rural credit delivery system matches the population of co-operative credit institutions, is a common saying in banking circles. As the agriculture sector becomes more commercial, there would be a greater need for credit. Banks need to change their strategy towards agriculture lending, from 'directed' credit to the one that is business opportunity- led. A substantial jump in the credit flow to agriculture is envisaged in the Tenth Plan at ₹7,36,570 crore, which is more than three times of what was achieved during the Ninth Plan. The contribution by commercial banks is projected at ₹3,81,652 crore. In order to achieve this target, the Government has directed banks to double the flow of farm credit from the level achieved as on 31.03.2004 in the next three years. In this context, the Government/ RBI needs to take a number of initiatives: Revitalising RRBs: Although, RRBs have established themselves as a strong alternative mechanism for rural credit delivery, their potential and relevance is rather neglected in the current scenario. The issue of capital infusion of RRBs assumes critical importance to enlarge the scope of RRB operations.

RRBs need to be provided with adequate capital support to enable them to have a net capital adequacy ratio (CAR) of 5 per cent. The share of sponsoring institutions in the capital structure of RRBs also needs to be enlarged to make them majority shareholders. By acquiring the majority shareholding in RRB, the sponsor banks/institutions can convert them into vibrant and professional subsidiaries and area-specific special business units (SBU). In the long run, they may merge all their agricultural and rural activities under the umbrella of these SBU. The government should further amalgamate regional rural banks (RRBs) with the sponsor banks to increase the reach of PSBs in rural areas.With the merger of RRBs with sponsor banks, the latter will get a wide branch network in rural areas.In the long term, however, a single independent owner of all RRBs with exclusive focus on rural and micro-credit, would be a great step towards channelising resources for the purpose for which RRBs were established.

Increasing the scope of NABARD: NABARD has evolved over the past two decades into a strong and rural-sensitive developmental institution with a complete understanding of the complexities of the agricultural and rural sectors. NABARD should thus become an apex development bank in the rural and agricultural sectors with direct equity participation in RRBs along with sponsoring institutions With presence on the boards of all RRBs and co-operatives, NABARD is fully equipped to emerge as a strong player in the rural credit system. NABARD's promotion of self-help group (SHGs) movements reflects its immense capability in capacity building and nurturing the rural credit delivery system.

Minimum CD Ratio: In order to obviate the regional or urban/rural imbalances, the minimum benchmark CD ratio provided (for example, 55 per cent) should be envisaged in all districts of the country. That will assist broad-based and equitable credit expansion, thereby contributing enhanced economic activity. The reason urban India is reflecting enhanced economic activity post-reforms is the availability and expansion of credit for housing and consumption purposes.

Reducing cost of rural credit: A different dispensation under CRR and SLR would help in making available more resources for rural credit deployment. The rate of interest paid on CRR balances held by these rural institutions might also be marginally (100 basis points) above what is paid to commercial banks.

Similarly, the Central Government and all State governments need to park their rural developmental funds with RRB to ensure cheaper flow of demand deposits. Regulation with respect to banking has been designed for delivery in urban India and distribution required more manpower to be deployed in rural areas. All rural financial institutions need special dispensation suited to their local potential and challenges.

Commodity Markets: The focus of the commodity exchanges has been confined to traditional future/derivative trading centres, and the farmers and actual commodity users are still not participating. Only traders and speculators are participating in it. Banks should be permitted to offer futures-based products to farmers in order to enable them to hedge against price or weather risk, etc. To mitigate the risk in the financing of agriculture, the Government should allow banks to operate on behalf of farmers and participate in commodity futures. Allowing banks entry into commodity futures trading will not only boost liquidity and turnover volumes but will also provide them with a protective cover against default on agricultural loans. In the new arrangement, banks can lend to farmers or cooperatives and simultaneously encourage them to sell into futures contracts. This can help reduce the risk of farmers defaulting on their loans in the event of a fall in spot commodity prices or unexpected weather conditions.

Crop Insurance: The Agriculture Insurance Company of India (AIC) should further spread crop insurance awareness level among the Indian farming community, which is abysmally low. The Union and State Governments should give time-bound subsidy on premiums of crop insurance to increase the coverage of the AIC.

Promoting Micro-finance/Micro enterprise: Micro-finance refers to the provision of small-scale savings, credit, insurance, and any other financial services to those who cannot access them from formal financial institutions. Due to issues of risk and cost associated with servicing the larger numbers of small low capital input businesses, the formal sector lending to micro enterprises is low. Banks offer a variety of potential advantages for financing micro-enterprises like commercial outlook and relatively sophisticated skills. Apart from acting as a credit provider, the banks should act as agents of change by helping people in acquiring the basic knowledge of business, policy environment, etc.

Well-defined investment policy: RBI/NABARD should also provide a well-defined investment policy for the above mentioned institutions. This will help these institutions in better deployment of surplus funds. In comparison to PSB's and Private Sector banks these institutions can't afford to have statistically sophisticated models for investment and treasury management. In that regard they seek the guidance and assistance from the supervisor in this area. Learning from other countries/ Adopting new models: Banks also need to look at the models followed by banks in other countries. For example, Bangladesh Grameen Bank model and micro-finance experience of Philippines are quite well-known. Banking Correspondents in Brazil is another successful model where banks can create a network of "banking correspondents". These banking correspondents are small outlets, which provide basic banking services, example drug stores, petrol pump, small stores in the neighbourhood, etc. The widely spread post-offices network in the country can also be used to deliver banking services. Banks and regulators need to look at these models and their feasibility in the Indian scenario to bridge the banking divide.

ROLE OF BANKS

Money lending in one form or the other has evolved along with the history of the mankind. Even in the ancient times there are references to the moneylenders. Shakespeare also referred to 'Shylocks' who made unreasonable demands in case the loans were not repaid in time along with interest. Indian history is also replete with the instances referring to indigenous money lenders, Sahukars and Zamindars involved in the business of money lending by mortgaging the landed property of the borrowers. Towards the beginning of the twentieth century, with the onset of modern industry in the country, the need for government regulated banking system was felt.

The British government began to pay attention towards the need for an organised banking sector in the country and Reserve Bank of India was set up to regulate the formal banking sector in the country. But the growth of modern banking remained slow mainly due to lack of surplus capital in the Indian economic system at that point of time. Modern banking institutions came up only in big cities and industrial centres. The rural areas, representing vast majority of Indian society, remained dependent on the indigenous money lenders for their credit needs. Independence of the country heralded a new era in the growth of modern banking. Many new commercial banks came up in various parts of the country. As the modern banking network grew, the government began to realise that the banking sector was catering only to the needs of the well-to-do and the capitalists.

The interests of the poorer sections as well as those of the common man were being ignored. In 1969, Indian government took a historic decision to nationalise 14 biggest private commercial banks. A few more were nationalised after a couple of years. This resulted in transferring the ownership of these banks to the State and the Reserve Bank of India could then issue directions to these banks to fund the national programmes, the rural sector, the plan priorities and the priority sector at differential rate of interest.

This resulted in providing fillip the banking facilities to the rural areas, to the under-privileged and the downtrodden. It also resulted in financial inclusion of all categories of people in almost all the regions of the country. However, after almost two decades of bank nationalisation some new issues became contextual. The service standards of the public sector banks began to decline. Their profitability came down and the efficiency of the staff became suspect. Non-performing assets of these banks began to rise. The wheel of time had turned a full circle by early nineties and the government after the introduction of structural and economic reforms in the financial sector, allowed the setting up of new banks in the private sector. The new generation private banks have now established themselves in the system and have set new standards of service and efficiency. These banks have also given tough but healthy competition to the public sector banks.

COMPETITIVE LANDSCAPE OF BANKS IN INDIA

Banks face competition from a wide range of financial intermediaries in the public and private sectors in the areas of financial intermediation and financial services (although the payments system is exclusively for banks). Such intermediaries form a diverse group in terms of size and nature of their activities, and play an important role in the financial system by not only competing with banks, but also complementing them in providing a wide range of financial services.

Some of these intermediaries include:

- Term-lending institutions
- Non-banking financial companies
- Insurance companies
- Mutual funds

TERM-LENDING INSTITUTIONS

Term lending institutions exist at both state and all-India levels. They provide term loans (*i.e.*, loans with medium to long-term maturities) to various industry, service and infrastructure sectors for setting up new projects and for the expansion of existing facilities and thereby compete with banks. At the all-India level, these institutions are typically specialized, catering to the needs of specific sectors, which make them competitors to banks in those areas. These include the Export Import Bank of India (EXIM Bank), Small Industries Development Bank of India (SIDBI), Tourism Finance Corporation of India Limited (TFCI), and Power Finance Corporation Limited (PFCL).

At the state level, various State Financial Corporations (SFCs) have been set up to finance and promote small and medium-sized enterprises. There are also State Industrial Development Corporations (SIDCs), which provide finance primarily to medium-sized and large-sized enterprises. In addition to SFCs and SIDCs, the North Eastern Development Financial Institution Ltd. (NEDFI) has been set up to cater specifically to the needs of the north-eastern states.

NON-BANKING FINANCE COMPANIES (NBFCS)

India has many thousands of non-banking financial companies, predominantly from the private sector. NBFCs are required to register with RBI in terms of the Reserve Bank of India (Amendment) Act, 1997. The principal activities of NBFCs include equipment-leasing, hirepurchase, loan and investment and asset finance. NBFCs have been competing with and complementing the services of commercial banks for a long time. All NBFCs together currently account for around nine per cent of assets of the total financial system.

Housing-finance companies form a distinct sub-group of the NBFCs. As a result of some recent government incentives for investing in the housing sector, these companies' business has grown substantially.

Housing Development Finance Corporation Limited (HDFC), which is in the private sector and the Government-controlled Housing and Urban Development Corporation Limited (HUDCO) are the two premier housing-finance companies. These companies are major players in the mortgage business, and provide stiff competition to commercial banks in the disbursal of housing loans.

INSURANCE COMPANIES

Insurance/reinsurance companies such as Life Insurance Corporation of India (LIC), General Insurance Corporation of India (GICI), and others provide substantial long-term financial assistance to the industrial and housing sectors and to that extent, are competitors of banks. LIC is the biggest player in this area.

MUTUAL FUNDS

Mutual funds offer competition to banks in the area of fund mobilization, in that they offer alternate routes of investment to households. Most mutual funds are standalone asset management companies. In addition, a number of banks, both in the private and public sectors, have sponsored asset management companies to undertake mutual fund business. Banks have thus entered the asset management business, sometimes on their own and other times in joint venture with others.

BANKING REFORM IN INDIA

Measured by share of deposits, 83 per cent of the banking business in India is in the hands of state or nationalized banks, which are banks that are owned by the government, in some, increasingly less clear-cut way. Moreover, even the non-nationalized banks are subject to extensive regulations on who they can lend to, in addition to the more standard prudential regulations.

Government control over banks has always had its fans, ranging from Lenin to Gerschenkron. While there are those who have emphasized the political importance of public control over banking, most arguments for nationalizing banks are based on the premise that profit maximizing lenders do not necessarily deliver credit where the social returns are the highest. The Indian government, when nationalizing all the larger Indian banks in 1969, argued that banking was "inspired by a larger social purpose" and must "sub serve national priorities and objectives such as rapid growth in agriculture, small industry and exports."

There is now a body of direct and indirect evidence showing that credit markets in developing countries often fail to deliver credit where its social product might be the highest, and both

- We thank the Reserve Bank of India, in particular Y.V. Reddy, R.B. Barman, and Abhiman Das, for generous assistance with technical and substantative issues. We also thank Abhiman Das for performing calculations which involved proprietary RBI data, as well as Saibal Ghosh and Petia Topalova for helpful comments. We are grateful to the staff of the public sector bank we study for allowing us access to their data. We gratefully acknowledge financial support from the Alfred P. Sloan Foundation.
- If nationalization succeeds in pushing credit into these sectors, as the Indian government claimed it would, it could indeed raise both equity and efficiency. The cross-country evidence on the impact of bank nationalization is not very encouraging. For example, find in a cross-country setting that govern-ment ownership of banks is negatively correlated with both financial development and economic growth.
- They interpret this as support for their view, which holds that the potential benefits of public ownership of banks, and public control over banks more generally, are swamped by the costs that come from the agency problems it creates: cronyism, leading to the deliberate misallocation of capital, bureaucratic lethargy, leading to less deliberate, but perhaps equally costly errors in the allocation of capital, as well as inefficiency in the process of mobilizing savings and transforming them into credit. Unfortunately the interpretation of this type of cross-country analysis is never easy, and never more so than the case of something like bank nationalization, which typically occurs as part of a package of other policies. For example, Bertrand et. al. study a 1985 banking deregulation in France, which gave banks much greater freedom to compete for clients.
- They find that deregulated banks respond more to profitability when making lending decisions. After the reform, firms that suffer a negative

shock are much more likely to undertake restructuring measures, and there is more entry and exit in bank-dependent industries. Micro studies of the effect of bank nationalization are rare: an important exception is Mian who examines the privatization of a large public bank in Pakistan in 1991.

- He finds that the privatized bank does a better job both at choosing profitable clients and monitoring existing clients, than the commercial banks that remained public. Micro data from a nationalized bank to evaluate the effectiveness of the Indian banking system in delivering credit.
- The Indian financial system is characterized by under-lending in the sense that there are many firms that could earn large profits if they were given access to credit at the current market prices.

The work with the aim of using that evidence and evidence from other research by ourselves and others, to come to an assessment of the appropriate role of the Indian government vis a vis the banking sector. We first provide a very brief history of banking in India.

We begin by presenting evidence that there is substantial under-lending in India. To understand what role public ownership of banks may play in underlending, we identify differences between public and private banks in the sectoral allocation of credit between public and private banks. In particular, we focus on the question of whether being nationalized has made these banks more responsive to what the Indian government wants them to do. We report results, based on work by Cole showing that on many of the declared objectives of "social banking," the private banks were no less responsive than the comparable nationalized banks, with the exception of agricultural lending.

Finally, the last sub-section compares the performance of public and private banks as financial intermediaries and concludes that the public banks have been less aggressive than private banks both in lending, in attracting deposits and in setting up branches, at least since 1990. We find that official lending policy is very rigid. Moreover, loan officers do not appear to use what little flexibility they have. We argue that the evidence suggests that bankers in the public sector have a preference for what we may call passive lending.

To understand why this is the case, we examine the incentives and constraints faced by public loan officers. We focus on whether vigilance activity impedes lending, and whether public sector banks prefer to lend to the government, rather than private firms. The penultimate part compares the performance of public and private banking in two other areas. First, we examine how nationalization of banks has affected the availability of bank branches in rural areas, and find that, if anything, nationalization appears to have inhibited the growth of rural branches. Second, we try to say something about the sensitive issue of NPAs and bailouts. While the dataset we have now is rather sparse, it appears that the bailouts of the public banks have proved more expensive for the government, but once we control for differences in size between the public and private banks, it is less clear-cut. We conclude in a short discussion of the implications of these results for the future of banking reform. Background India has a long history of both public and private banking. Modern banking in India began in the 18th century, with the founding of the English Agency House in Calcutta and Bombay. In the first half of the 19th century, three Presidency banks were founded. After the 1860 introduction of limited liability, private banks began to appear, and foreign banks entered the market.

The beginning of the 20th century saw the introduction of joint stock banks. In 1935, the presidency banks were merged together to form the Imperial Bank of India, which was subsequently renamed the State Bank of India. Also that year, India's central bank, the Reserve Bank of India (RBI), began operation. Following independence, the RBI was given broad regulatory authority over commercial banks in India. In 1959, the State Bank of India acquired the state-owned banks of eight former princely states. Thus, by July 1969, approximately 31 per cent of scheduled bank branches throughout India were government controlled, as part of the State Bank of India. The post-war development strategy was in many ways a socialist one, and the Indian government felt that banks in private hands did not lend enough to those who needed it most.

In July 1969, the government nationalized all banks whose nationwide deposits were greater than ₹.500 million, resulting in the nationalization of 54 per cent more of the branches in India, and bringing the total number of branches under government control to 84 per cent. Prakesh Tandon, a former chairman of the Punjab National Bank (nationalized in 1969) describes the rationale for nationalization as follows: Many bank failures and crises over two centuries, and the damage they did under 'laissez faire' conditions; the needs of planned growth and equitable distribution of credit, which in privately owned banks was concentrated mainly on the controlling industrial houses and influential borrowers; the needs of growing small scale industry and farming regarding finance, equipment and inputs; from all these there emerged an inexorable demand for banking legislation, some government control and a central banking authority, adding up, in the final analysis, to social control and nationalization.

After nationalization, the breadth and scope of the Indian banking sector expanded at a rate perhaps unmatched by any other country. Indian banking has been remarkably successful at achieving mass participation. Between the time of the 1969 nationalizations and the present, over 58,000 bank branches were opened in India; these new branches, as of March 2003, had mobilized over 9 trillion Rupees in deposits, which represent the overwhelming majority of deposits in Indian banks. This rapid expansion is attributable to a policy which required banks to open four branches in unbanked locations for every branch opened in banked locations. Between 1969 and 1980, the number of private branches grew more quickly than public banks, and on April 1, 1980, they accounted for approximately 17.5 per cent of bank branches in India.

INSTITUTIONAL EVOLUTION OF THE INDIAN BANKING

As most of you would, no doubt, be aware, the indigenous system of banking had existed in India for many centuries, and catered to the credit needs of the economy of that time. The famous *Kautilya Arthashastra*, which is ascribed to be dating back to the 4th century BC, contains references to creditors and lending. For instance, it says "*If anyone became bankrupt, debts owed to the state had priority over other creditors*". Similarly, there is also a reference to "*Interest on commodities loaned*" to be accounted as revenue of the state. Thus, it appears that lending activities were not entirely unknown in the medieval India and the concepts such as 'priority of claims of creditors' and 'commodity lending' were established business practices.

During the period of modern history, however, the roots of commercial banking in India can be traced back to the early eighteenth century when the Bank of Calcutta was established in June 1806 – which was renamed as Bank of Bengal in January 1809 – mainly to fund General Wellesley's wars. This was followed by the establishment of the Bank of Madras in July 1843, as a joint stock company, through the reorganisation and amalgamation of four banks *viz.*, Madras Bank, Carnatic Bank, Bank of Madras and the Asiatic Bank. This bank brought about major innovations in banking such as use of joint stock system, conferring of limited liability on shareholders, acceptance of deposits from the general public, etc. The Bank of Bombay, the last bank to be set up under the British Raj pursuant to the Charter of the then British East India Company, was established in 1868, about a decade after the India's first war of independence.

The three Presidency Banks, as these were then known, were amalgamated in January 1921 to form the Imperial Bank of India, which acquired the three-fold role: of a commercial bank, of a banker's bank and of a banker to the government.

It is interesting to note here that merger of banks and consolidation in the banking system in India, is not as recent a phenomenon as is often thought to be, and dates back to at least 1843 – and the process, of course, still continues. With the formation of the Reserve Bank of India in 1935, some of the central banking functions of the Imperial Bank were taken over by the RBI and subsequently, the State Bank of India, set up in July 1955, assumed the other functions of the Imperial Bank and became the successor to the Imperial Bank of India.

EVOLUTION OF LEGISLATIVE REGULATION OF BANKING IN INDIA

In the very early phase of commercial banking in India, the regulatory framework was somewhat diffused and the Presidency Banks were regulated and governed by their Royal Charter, the East India Company and the Government of India of that time. Though the Company law was introduced in India way back in 1850, it did not apply to the banking companies. The banking crisis of 1913, however, had revealed several weaknesses in the Indian banking system, such as the low proportion of liquid assets of the banks and connected lending practices, resulting in large-scale bank failures. The recommendations of the Indian Central Banking Enquiry Committee, which looked into the issue of bank failures, paved the way for a legislation for banking regulation in the country.

Though the RBI, as part of its monetary management mandate, had, from the very beginning, been vested with the powers, under the RBI Act, 1934, to regulate the volume and cost of bank credit in the economy through the instruments of general credit control, it was not until 1949 that a comprehensive enactment, applicable only to the banking sector, came into existence. Prior to 1949, the banking companies, in common with other companies, were governed by the Indian Companies Act, 1913, which itself was a comprehensive re-enactment of the earlier company law of 1850.

This Act, however, contained a few provisions specially applicable to banks. There were also a few *ad hoc* enactments, such as the Banking Companies (Inspection) Ordinance, 1946, and the Banking Companies (Restriction of Branches) Act, 1946, covering specific regulatory aspects.

In this backdrop, in March 1949, a special legislation, called the Banking Companies Act, 1949, applicable exclusively to the banking companies, was passed; this Act was renamed as the Banking Regulation Act from March 1966.

The Act vested in the Reserve Bank the responsibility relating to licensing of banks, branch expansion, liquidity of their assets, management and methods of working, amalgamation, reconstruction and liquidation. Important changes in several provisions of the Act were made from time to time, designed to enlarge or amplify the responsibilities of the RBI or to impart flexibility to the relative provisions, commensurate with the imperatives of the banking sector developments.

It is interesting to note that till March 1966, the Reserve Bank had practically no role in relation to the functioning of the urban co-operative banks. However, by the enactment of the Banking Laws (Application to Co-operative Societies) Act, 1965, certain provisions of the Banking Regulation Act, regarding the matters *relating to banking business*, were extended to the urban cooperative banks also. Thus, for the first time in 1966, the urban co-operative banks too came within the regulatory purview of the RBI.

MODERN DAY ROLE

Banking system and the Financial Institutions play very significant role in the economy. First and foremost is in the form of catering to the need of credit for all the sections of society. The modern economies in the world have developed primarily by making best use of the credit availability in their systems. An efficient banking system must cater to the needs of high end investors by making available high amounts of capital for big projects in the industrial, infrastructure and service sectors. At the same time, the medium and small ventures must also have credit available to them for new investment and expansion of the existing units. Rural sector in a country like India can grow only if cheaper credit is available to the farmers for their short and medium term needs. Credit availability for infrastructure sector is also extremely important.

The success of any financial system can be fathomed by finding out the availability of reliable and adequate credit for infrastructure projects. Fortunately, during the past about one decade there has been increased participation of the private sector in infrastructure projects. The banks and the financial institutions also cater to another important need of the society *i.e.* mopping up small savings at reasonable rates with several options.

The common man has the option to park his savings under a few alternatives, including the small savings schemes introduced by the government from time to time and in bank deposits in the form of savings accounts, recurring deposits and time deposits. Another option is to invest in the stocks or mutual funds.

The banks and the financial institutions also perform certain new-age functions which could not be thought of a couple of decades ago. The facility of internet banking enables a consumer to access and operate his bank account without actually visiting the bank premises. The facility of ATMs and the credit/ debit cards has revolutionised the choices available with the customers. The banks also serve as alternative gateways for making payments on account of income tax and online payment of various bills like the telephone, electricity and tax.

The bank customers can also invest their funds in various stocks or mutual funds straight from their bank accounts. In the modern day economy, where people have no time to make these payments by standing in queue, the service provided by the banks is commendable. While the commercial banks cater to the banking needs of the people in the cities and towns, there is another category of banks that looks after the credit and banking needs of the people living in the rural areas, particularly the farmers. Regional Rural Banks (RRBs) have been sponsored by many commercial banks in several States. These banks, along with the cooperative banks, take care of the farmer-specific needs of credit and other banking facilities.

FUTURE

Till a few years ago, the government largely patro-nized the small savings schemes in which not only the interest rates were higher, but the income tax rebates and incentives were also in plenty. The bank deposits, on the other hand, did not entail such benefits. As a result, the small savings were the first choice of the investors. But for the last few years the trend has been reversed. The small savings, the bank deposits and the mutual funds have been brought at par for the purpose of incentives under the income tax.

Moreover, the interest rates in the small savings schemes are no longer higher than those offered by the banks. Banks today are free to determine their interest rates within the given limits prescribed by the RBI. It is now easier for the banks to open new branches. But the banking sector reforms are still not complete. A lot more is required to be done to revamp the public sector banks. Mergers and amalgamation is the next measure on the agenda of the government. The government is also preparing to disinvest some of its equity from the PSU banks. The option of allowing foreign direct investment beyond 50 per cent in the Indian banking sector has also been under consideration. Banks and financial intuitions have played major role in the economic development of the country and most of the credit- related schemes of the government to uplift the poorer and the under-privileged sections have been implemented through the banking sector. The role of the banks has been important, but it is going to be even more important in the future.

ECONOMIC FUNCTIONS

The economic functions of banks include:

- Issue of money, in the form of banknotes and current accounts subject to cheque or payment at the customer's order. These claims on banks can act as money because they are negotiable and/or repayable on demand, and hence valued at par and effectively transferable by mere delivery in the case of banknotes, or by drawing a cheque, delivering it to the payee to bank or cash.
- Netting and settlement of payments — banks act both as collection agent and paying agents for customers, and participate in inter-bank clearing and settlement systems to collect, present, be presented with, and pay payment instruments. This enables banks to economise on reserves held for settlement of payments, since inward and outward

payments offset each other. It also enables payment flows between geographical areas to offset, reducing the cost of settling payments between geographical areas.

- Credit intermediation — banks borrow and lend back-to-back on their own account as middle men
- Credit quality improvement — banks lend money to ordinary commercial and personal borrowers (ordinary credit quality), but are high quality borrowers. The improvement comes from diversification of the bank's assets and the bank's own capital which provides a buffer to absorb losses without defaulting on its own obligations. However, since banknotes and deposits are generally unsecured, if the bank gets into difficulty and pledges assets as security to try to get the funding it needs to continue to operate, this puts the note holders and depositors in an economically subordinated position.
- Maturity transformation — banks borrow more on demand debt and short term debt, but provide more long term loans. Bank can do this because they can aggregate issues (*e.g.* accepting deposits and issuing banknotes) and redemptions (*e.g.* withdrawals and redemptions of banknotes), maintain reserves of cash, invest in marketable securities that can be readily converted to cash if needed, and raise replacement funding as needed from various sources (*e.g.* wholesale cash markets and securities markets) because they have a high and more well known credit quality than most other borrowers.

LAW OF BANKING

Banking law is based on a contractual analysis of the relationship between the bank and the customer. The definition of bank is given above, and the definition of customer is any person for whom the bank agrees to conduct an account.

The law implies rights and obligations into this relationship as follows:

- The bank account balance is the financial position between the bank and the customer, when the account is in credit, the bank owes the balance to the customer, when the account is overdrawn, the customer owes the balance to the bank.
- The bank engages to pay the customer's cheques up to the amount standing to the credit of the customer's account, plus any agreed overdraft limit.
- The bank may not pay from the customer's account without a mandate from the customer, *e.g.* a cheque drawn by the customer.
- The bank engages to promptly collect the cheques deposited to the

customer's account as the customer's agent, and to credit the proceeds to the customer's account.

- The bank has a right to combine the customer's accounts, since each account is just an aspect of the same credit relationship.
- The bank has a lien on cheques deposited to the customer's account, to the extent that the customer is indebted to the bank.
- The bank must not disclose the details of the transactions going through the customer's account unless the customer consents, there is a public duty to disclose, the bank's interests require it, or under compulsion of law.
- The bank must not close a customer's account without reasonable notice to the customer, because cheques are outstanding in the ordinary course of business for several days.

These implied contractual terms may be modified by express agreement between the customer and the bank. The statutes and regulations in force in the jurisdiction may also modify the above terms and/or create new rights, obligations or limitations relevant to the bank-customer relationship.

ENTRY REGULATION

Currently in most jurisdictions commercial banks are regulated by government entities and require a special bank licence to operate. Usually the definition of the business of banking for the purposes of regulation is extended to include acceptance of deposits, even if they are not repayable to the customer's order, however money lending, by itself, is generally not included in the definition. Unlike most other regulated industries, the regulator is typically also a participant in the market, *i.e.* government owned bank (a central bank). Central banks also typically have a monopoly on the business of issuing banknotes. However, in some countries this is not the case, *e.g.* in the UK the Financial Services Authority licences banks and some commercial banks, such as the Bank of Scotland, issue their own banknotes in competition with the Bank of England, the UK government's central bank. Some types of entity may be partly or wholly exempt from bank licence requirements and are regulated by separate regulators, *e.g.* building societies and credit unions.

The requirements for the issue of a bank licence vary between jurisdictions but typically incude:

- Minimum capital
- Minimum capital ratio
- 'Fit and Proper' requirements for the bank's controllers, owners, directors, and/or senior officers

- Approval of the bank's business plan as being sufficiently prudent and plausible.

FINANCIAL INSTITUTION

In financial economics, a financial institution is an institution that provides financial services for its clients or members. Probably the most important financial service provided by financial institutions is acting as financial intermediaries. Most financial institutions are regulated by the government.

Broadly speaking, there are three major types of financial institutions:

- Deposit-taking institutions that accept and manage deposits and make loans, including banks, building societies, credit unions, trust companies, and mortgage loan companies
- Insurance companies and pension funds; and
- Brokers, underwriters and investment funds.

FUNCTION

Financial institutions provide service as intermediaries of financial markets. They are responsible for transferring funds from investors to companies in need of those funds. Financial institutions facilitate the flow of money through the economy. To do so, savings arisk brought to provide funds for loans. Such is the primary means for depository institutions to develop revenue. Should the yield curve become inverse, firms in this arena will offer additional fee-generating services including securities underwriting, and pre. fds

CORPORATE VALUATION

- *Relative metrics:* = Firm wields capital machinery (asset) and the loans (liabilities) it used to finance that asset. The line is blurred in Financial Institutions, which must hold deposit accounts (liabilities) to fuel the issuance of loans (assets). The same accounts are considered loans as they are held in ownership not of the bank, but of the individual client.
- *Dividend Discount Model:* Earnings-per-share
- Dividends-per-share
- *Discounted Cash Flow (DCF) Model:* You'll need the FCFE (Free Cash Flow for Equity), which is the amount of money that is returned to shareholders. Calculate an FCFF (Free Cash Flow to the Firm): EBIT (1-tax rate) -Capital Expenditures+ (Depreciation and Amortization) - (Net increase in working capital)= FCFF (FCFF-Debt+Cash=FCFE)
- Use the Capital Asset Pricing Model, not the Weighted Average Cost

of Capital (for the same reasons one uses Equity Multiples in relative valuation) to determine the cost of equity (the return required by shareholders to make the decision to invest in a financial institutions)

- *Excess Return Model:* A model where valuation is expressed as the sum of capital invested currently in the firm and the present value of dollar excess returns that the firm expects to make in the future.

STANDING SETTLEMENT INSTRUCTIONS

Standing Settlement Instructions (SSIs) are the agreements between two financial institutions which fix the receiving agents of each counterparty in ordinary trades of some type. These agreements allow traders to make faster trades since time used to settle the receiving agents is conserved. Limiting the trader to an SSI also lowers the likelihood of a fraud.

REGULATION

Financial institutions in most countries operate in a heavily regulated environment as they are critical parts of countries' economies. Regulation structures differ in each country, but typically involve prudential regulation as well as consumer protection and market stability. Some countries have one consolidated agency that regulates all financial institutions while others have separate agencies for different types of institutions such as banks, insurance companies and brokers. Countries that have separate agencies include the United States, where the key governing bodies are the Federal Financial Institutions Examination Council (FFIEC), Office of the Comptroller of the Currency - National Banks, Federal Deposit Insurance Corporation (FDIC) State "non-member" banks, National Credit Union Administration (NCUA) - Credit Unions, Federal Reserve (Fed) - "member" Banks, Office of Thrift Supervision - National Savings and Loan Association, State governments each often regulate and charter financial institutions.

Countries that have one consolidated financial regulator include United Kingdom with the Financial Services Authority, Norway with the Financial Supervisory Authority of Norway, Hong Kong with Hong Kong Monetary Authority and Russia with Central Bank of Russia.

FRACTIONAL RESERVE BANKING

Fractional-reserve banking is a form of banking where banks maintain reserves (of cash and coin or deposits at the central bank) that are only a fraction of the customer's deposits. Funds deposited into a bank are mostly lent out, and a bank keeps only a fraction (called the reserve ratio) of the quantity of deposits as reserves. Some of the funds lent out are subsequently deposited with another bank, increasing deposits at that second bank and allowing further lending.

As most bank deposits are treated as money in their own right, fractional reserve banking increases the money supply, and banks are said to create money. Due to the prevalence of fractional reserve banking, the broad money supply of most countries is a multiple larger than the amount of base money created by the country's central bank. That multiple (called the money multiplier) is determined by the reserve requirement or other financial ratio requirements imposed by financial regulators, and by the excess reserves kept by commercial banks. Central banks generally mandate reserve requirements that require banks to keep a minimum fraction of their demand deposits as cash reserves.

This both limits the amount of money creation that occurs in the commercial banking system, and ensures that banks have enough ready cash to meet normal demand for withdrawals. Problems can arise, however, when depositors seek withdrawal of a large proportion of deposits at the same time; this can cause a bank run or, when problems are extreme and widespread, a systemic crisis.

To mitigate this risk, the governments of most countries (usually acting through the central bank) regulate and oversee commercial banks, provide deposit insurance and act as lender of last resort to commercial banks. Fractional-reserve banking is the most common form of banking and is practiced in almost all countries. Although Islamic banking prohibits the making of profit from interest on debt, a form of fractional-reserve banking is still evident in most Islamic countries.

HISTORY

Savers looking to keep their valuables in safekeeping depositories deposited gold coins and silver coins at goldsmiths, receiving in turn a note for their deposit. Once these notes became a trusted medium of exchange an early form of paper money was born, in the form of the goldsmiths' notes. As the notes were used directly in trade, the goldsmiths observed that people would not usually redeem all their notes at the same time, and they saw the opportunity to invest their coin reserves in interest-bearing loans and bills.

This generated income for the goldsmiths but left them with more notes on issue than reserves with which to pay them. A process was started that altered the role of the goldsmiths from passive guardians of bullion, charging fees for safe storage, to interest-paying and interest-earning banks. Thus fractional-reserve banking was born. However, if creditors (note holders of gold originally deposited) lost faith in the ability of a bank to redeem (pay) their notes, many would try to redeem their notes at the same time. If in response a bank could not raise enough funds by calling in loans or selling bills, it either went into insolvency or defaulted on its notes.

Such a situation is called a *bank run* and caused the demise of many early banks. Repeated bank failures and financial crises led to the creation of central banks – public institutions that have the authority to regulate commercial banks, impose reserve requirements, and act as lender-of-last-resort if a bank runs low on liquidity. The emergence of central banks mitigated the dangers associated with fractional reserve banking. From about 1991 a consensus had emerged within developed economies about the optimum design of monetary policy. In essence central bankers gave up attempts to directly control the amount of money in the economy and instead moved to indirect means by targeting interest rates. This consensus is criticized by some economists.

Reason for Existence

Fractional reserve banking allows people to invest their money, without losing the ability to use it on demand. Since most people do not need to use all their money all the time, banks lend out that money, to generate profit for themselves. Thus, banks can act as financial intermediaries — facilitating the investment of savers' funds. Full reserve banking, on the other hand, does not allow any money in such demand deposits to be invested (since all of the money would be locked up in reserves) and less liquid investments (such as stocks, bonds and time deposits) lock up a lender's money for a time, making it unavailable for the lender to use. According to mainstream economic theory, regulated fractional-reserve banking also benefits the economy by providing regulators with powerful tools for manipulating the money supply and interest rates, which many see as essential to a healthy economy.

HOW IT WORKS

The nature of modern banking is such that the cash reserves at the bank available to repay demand deposits need only be a fraction of the demand deposits owed to depositors. In most legal systems, a demand deposit at a bank (*e.g.*, a checking or savings account) is considered a loan to the bank (instead of a bailment) repayable on demand, that the bank can use to finance its investments in loans and interest bearing securities.

Banks make a profit based on the difference between the interest they charge on the loans they make, and the interest they pay to their depositors (aggregately called the net interest margin (NIM)). Since a bank lends out most of the money deposited, keeping only a fraction of the total as reserves, it necessarily has less money than the account balances of its depositors.

The main reason customers deposit funds at a bank is to store savings in the form of a demand claim on the bank. Depositors still have a claim to full repayment of their funds on demand even though most of the funds have already been invested by the bank in interest bearing loans and securities. Holders of demand deposits can withdraw all of their deposits at any time. If all the depositors of a bank did so at the same time a bank run would occur, and the bank would likely collapse.

Due to the practice of central banking, this is a rare event today, as central banks usually guarantee the deposits at commercial banks, and act as lender of last resort when there is a run on a bank. However, there have been some recent bank runs: the Northern Rock crisis of 2007 in the United Kingdom is an example.

The collapse of Washington Mutual bank in September 2008, the largest bank failure in history, was preceded by a "silent run" on the bank, where depositors removed vast sums of money from the bank through electronic transfer. However, in these cases, the banks proved to have been insolvent at the time of the run. Thus, these bank runs merely precipitated failures that were inevitable in any case.

In the absence of crises that trigger bank runs, fractional-reserve banking usually functions smoothly because at any one time relatively few depositors will make cash withdrawals simultaneously compared to the total amount on deposit, and a cash reserve can be maintained as a buffer to deal with the normal cash demands from depositors seeking withdrawals. In addition, in a normal economic environment, cash is steadily being introduced into the economy by the central bank, and new funds are steadily being deposited into the commercial banks. However, if a bank is experiencing a financial crisis, and net redemption demands are unusually large over a period of time, the bank will run low on cash reserves and will be forced to raise additional funds to avoid running out of reserves and defaulting on its obligations.

A bank can raise funds from additional borrowings (*e.g.*, by borrowing from the money market or using lines of credit held with other banks), or by selling assets, or by calling in short-term loans. If creditors are afraid that the bank is running out of cash or is insolvent, they have an incentive to redeem their deposits as soon as possible before other depositors access the remaining cash reserves before they do, triggering a cascading crisis that can result in a full-scale bank run.

As an example for a very simple idea of how the fractional reserve system can work if there is only one bank, for a Reserve Fraction of 10 per cent, a bank can turn a $1000 deposit of "M0" money, into $18,997 of "M1" money. Ignoring interest and fees, which makes banks even more profitable, this is how a bank can copy 90 per cent of "M0" money to make "M1" money, where in this example the money loaned out is simply re-deposited in the bank and loaned out again, and so on, that is how the $18,997 "M1" money comes from the $1000 of "M0" money. Banks do this by accumulating loans and deposits (effectively multiplying) the "M0" supply to make a larger "M1" supply.

Banks can collect interest on the spread of the higher loan interest from the lower deposit interests. Return On Investment (ROI) for a bank is theoretically infinite considering the bank is using none of its own money, if one excludes the cost of setting up and maintaining the accounting system.

MONEY CREATION

Modern central banking allows banks to practice fractional reserve banking with inter-bank business transactions with a reduced risk of bankruptcy. The process of fractional-reserve banking expands the money supply of the economy but also increases the risk that a bank cannot meet its depositor withdrawals.

Though not a mainstream economic belief, a number of central bankers, monetary economists, and text books, have said that banks create money by 'extending credit', where banks obligate themselves to borrowers, and then later manage whatever liabilities this creates for them, where if the central bank targets interest rates, it must supply base money on demand to meet the banks reserve requirements, *after* the banks have begun the lending process and that rather than deposits leading to loans, causality is reversed, and loans lead to deposits.

There are two types of money in a fractional-reserve banking system operating with a central bank:

1. *Central bank money:* Money created or adopted by the central bank regardless of its form -- precious metals, commodity certificates, banknotes, coins, electronic money loaned to commercial banks, or anything else the central bank chooses as its form of money
2. *Commercial bank money:* Demand deposits in the commercial banking system; sometimes referred to as chequebook money

When a deposit of central bank money is made at a commercial bank, the central bank money is removed from circulation and added to the commercial banks' reserves (it is no longer counted as part of M1 money supply). Simultaneously, an equal amount of new commercial bank money is created in the form of bank deposits. When a loan is made by the commercial bank (which keeps only a fraction of the central bank money as reserves), using the central bank money from the commercial bank's reserves, the m1 money supply expands by the size of the loan. This process is called deposit multiplication.

Example of Deposit Multiplication

The mainstream economics relending model of how loans are funded and how the money supply is affected. It also shows how central bank money is used to create commercial bank money from an initial deposit of $100 of central bank money. In the example, the initial deposit is lent out 10 times with a fractional-reserve rate of 20 per cent to ultimately create $500 of commercial bank money. Each successive bank involved in this process creates new commercial bank money on a diminishing portion of the original deposit of central bank money. This is because banks only lend out a portion of the central bank money deposited, in order to fulfill reserve requirements and to ensure that they always have enough reserves on hand to meet normal transaction demands.

The relending model begins when an initial $100 deposit of central bank money is made into Bank A. Bank A takes 20 per cent of it, or $20, and sets it aside as reserves, and then loans out the remaining 80 per cent, or $80. At this point, the money supply actually totals $180, not $100, because the bank has loaned out $80 of the central bank money, kept $20 of central bank money in reserve (not part of the money supply), and substituted a newly created $100 IOU claim for the depositor that *acts equivalently to and can be implicitly redeemed for* central bank money (the depositor can transfer it to another account, write a check on it, demand his cash back, etc.). These claims by depositors on banks are termed *demand deposits* or *commercial bank money* and are simply recorded in a bank's accounts as a liability (specifically, an IOU to the depositor). From a depositor's perspective, commercial bank money is equivalent to central bank money – it is impossible to tell the two forms of money apart unless a bank run occurs (at which time everyone wants central bank money).

At this point in the relending model, Bank A now only has $20 of central bank money on its books. The loan recipient is holding $80 in central bank money, but he soon spends the $80. The receiver of that $80 then deposits it into Bank B. Bank B is now in the same situation as Bank A started with, except it has a deposit of $80 of central bank money instead of $100. Similar to Bank A, Bank B sets aside 20 per cent of that $80, or $16, as reserves and lends out the remaining $64, increasing money supply by $64. As the process continues, more commercial bank money is created. To simplify the table, a different bank is used for each deposit. In the real world, the money a bank lends may end up in the same bank so that it then has more money to lend out.

The expansion of $100 of central bank money through fractional-reserve lending with a 20 per cent reserve rate. $400 of commercial bank money is created virtually through loans. Although no new money was physically created in addition to the initial $100 deposit, new commercial bank money is created through loans. The 2 boxes marked in red show the location of the original $100 deposit throughout the entire process. The total reserves plus the last deposit (or last loan, whichever is last) will always equal the original amount, which in this case is $100. As this process continues, more commercial bank money is created. The amounts in each step decrease towards a limit. If a graph is made showing the accumulation of deposits, one can see that the graph is curved and approaches a limit.

Individual Bank	Amount Deposited	Lent Out	Reserves
A	100	80	20
B	80	64	16
C	64	51.20	12.80
D	51.20	40.96	10.24
E	40.96	32.77	8.19
F	32.77	26.21	6.55
G	26.21	20.97	5.24
H	20.97	16.78	4.19
I	16.78	13.42	3.36
J	13.42	10.74	2.68
K	10.74		
			Total Reserves:
			89.26
	Total Amount of Deposits:	Total Amount Lent Out:	Total Reserves + Last Amount Deposited:
	457.05	357.05	100

This limit is the maximum amount of money that can be created with a given reserve rate. When the reserve rate is 20 per cent, the maximum amount of total deposits that can be created is $500 and the maximum increase in the money supply is $400. For an individual bank, the deposit is considered a *liability* whereas the loan it gives out and the reserves are considered *assets*. Deposits will always be equal to loans plus a bank's reserves, since loans and reserves are created from deposits. This is the basis for a bank's *balance sheet*. Fractional reserve banking allows the money supply to expand or contract. Generally the expansion or contraction of the money supply is dictated by the balance between the rate of new loans being created and the rate of existing loans being repaid or defaulted on.

The balance between these two rates can be influenced to some degree by actions of the central bank. This table gives an outline of the makeup of money supplies worldwide. Most of the money in any given money supply consists of commercial bank money.

The value of commercial bank money is based on the fact that it can be exchanged freely at a bank for central bank money. The actual increase in the money supply through this process may be lower, as (at each step) banks may choose to hold reserves in excess of the statutory minimum, borrowers may let some funds sit idle, and some members of the public may choose to hold cash, and there also may be delays or frictions in the lending process. Government regulations may also be used to limit the money creation process by preventing banks from giving out loans even though the reserve requirements have been fulfilled.

Money multiplier

The most common mechanism used to measure this increase in the money supply is typically called the money multiplier. It calculates the maximum amount of money that an initial deposit can be expanded to with a given reserve ratio.

Formula

The money multiplier, *m*, is the inverse of the reserve requirement, *R*:

$$m = \frac{1}{R}$$

Example:

For example, with the reserve ratio of 20 per cent, this reserve ratio, *R*, can also be expressed as a fraction:

$$R = \frac{1}{5}$$

So then the money multiplier, *m*, will be calculated as:

$$m = \frac{1}{1/5} = 5$$

This number is multiplied by the initial deposit to show the maximum amount of money it can be expanded to. The money creation process is also affected by the currency drain ratio (the propensity of the public to hold banknotes rather than deposit them with a commercial bank), and the safety reserve ratio (excess reserves beyond the legal requirement that commercial banks voluntarily hold—usually a small amount). Data for "excess" reserves and vault cash are published regularly by the Federal Reserve in the United States.

In practice, the actual money multiplier varies over time, and may be substantially lower than the theoretical maximum. Confusingly there are many different "money multipliers", some referring to ratios of rates of change of different money measures and others referring to ratios of absolute values of money measures.

Reserve requirements

The modern mainstream view of reserve requirements is that they are intended to prevent banks from:

- Generating too much money by making too many loans against the narrow money deposit base;
- Having a shortage of cash when large deposits are withdrawn

(although the reserve is thought to be a legal minimum, it is understood that in a crisis or bank run, reserves may be made available on a temporary basis).

In practice, some central banks do not require reserves to be held, and in some countries that do, such as the USA and the EU they are not required to be held during the day when the banks are lending, and banks can borrow from other banks at near the central bank policy rate to ensure they have the necessary amount of required reserves by the close of business. *Required* reserves are therefore considered by some central bankers, monetary economists and textbooks to only play a very small role in limiting money creation in these countries. Most commentators agree however, that they help the banks have sufficient supplies of highly liquid assets, so that the system operates in an orderly fashion and maintains public confidence.

The UK for example, which does not have required reserves, does have requirements that the banks keep a certain amount of cash, and in Australia while there are no reserve requirements, there *are* a variety of requirements to ensure the banks have a stabilising ratio of liquid assets, such as deposits held with local banks.

Individual countries adhere to varying required reserve ratios which have changed over time. In addition to reserve requirements, there are other required financial ratios that affect the amount of loans that a bank can fund. The capital requirement ratio is perhaps the most important of these other required ratios. When there are no mandatory reserve requirements, which are considered by some mainstream economists to restrict lending, the capital requirement ratio acts to prevent an infinite amount of bank lending.

Alternative views

Theories of *endogenous money* date to the 19th century, and were described by Joseph Schumpeter, and later the post-Keynesians. Endogenous money theory states that the supply of money is credit-driven and determined endogenously by the demand for bank loans, rather than exogenously by monetary authorities.

Charles Goodhart worked for many years to encourage a different approach to money supply analysis and said the base money multiplier model was "such an incomplete way of describing the process of the determination of the stock of money that it amounts to misinstruction" Ten years later he said: "Almost all those who have worked in a [central bank] believe that this view is totally mistaken; in particular, it ignores the implications of several of the crucial institutional features of a modern commercial banking system...". Goodhart has characterized the money stock as a dependent endogenous variable. In 1994, Mervyn King said that the causation between money and demand is a contentious issue, because although textbooks assume that money is exogenous, in the United Kingdom money is endogenous, as the Bank of England provides base money on demand and broad money is created by the banking system.

Seth B. Carpenter and Selva Demiralp concluded the simple textbook base money multiplier is implausible in the United States.

MONEY SUPPLIES AROUND THE WORLD

Fractional-reserve banking determines the relationship between the amount of central bank money (currency) in the official money supply statistics and the total money supply. Most of the money in these systems is commercial bank money. Fractional reserve banking involves the issuance and creation of commercial bank money, which increases the money supply through the deposit creation multiplier.

The issue of money through the banking system is a mechanism of monetary transmission, which a central bank can influence indirectly by raising or lowering interest rates (although banking regulations may also be adjusted to influence the money supply, depending on the circumstances).

REGULATION

Because the nature of fractional-reserve banking involves the possibility of bank runs, central banks have been created throughout the world to address these problems.

Central banks

Government controls and bank regulations related to fractional-reserve banking have generally been used to impose restrictive requirements on note issue and deposit taking on the one hand, and to provide relief from bankruptcy and creditor claims, and/or protect creditors with government funds, when banks defaulted on the other hand.

Such measures have included:

- Minimum required reserve ratios (RRRs)
- Minimum capital ratios
- Government bond deposit requirements for note issue
- 100 per cent Marginal Reserve requirements for note issue, such as the Bank Charter Act 1844 (UK)
- Sanction on bank defaults and protection from creditors for many months or even years, and
- Central bank support for distressed banks, and government guarantee funds for notes and deposits, both to counteract bank runs and to protect bank creditors.

Liquidity and Capital Management for a Bank

To avoid defaulting on its obligations, the bank must maintain a minimal reserve ratio that it fixes in accordance with, notably, regulations and its liabilities. In practice this means that the bank sets a reserve ratio target and responds when the actual ratio falls below the target.

Such response can be, for instance:

- Selling or redeeming other assets, or securitization of illiquid assets,
- Restricting investment in new loans,
- Borrowing funds (whether repayable on demand or at a fixed maturity),
- Issuing additional capital instruments, or
- Reducing dividends.

Because different funding options have different costs, and differ in reliability, banks maintain a stock of low cost and reliable sources of liquidity such as:

- Demand deposits with other banks
- High quality marketable debt securities
- Committed lines of credit with other banks

As with reserves, other sources of liquidity are managed with targets. The ability of the bank to borrow money reliably and economically is crucial, which is why confidence in the bank's creditworthiness is important to its liquidity.

This means that the bank needs to maintain adequate capitalisation and to effectively control its exposures to risk in order to continue its operations. If creditors doubt the bank's assets are worth more than its liabilities, all demand creditors have an incentive to demand payment immediately, a situation known as a run on the bank.

Contemporary bank management methods for liquidity are based on maturity analysis of all the bank's assets and liabilities (off balance sheet exposures may also be included). Assets and liabilities are put into residual contractual maturity buckets such as 'on demand', 'less than 1 month', '2–3 months' etc. These residual contractual maturities may be adjusted to account for expected counter party behaviour such as early loan repayments due to borrowers refinancing and expected renewals of term deposits to give forecast cash flows.

This analysis highlights any large future net outflows of cash and enables the bank to respond before they occur. Scenario analysis may also be conducted, depicting scenarios including stress scenarios such as a bank-specific crisis.

Risk and Prudential Regulation

In a fractional-reserve banking system, in the event of a bank run, the demand depositors and note holders would attempt to withdraw more money than the bank has in reserves, causing the bank to suffer a liquidity crisis and, ultimately, to perhaps default.

In the event of a default, the bank would need to liquidate assets and the creditors of the bank would suffer a loss if the proceeds were insufficient to pay its liabilities. Since public deposits are payable on demand, liquidation may require selling assets quickly and potentially in large enough quantities to affect the price of those assets. An otherwise solvent bank (whose assets are worth more than its liabilities) may be made insolvent by a bank run.

This problem potentially exists for any corporation with debt or liabilities, but is more critical for banks as they rely upon public deposits (which may be redeemable upon demand). Although an initial analysis of a bank run and default points to the bank's inability to liquidate or sell assets (*i.e.* because the fraction of assets not held in the form of liquid reserves are held in less liquid investments such as loans), a more full analysis indicates that depositors will cause a bank run only when they have a genuine fear of loss of capital, and that banks with a strong risk adjusted capital ratio should be able to liquidate assets and obtain other sources of finance to avoid default.

For this reason, fractional-reserve banks have every reason to maintain their liquidity, even at the cost of selling assets at heavy discounts and obtaining finance at high cost, during a bank run (to avoid a total loss for the contributors of the bank's capital, the shareholders).

Many governments have enforced or established deposit insurance systems in order to protect depositors from the event of bank defaults and to help maintain public confidence in the fractional-reserve system. Responses to the problem of financial risk described above include:

- Proponents of prudential regulation, such as minimum capital ratios, minimum reserve ratios, central bank or other regulatory supervision, and compulsory note and deposit insurance;
- Proponents of free banking, who believe that banking should be open to free entry and competition, and that the self-interest of debtors, creditors and shareholders should result in effective risk management; and,
- Withdrawal restrictions: some bank accounts may place a limit on daily cash withdrawals and may require a notice period for very large withdrawals. Banking laws in some countries may allow restrictions to be placed on withdrawals under certain circumstances, although these restrictions may rarely, if ever, be used;

- Opponents of fractional reserve banking who insist that notes and demand deposits be 100 per cent reserved.

Example of a Bank Balance Sheet and Financial Ratios

An example of fractional reserve banking, and the calculation of the reserve ratio is shown in the balance sheet below:

Table. ANZ National Bank Limited
Balance Sheet as at 30 September 2007

Assets	NZ$m	Liabilities	NZ$m
Cash	201	Demand Deposits	25482
Balance with Central Bank	2809	Term Deposits and other borrowings	35231
Other Liquid Assets	1797	Due to Other Financial Institutions	3170
Due from other Financial Institutions	3563	Derivative financial instruments	4924
Trading Securities	1887	Payables and other liabilities	1351
Derivative financial instruments	4771	Provisions	165
Available for sale assets	48	Bonds and Notes	14607
Net loans and advances	87878	Related Party Funding	2775
Shares in controlled entities	206	[subordinated] Loan Capital	2062
Current Tax Assets	112	Total Liabilities	99084
Other assets	1045	Share Capital	5943
Deferred Tax Assets	11	[revaluation] Reserves	83
Premises and Equipment	232	Retained profits	2667
Goodwill and other intangibles	3297	Total Equity	8703
Total Assets	107787	Total Liabilities plus Net Worth	107787

In this example the cash reserves held by the bank is $3010m ($201m currency + $2809m held at central bank) and the demand liabilities of the bank are $25482m, for a cash reserve ratio of 11.81 per cent.

Other Financial Ratios

The key financial ratio used to analyze fractional-reserve banks is the cash reserve ratio, which is the ratio of cash reserves to demand deposits. However, other important financial ratios are also used to analyze the bank's liquidity, financial strength, profitability etc.

For example the ANZ National Bank Limited balance sheet above gives the following financial ratios:

The cash reserve ratio is $3010m/$25482m, *i.e.* 11.81 per cent.

The liquid assets reserve ratio is ($201m+$2809m+$1797m)/$25482m, *i.e.* 18.86 per cent.

The equity capital ratio is $8703m/107787m, *i.e.* 8.07 per cent.

The tangible equity ratio is (\$8703m-\$3297m)/107787m, *i.e.* 5.02 per cent

The total capital ratio is (\$8703m+\$2062m)/\$107787m, *i.e.* 9.99 per cent.

It is very important how the term 'reserves' is defined for calculating the reserve ratio, as different definitions give different results. Other important financial ratios may require analysis of disclosures in other parts of the bank's financial statements. In particular, for liquidity risk, disclosures are incorporated into a note to the financial statements that provides maturity analysis of the bank's assets and liabilities and an explanation of how the bank manages its liquidity.

Critics of fractional reserve banking have argued one or more of the following: that it is unstable, that it exacerbates business cycles, that it causes inflation, or that it leads to environmental degradation. "The Federal Reserve Idea was doubtless right; if it had not been, it could not have been established. But it has been manipulated. It has not been a 'federal' reserve; it has been a private reserve.

RURAL WOMEN, FOOD SECURITY AND AGRICULTURAL COOPERATIVES

Regardless of the level of development achieved by the respective economies, women play a pivotal role in agriculture and in rural development in most countries of the Asia-Pacific Region. Evidently there are serious constraints which militate against the promotion of an effective role for women in development in those societies which were bound by age-old traditions and beliefs.

Patriarchal modes and practices motivated by cultures and/or interpretations of religious sanctions and illiteracy hinder women's freedom to opt for various choices to assert greater mobility in social interactions. Resulting from these situations, women's contribution to agriculture and other sectors in the economy remain concealed and unaccounted for in monitoring economic performance measurement.

Consequently, they are generally invisible in plans and programmes. They were, in fact, discriminated against by stereotypes which restrict them to a reproductive role, and denied access to resources which could eventually enhance their social and economic contribution to the society. In developing countries, among the poor, rural women are the poorest and more vulnerable. Empirical evidences suggest that women in rural areas are more adversely affected by poverty than men. The incidence of poverty among rural women is on the rise in most of the developing countries. The issues of gender bias and equity point to the double burden women have to bear - that on being poor and being a woman. Further strategies and programmes for development had largely overlooked the question of gender equity. Projects aiming to reduce poverty view the poor rural women as the recipient of benefits of development, instead of active participant and still poor rural women have the least access to basic needs such as food, health and education.

HUNGER AND POVERTY

Hunger, which usually follows food shortages, is caused by a complex set of events and circumstances [social, economic and political factors] that differ depending on the place and time. Although hunger has been a part of human experience for centuries and a dominant feature of life in many low-income countries, the causes of hunger and starvation are not very well understood. Our understanding of the main causes of hunger and starvation has been hampered by myths and misconceptions about the interplay between hunger and population growth, land use, farm size, technology, trade, environment and other factors.

Poverty cannot be defined simply in terms of lacking access to sufficient food. It is also closely associated with a person's lack of access to productive assets, services and markets. Without access to these, it is unlikely that production and incomeearning capacities can be improved on a sustainable basis. Rural poverty is related to food insecurity, access to assets, services and markets: income-earning opportunities; and the organisational and institutional means for achieving those ends.

Throughout the history and in many societies, inequalities of women and men were part and parcel of an accepted male-dominated culture. It is a complex historical process, which requires detailed study before one can conceive of a viable strategy to improve and sustain the status of women in society. One of the basic factors causing unequal share of women in development relates to the division of labour between the sexes. This division of labour has been justified on the basis of the childbearing function of women and this is biologically important for survival. Consequently, distribution of tasks and responsibilities between men and women in a given society has mainly restricted women to the domestic sphere. Mass poverty and general backwardness has further aggravated the inequalities.

While the women's childbearing and child-rearing functions are respected in many countries, there has been very little recognition of women's actual or potential contribution to the economic, social and cultural states. The role of women within the family combined with high level of unemployment and under-employment of the population in general, has led to the unequal state of priority to men in matters of employment. It is understandable that women cannot be expected to join the army, for instance, as foot soldiers but Israel's well-known and rightfully feared sabrahs or women commandos have shattered the myth of man's physical superiority and thus priority for most jobs.

DISCRIMINATION AND UNDERDEVELOPMENT

It is relevant to consider some aspects of the marginalisation of the status of women in the world by having a look at the figures which are based on the documents of the United Nations.

Some of the findings are:

- *Agriculture*: Women grow about half of the world's food, but own hardly any land, have difficulty in obtaining credit and are overlooked by agricultural advisors and projects. In Africa, three-quarters of the agricultural work is done by women while in Asia, Latin America and the Middle-East, women comprise half of the agricultural labour force;
- *Domestic Work*: Women do almost all the world's domestic work and coupled with their additional work in the productive spheres - this means most women work a double day. Unpaid domestic work is regarded as women's work. Though it is vital work, it is invisible work, unpaid, undervalued and unrecognised. Yet, the women's contribution to society in this regard is enormous;
- *Education*: Women continue to outnumber men among the world's illiterates by about 3:2 ratio, but school enrollment boom is closing the education gap between boys and girls;
- *Health*: Women provide more health care than all health services combined and have been major beneficiaries of a new global shift in priorities towards prevention of disease and promotion of good health;
- *Inequality in Pay*: All over the world women earn only two-thirds of men's pay and earn less than three-quarters of the wages of men doing similar jobs. Women form a third of the world's official labour force, but are concentrated in the lowest-paid jobs and are more vulnerable to unemployment than men;
- *Political Affairs*: Due to poorer education, lack of confidence and greater workload, women are still under-represented in the decision-making bodies of their countries.
- *Unemployment Rate*: Male unemployment rate decreased by 11% from 1984 to 1988 while that of women, unemployment rate increased by 0.5% during the same period;
- *Women in the Informal Sector*: Without legal protection or security, women depend on informal trade for their survival. In Third World countries, a high percentage of food vendors were women: in Nigeria 94%, Thailand 80%, 63% in the Philippines;

The effects of the long-term cumulative process of discrimination against women have been accentuated by underdevelopment. Graphically, while women represent nearly 50% of the world's adult population and one-third of the total labour force, they labour nearly two-thirds of the total working hours but receive only one-tenth of world income and own less than one per cent of property. The story of overworked women in the rural areas of the developing and underdeveloped countries of the world is too well known. The type of agricultural activities generally expected of women is highly labour-intensive and the rural women generally do not enjoy the benefits of new technologies. Their wages are generally less because it is assumed that the efficiency of women's labour is poor compared to that of men. Regarding ownership of land, women do not enjoy equal rights, particularly in the developing countries where most of the production, processing, storage and preparation of food is carried out by the women.

These account for 50% of the total labour required for food production. Many of these tasks are performed by children, especially the girls. Besides helping the menfolk in many farm operations, women have to shoulder the entire responsibilities for household chores. Bringing water from far-off wells and rivers and gathering fuel wood from forests are also part of their daily duties. Such enormous waste of human energy is unnecessary in this technological age.

GENDER DIVISION OF LABOUR IN AGRICULTURE

The particular tasks done on farms by men and women have certain common patterns. In general, men undertake the heavy physical labour of land preparation and jobs which are specific to distant locations, such as livestock herding, while women carry out the repetitious, time-consuming tasks like weeding and those which are located close to home, such as care of the kitchen garden. In most cultures the application of pesticides is considered a male task, as women are aware of the danger to their unborn children of exposure to chemicals. Women do a major part of the planting and weeding of crops. Care of livestock is shared, with men looking after the larger animals and women the smaller ones.

Marketing is often seen as a female task, although men are most likely to negotiate the sale of crops. Some jobs are gender neutral. The introduction of a new tool may cause a particular job to be reassigned to the opposite sex and men tend to assume tasks that become mechanised. The impact on women of the modernisation of agriculture is both complex and contradictory. Women have often been excluded from agrarian reform and training programmes in new agricultural methods.

Where both men and women have equal access to modern methods and inputs there is no evidence that either sex is more efficient than the other. Technological changes in post-harvest processing may even deprive women of a traditional income-earning task.

WOMEN AND FOOD SECURITY ISSUES

Not only do women produce and process agricultural products but they are also responsible for much of the trade in these and other goods in many parts of the third world. In many parts of the world, women continue to play an important role as rural information sources and providers of food to urban areas. This may involve food from the sea as well as from the land. Although women rarely work as fisherpeople they are often involved in net-making and the preparation and sale of the catch.

Women's roles and status all over the world are generally determined by social institutions and norms, religious ideologies, eco-systems and by class positions. The Indian social systems exhibit such grave disparities. Indian women are not a homogeneous group. Their traditional roles are not identical in all strata of society. Norms and taboos governing their roles and behaviours within and outside the family, the structure of family organisations and social practices and the positions accorded to women in a community differ considerably across regions, cultures and levels of socio-economic development.

It is needless to emphasise on the significant contribution of women to agricultural production and household food security. In the process of production, handling and preparation of food, women play a multiple role throughout the sequence. They are said to be "feeding the world". Do women really feed the world? Let us consider the evidence. On a global scale, women produce more than half of all the food that is grown. In sub-Sahara Africa and the Caribbean, they produce up to 80% of basic foodstuffs. In Asia, they provide from 50 to 90% of the labour for rice cultivation. And in Southeast Asia and the Pacific as well as Latin America, women's home gardens represent some of the most complex agricultural systems known. In countries in transition, the percentage of rural women working in agriculture ranges from about a third in Bosnia and Herzegovina to more than half in Poland. Across much of the developing world, rural women provide most of the labour for farming, from soil preparation to harvest.

After the harvest, they are almost entirely responsible for operations such as storage, handling, stocking, marketing and processing. Women in rural areas generally bear primary responsibility for the nutrition of their children, from gestation through weaning and throughout the critical period of growth. In addition, they are the principal food producers and preparers for the rest of the family. Despite their contributions to food security, women tend to be invisible actors in development. All too often, their work is not recorded in statistics. As a result, their contribution is poorly understood and often underestimated.

There are many reasons for this. Work in the household is often considered to be part of a woman's duties as wife and mother, rather than an occupation to be accounted for in both the household and the national economy. Outside the household, a great deal of rural women labour - whether regular or seasonal - goes unpaid and is, therefore, rarely taken into account in official statistics. In most countries, women do not own the land they cultivate. Discriminatory laws and practices for inheritance of and access and ownership to land are still widespread.

Land that women do own tends to consist of smaller, less valuable plots that are also frequently overlooked in statistics. Furthermore, women are usually responsible for the food crops destined for immediate consumption by the household, that is, for subsistence crops rather than cash crops. Also, when data is collected for national statistics, gender is often ignored or the data is biased in the sense that it is collected only from males, who are assumed to be the heads of households. These handicaps have contributed to an increasing "faminisation" of poverty. Since the 1970s, the number of women living below the poverty line has increased by 50%, in comparison with 30% for their male counterparts.

Women may feed the world today, but, given this formidable lists of obstacles placed in their path, will they be able to produce the additional food needed for a world population expected to grow by three billion in 2030? During the FAO-sponsored World Food summit of 1996, world leaders from 186 countries adopted the Rome Declaration on World Food Security and a Plan of Action.

These international agreements specified that the role of women in agriculture and food security must be emphasised, in order to create the enabling political, social and economic environment required for the eradication of hunger ad poverty. Under Commitment-I of the World Food Summit Plan of Action agenda, governments committed themselves to:

- Ensure that institutions provide equal access for women;
- Focus research efforts on the division of labour and on income access and control within the household; and
- Gather information on women's traditional knowledge and skills in agriculture, fisheries, forestry and natural resources management.
- Improve the collection, dissemination and use of gender-disaggregated data [which distinguishes between males and females];
- Promote women's full and equal participation in the economy...including secure and equal access to and control over credit, land and water;
- Provide equal gender opportunities for education and training in food production, processing and marketing;
- Support and implement commitments made at the 4th World

Conference on Women that a gender perspective is mainstreamed in all policies;

- Tailor extension and technical services to women producers and increase the number of women advisors and agents;

FAO's Plan of Action for Women in Development ensures that gender issues are considered in its development work. Objectives include giving women equal access to and control of land and other productive resources, increasing their participation in decision-making and policy-making, reducing the workloads of women and enhancing their opportunities for paid employment and income.

GENDER EQUALITY AND SHARING OF OPPORTUNITIES

The Universal Declaration of Human Rights recognised several dimensions of human rights for all people. Some are tangible and quantifiable, such as access to education, health and a decent standard of living and ability to take part in the government of the country. Others are intangible, such as freedom, dignity, and security of person and participation in the cultural life of the community.

The goals of gender equality differ from one country to another, depending on the social, cultural and economic contexts. So, in the struggle for equality, different countries may set different priorities, ranging from more education for girls, to better maternal health, to equal pay for equal work, to more seats in parliament, to removal of dissemination in employment, to protection against violence in the home, to changes in family law, to having men take more responsibility for family life.

Equality is not a technocratic goal - it is a wholesale political commitment. Achieving it requires a long-term process in which all cultural, social, political and economic norms undergo fundamental change. The UNDP Human Development Report-1995 outlines a vision for the 21st century that should build a world order that:

- Eliminates the prevailing disparities between men and women and creates an enabling environment for the full flowering of the productive and creative potential of both sexes;
- Embraces full equality of opportunity between women and men as a fundamental concept;
- Promotes more sharing of work and experience between women and men in the workplace as well as in the household;
- Puts people - both women and men - clearly at the centre of all development processes.
- Regarding women as essential agents of change and development and

opens many more doors to women to participate more equally in economic and political opportunities;

- Values the work and contribution of women in all fields on par with those of men, solely on merit, without making any distinction;

The UNDP Report-1995 also states that the GDI [Gender-related Development Index] ranking can be different in different situations, as is shown by the following conclusions of a recent survey:

- Gender equality does not depend on the income level of a society. What it requires is a firm political commitment, not enormous financial wealth;
- No society treats its women as well as its men. Substantial progress on gender equality has been made in only a few societies;
- Significant progress has been achieved over the past two decades, though there is still a long way to go. Not a single country has slipped back in the march towards greater gender equality at higher levels of capabilities, though the pace of progress has been extremely uneven and slow.

Much progress remains to be made in gender equality in almost every country. And in equality of choice in economic and political participation, industrial countries are not necessarily taking the lead.

The areas showing the least progress are parliamentary representation and percentage share of administrators and managers. The clear policy message from this simple exercise is this: "In most countries, industrial or developing, women are not yet allowed into the corridors of economic and political power. In exercising real power or decision-making authority, women are a distinct minority throughout the world."

WOMEN IN AGRICULTURE

Women play an indispensable role in farming and in improving the quality of life in rural areas. However, their contributions often remain concealed due to some social barriers and gender bias. Even government programmes often fail to focus on women in agriculture.

This undermines the potential benefits from programmes, especially those related to food production, household income improvements, nutrition, literacy, poverty alleviation and population control. Equitable access for rural women to educational facilities would certainly improve their performance and liberate them from their marginalised status in the society.

Other areas where women's potential could be effectively harnessed are agricultural extension, farming systems development, land reform and rural welfare. Landmark improvements have been recorded in such cases as the extension of institutional credit and domestic water supplies where women's potential have been consciously tapped. Socio-economic goals of productivity, equity and environment stability are closely woven around the agriculture sector policies and new dimensions in programmes implemented are already emerging as new values.

Regardless of the level of development achieved by the respective economies, women play a pivotal role in agriculture and in rural development in most countries of the Asia-Pacific Region. Asia-Pacific region had witnessed spectacular development in crop yields which even surpassed the population growth rate in the past decade.

However, pockets of hunger remain when landless or small farm rural population lack economic access to food because of a lack of remunerative non-farm employment in rural areas, where 80% of Asia-Pacific's 400 million poor live. It has also been suggested that with the acceleration of crop-diversification programmes and the transformation of agriculture to commercial production levels, women's lot had been even further worsened by the addition of new burdens which they have to shoulder in order to realise profits in farm operations. Rural women who are obliged to attend to all the household chores, children's welfare, nutrition and family cohesion along with farm work, are desperately driven to adopt a survival strategy to save the family food security from total collapse.

Rural poverty has increased in the region particularly for farmers as priority has been accorded to the industrial and service sectors: this is both the cause and an effect of rural-urban migration leading to the "feminisation of farming". Thus the numbers and the proportion of rural women among the absolutely poor and destitute, currently around 60%, is expected to increase to 65 to 70% by the year 2000. In spite of social, political and economic constraints, women farmers have proved extremely resourceful and hardworking in their attempt to ensure household food security.

Social constraints place barriers around their access to scientific and technological information. Lack of collateral denies them access to agricultural credit. Culture or traditions accord membership of cooperatives only to heads of households - usually a man. Many rural women, even in highly mechanised farming systems such as the Republic of Korea and Japan would have agriculture for work in other sectors if choices were available.

After some decades of development, global problems and issues concerning environment, women in development, and poverty have reappeared. All these have emerged in rural communities and threatening their sustainability. Rural communities with norms developed for managing resources are important for the stability of community life. Gender-oriented rural development programmes which focus on role of women to guarantee the stability of life provide a sound basis for integrated development of the quality of life. In progressive economies like Japan, rural women have shown anxieties over several concerns affecting their livelihood. Some of the priority items include measures for success in agricultural enterprises, expansion of periodic farming resulting in reduced holidays, the need to reduce agricultural work, changes in awareness of rural societies and reduction in the work connected with caring for elderly people. In order to redress these problems, five tasks have been identified for promotion which will result in making rural living more pleasant and comfortable.

These tasks include:

- Acquiring skills to diversify areas of involvement by women supporting women in entrepreneurial roles; and
- Adopt a structured approach to execute the vision to improve rural conditions.
- Appreciating the positive aspects of living in rural areas and creating a conducive environment which will contribute towards better rural life;
- Creating awareness of changes and measures pursued to change the status of women by their active participation in agricultural and fisheries cooperatives;
- Improving working conditions and environment;

CONCLUSION

Women have been the focus of attention of all international and national development programmes. Efforts have been directed at empowering them in all fields of activity. Special programmes have been instituted to improve their social and economic status through provision of education, employment, health-care and involvement in social and economic institutions, including cooperatives.

Cooperative institutions and especially the agricultural cooperatives are the agencies which hold enormous potential for the development of women, and more particularly the rural women. Rural women are actively involved in the process of food production, processing and marketing. They often lack the legal status which prohibits them to have access to credit, education and technology.

Cooperative institutions can help accelerate the process of development and participation of women in their organisational and business activities. Institutions like the International Cooperative Alliance [ICA] and the Institute for the Development of Agricultural Cooperation in Asia-Japan [IDACA] together with the support of other international organisations and national level institutions can develop and sponsor programmes which are aimed at improving the lot of rural women.

In the past some efforts have been made through which member-organisations, cooperative and agricultural departments all over Asia and Africa have been requested to make special programmes for rural women and set aside budgets for their implementation. In some cases some good responses have been received. While it is generally agreed that education is central to women's development the participation of girls in the national educational system continues to lag well behind that of boys at every level. Among the factors that are believed to contribute to this gap are women's self-perpetuating negative social status, economic constraints and male-oriented biases in the design and delivery of primary and secondary education.

These limitations have meant that millions of women have not received formal education and that millions more are deprived of the opportunity for more than token participation. Women, however, retain a strong orientation to self-help and group cooperation. They look to their own resources and to other women when faced with a problem of opportunity. This perhaps is the key factor on which women's development programme could be developed. This is their greatest asset. They have kept folk art, family bonds, religious traditions, cultural heritage alive, thriving and vibrant. They have played significant role in food security efforts and rural and small industrial sectors.

8

Regional Banks for Rural Development

The main objective of the Regional Rural Banks is to provide credit and other facilities particularly to the small and marginal farmers, agricultural labourers, artisans and small entrepreneurs so as to develop agriculture, trade, commerce, industry and other productive activities in the rural areas.

Initially, five regional rural banks were set up on October 2, 1975 at Moradabad and Gorahpur in Uttar Pradesh, Bhiwani in Haryana, Jaipur in Rajasthan and Malda in West Bengal. These banks were sponsored by the syndicate Bank, United Commercial Bank and United Bank of India respectively. Each Regional Rural Bank has an authorized capital of ₹ 1 Crore and issued and paid-up capital of ₹ 25 lakhs. The share capital of the Regional Rural Bank is subscribed by the Central Government (5.0 per cent), the State Government concerned (15 per cent), and the sponsoring commercial Bank (35 per cent). The Regional Banks, thought basically scheduled commercial Banks, differ from the latter in certain aspects.

(a) The area of regional rural banks is limited to a specified region comprising one or more districts of a state.

(b) The regional rural banks grant direct loans and advances only to small and marginal farmers, rural artisans and agricultural labourers and other of small means for productive purpose.

(c) The lending rates of the regional rural banks should not be higher than the prevailing lending rates of co-operative societies in any particular State. The sponsoring banks and concessions to RRBs to enable the later to function effectively.

BANK CREDIT TO SELF HELP GROUPS

Micro Finance is a useful tool in building the capacity of the poor in Management of sustainable self employment activities, besides providing other financial services like savings, hosings, consumption credit, insurance cover etc. The mission of NABARD is to link on million SHGs with the overall banking system by the year 2008, facilitating access of 100 million rural poor to formal credit system.

KISAN CREDIT CARD SCHEME:

Kisan Credit Card Scheme Primarily Caters to farmers who are eligible for sanction of production credit for cultivation purposes. The scheme is implemented by Commercial banks. RRBs and Cooperative banks in all the States and Union Territories. The Credit extended under the KCC is in the nature of resolving cash credit and provides for any number of drawals and repayments within the limit, while fixing the limits, the bank takes into account the entire production credit card is normally valid for 3 years subject to an annual review.

As on March 2004, 4.14 crore Kisan Credit cards had been issued.

Cumulative Agency wise all India position of KCC as on 31 St March 2004.

Agency	No. of SHGs Financed Rs. In lakh	Bank Loan
Commercial Banks	538,422	225,480
Co-operative Banks	134,671	37,110
RPBs	405,998	127,820
Total	1,079,091	390,410

Agency	No. of Cards issued (Lakhs)
Commercial Banks	132.22
Co-operative Banks	242.59
RPBs	38.99
Total	413.8

It is the farmers who by and large avail some kinds of institutional credit. The other farm households have to obtain credit from non-institutional sources. Hence every effort must be made to enhance coverage of institutional credit, including through Kisan Credit Cards, in line with the higher goals of agricultural credit in the coming years. Scheduled commercial banks have 33,029 branched (Rural and Semi Urban) RRBs have 14,051 of such branches and these outlets have to be energized to enhance the flow of agricultural credit. It was envisaged that by 31 st March 2004 all eligible agricultural borrowers will be covered under the Kisan Credit Cards Scheme. However, due to some constraints, impediments and operational difficulties, the lofty objective could not be fulfilled.

The RRBs were set up with a view to develop rural economy by providing credit facilities for the development of agriculture, trade, commerce, industry and other productive activities in the rural areas. Such facility was intended mainly for small and marginal farmers, agricultural labourers, artisans and small entrepreneurs. These banks are expected to provide cheap and liberal credit inculcate banking habits, create employment opportunities among these people and save them from the clutches of money lenders.

PERFORMANCE INDICATORS OF RRBS:

EXPANSION:

Particulars	2000	2001	2002	2003
Branch Network (No.)	14311	14311	14390	14433
Share Capital	195.60	195.66	195.81	195.85
Share Capital Deposited	2003.31	2054.33	2080.62	2112.74
Reserves	848.48	1270.86	1782.40	2357.41
Deposits	32204.34	38271.87	44539.15	50098.34
Borrowings	3756.75	4064.46	4524.37	4798.69
Investments	22944.75	27636.14	30531.73	33063.42
Loan and Advances	13814.89	15816.30	18629.22	22157.85
RRB's earnings Profit No.	162	170	167	156
Amount of Profit	543.52	676.48	699.93	733.97
RRB's incurring loss (No)	34	26	29	40
Amount of Losses	113.55	75.86	92.05	214.68
Accumulated losses	2978.90	2792.59	2694.06	2752.25

Viability Status

The net profit of 196 RRBs decreased to ₹ 519.29 crore as on 31st March 2003, 15 per cent less than the previous year. In all, 103 RIRBs showed improvement in their performance either by way of increase in profits or reduction in losses @by shifting from loss to profit as at ends March 2003 as compared to 121 as at ends of March 2002.

The number of RRBs which had wiped off accumulated losses to ₹ 1202.59 crore as at end of March 2003 from ₹ 1640.75 crore as at end of previous year.

RECOVERY PERFORMANCE

During the year ending June 2003, recovery performance of RRBs at the aggregate level improved futher as compared to the previous year. In absolute terms, the amount of recovery increased from ₹ 6789.53 crore (June 2001) to ₹ 9738.80 crore (June 2003) *i.e.* by 40 per cent (see table).

PROBLEMS FACED

RRBs face multifarious problems due to their peculiar nature and tasks involved.

The main issues are as follows.

- Poor recovery rate and the resultant, mounting losses.
- Delay in decision making on account of different agencies being involved in the management process.
- Capital inadequacy.

- Staff incompatibility as they find it difficult to cope with rural surroundings and business opportunities.
- Restrictions in respect of deposit mobilization and scope for investment.

CORPORATE GOVERNANCE

Corporate governance is of crucial importance for banks. The corporate governance philosophy of banks has to be based on the pursuit of sound business ethics and strong professionalism that aligns the interests of all stakeholders and the society at large. It is therefore necessary to constantly strengthen the corporate governance mechanism in all banks.

Disclosure of reliable information facilitates market discipline, strengthens confidence and reduces the chances for rumours and creation of atmosphere of suspicion and misleading information that may bring about market instability. Indian accounting standards still lag behind global practices in many respects. This has to be addressed effectively at the earliest.

INNOVATIVE BUSINESS MODEL

The introduction of innovative business models and financial technologies the world over has received an impetus through slashing operating cost through higher labour productivity, innovation and business process re-engineering, further reduction of NPAs, micro planning, branch-centric profit planning, effective implementation of plans and monitoring of results CBS and market centric HRM policies and manpower planning. Very high average age of staff, requirement of new skills and talents, working in a computerized environment, foray into new and emerging areas require recruitment of new staff and specialists, extensive training, etc. Although 86 per cent of PSBs are fully computerized only 44 per cent are actually functioning under CBS platform. Covering all branches of all banks under CBS will be a challenge for banks.

Increased customer-orientation and customer focus, product innovation, greater use of multiple channels like ATMs internet and mobile banking, etc. efficient credit delivery besides building up sound financial are vital for banks for facing emerging challenges and obstacles.

Camping of Human Resource Management: Staff at banks irrespective of their functional domain needs to add value to acquire an extra cutting edge. Human resources policies and Human resource management should be revamped so as to convert human resource management from a support function to a strategic partner to the banking business. This must happen in all banks. It is, therefore, necessary to develop a proper recruitment strategy and ensure that it dovetails with identified objectives of banks and helps attract and retain talent through flexible compensation packages and an institutional mechanism of recognition and reward.

FINANCIAL INCLUSION:

There are abundant opportunities for intermediation and mobilisation of savings and extension of bank credit at the bottom of the pyramid. About 60 to 70 per cent of enterprises and individuals do not have access to basic financial services such as savings and credit. Hence, increased financial inclusion of all those who presently stand excluded is of paramount importance. Bank linkage with SHGs, financing of SMEs, rural artisans, rural non-farm activities, etc will be great business opportunities for banks. Emphasis on volume-led growth in competitive balance sheet size, shift of focus from interest income to non-interest income and from capital adequacy to capital efficiency, etc. are vital from the point of view of maintaining benchmarks of return on assets, return on owning funds, net NPAs, capital adequacy, cost to income ratio, net interest margin and intermediation cost.

In bracing for tomorrow a paradigm shift in bank financing through innovative mechanism such as, templates for assessing customer risk and pricing products and services credit scoring, ensuring availability and use of information etc are absolutely essential. Retail banking requires product development and differentiation innovation and business process re-engineering, micro-planning marketing prudent pricing customization technology upgradation home, electronic and mobile banking cost-reduction and cross selling. All these must be given adequate attention. Banking success requires imaginative strategic planning organizational restructuring streamlining and revamping of human resources management, etc.

Developing Immunity: Banks have to adopt and implement strategies to ensure immunity of their balance sheets from interest rate fluctuations by paying greater attention to non-interest income. Growing services sector and financial markets have created new avenues for fee based income. Merchant banking international trade, funds transfer, payment and settlements, consultancy services financial derivatives utility service etc opened up new income sources for banks. But, what is required is a total transition from branch banking to virtual banking, market segmentation to customer-profitability and these are real challenges for banks. Many new challenges may also crop up in the years ahead.

Areas of continues challenge: The areas of continued challenge for banks would be risk management, full implementation of Basel II norms, achievement of full and meaningful financial inclusion an availment of rural business opportunities and opportunities at the bottom of the pyramid, rural credit delivery system, enhancing customer satisfaction, technology upgradation on a continual basis, expansion of CBS platform to all branches including rural branches, further reduction of NPAs reducing intermediation cost increasing non-interest income and fee based income for improving profitability staff involvement in all bank functions, revamping of human resource management – increasing volumes of business despite competition from other banks and other dis-in-termedition sources and participative and strategic planning.

As all the existing and future challenges have to be faced through staff banks have to give top priority to revamping of human resources management and development of human resources. Development of human resources through training, inducing participation and full involvement of all staff in bank functions and activities etc are very vital. Streamlining of audit and inspection, strict internal control and house-keeping, improved risk management, increasing capital efficiency and mobiisation of fresh equity from time to time, asset-liability management and balance sheet management are real challenges, requiring utmost attention.

Ensuring optimum performance: Developing concern for results and performance on the part of entire personnel in banks is a vital requirement. This too will be a challenge. Future of banks will depend on their alertness, operational and capital efficiency, customer orientation and standard of service creation of larger and larger volumes of performing assets, attainment of optimum levels of productivity profitability and overall performance.

Future of banks hinges on these and also on their ability to build up large volumes of quality assets with lesser capital charge thereon that perform on an enduring basis. Ensuring optimum performance of each manager, officer and staff will be crucial. Only those banks which are pro-active and which respond quickly to changing customer needs and changing environment and which give adequate attention to the above issues alone can successfully face the future challenges, perform well and grow as strong, vibrant, efficient and sound financial institutions.

WHAT IS RURAL BANKING?

Rural banking in our country refers to a set up of credit institutions for economic development of rural areas. There are three streams of such institutions- the cooperative banks which were initiated with the onset of the 20th century; the commercial banks which were involved in rural banking from late sixties onwards; and , Regional Rural Banks which were especially created as a new breed of banks in 1975, further intensifying the structure of rural banking.

The expansion of the network of branches has been rather more in rural areas especially after nationalization and with the set up of Regional Rural Banks, it has now brought down the average population covered per branch to approx.

13000 from 65000 in 1969. It has reduced regional imbalances in the spread of bank's branches to a great extent. However, population per branch is still high in North Eastern States- Assam, Manipur, Meghalaya, etc. Efforts are on to ensure availability of more bank branches in these areas.

Various studies on financial flow bring out the impressive widening and deepening of India's financial infrastructure. AS on March 31st 2003, out of total 66436 branches of scheduled commercial banks, 32244 braches were functioning in rural areas, apart from 14813 branches located in semi-urban areas. The Reserve Bank of India, as per its guidelines on 24th August 1996, decided to allow the establishment of new, local banks in the private sector in order to give encouragement to rural and semi-urban savings and to provide institutional credit for viable economic activities in the local areas. Local Banks are supposed to cater to the needs of local people and to provide efficient and competitive financial inter mediation services in the areas of operation.

FARM CREDIT

The role of credit in promoting agricultural growth is to provide the wherewithal for private investment in inputs and fixed capital to enable farmers to switch over to a superior production function. A product oriented lending system advocated by the Reserve Bank of India implies providing credit for such investments on the basis of its techno-economic feasibility rather than loan collateral and focusing particularly on those farmers with low income saving base which precludes their undertaking investments without credit. The role investments without credit.The role of credit growth in indirect but positive and its productivity is no different from that of investment financed by it. Large scale financing for farm machineries and minor irrigation has greatly facilitated increased agricultural production. As a result of private investment in credit, there has been drastic increase in the quantum of farm credit.

While the movement is poised for big growth, we have to ensure that the agriculture sector attains necessary resilience to show sustained growth to sustain the same. This calls for widening of agricultural production credit, rapid increase in the capital formation in agriculture enhancing access to credit by small farmers/marginal farmers and ensuring highest participation of farmers in the credit programmers. The economic participation of rural masses is critical to attain the equitable development of the country. The Government is also of the view that the full potential of agriculture as a profitable activity must be realized at the earliest to benefit the farmers. Among the factors that will help in realizing this potential are access to institutional credit to more farmers and appropriate quantity and quality of agricultural credit. Lending institutions must view agriculture as a sector where there are commercial opportunities to lend and earn reasonable profits. Failure to deliver adequate credit in a timely manner will be detrimental to interests of both the banks and the large community of farmers.

The Government of India estimated the credit flow from all lending institutions for the year 2003-04 at ₹ 80,000 crores and plans have been prepared by lending institutions to enhance the level of flow of ₹ 1,05,000 crores for the year 2004-05. This represents a 30 per cent increase over the previous year. To double the credit in the next 3 years, an agricultural credit growth of 30 per cent by Commercial Banks, 30 per cent by Cooperative Banks and 40 per cent of Regional Rural Banks is suggested.

Under a broad framework of a special Agricultural Credit plan, commercial banks will make an effort to bring into their fold on an average at least 100 new farmers at each rural and semi-urban branch during the current year. The goal is to enlarge the universe of new farmer borrowings from banks by about 50 lakhs.

STRATEGY

Each rural and semi urban branch of commercial bank on an average will take up at least two or three new investment project in the area of plantation and horticulture, fisheries, organic farming, agro processing, livestock farming, micro irrigation, sprinkler irrigation, watershed management, village ponds development and other agricultural activities.

Cumulative Agency-wise all India position of progress under SHG-Bank Linkage programme as on 31st March 2004.

(Rs. In Lakh)

Agency	No. of SHGs Financed	Bank Loan
Commercial Banks	538,422	225,480
Cooperative Banks	134,671	37,110
RRBs	405,998	127,820
Total	1079091	390410

(Lakh)

Agency	No. of cards Issued
Commercial Banks	13222
Cooperative Banks	24259
RRBs	3899
Total	4138

In every district on an average, all commercial banks put together will finance ten agro clinics during the current year. NABARD will finalise a programme for agro clinics. Public sector banks have been advised to lend more to small and marginal farmers and their progress on this behalf will be monitored. Emphasis has been laid to implement and monitor the branch credit plans.

KISAN CREDIT CARD SCHEME

Kisan Credit Card scheme primarily caters to farmers who are eligible for sanction of production credit for cultivation purposes. The scheme is implemented by commercial banks, RRBs and Cooperative banks in all states and Union Territories. The Credit extended under the KCC is in the nature of revolving cash credit and provides for any number of drawals and repayments within the limit. While fixing the limits, the bank takes into account the entire, production credit requirements of farmers for the full year. The credit card is normally valid for 3 years subject to an annual review.

As on March 2004, 4.14 crore Kisan Credit Cards had been issued.

Cumulative Agency wise All India Position of KCC as on 31st March 2004.

It is the farmers who by and large avail of some kinds of institutional credit. The other farm households have to obtain credit from non-institutional sources. Hence every effort must be made to enhance coverage of institutional credit, including through Kisan Credit Cards, in line with the higher goals of agricultural credit in the coming years. Scheduled Commercial banks have 33,029 branches (rural and semi urban). RRBs have 14,051 of such branches and these outlets have to be energized to enhance the flow of agricultural credit.

It was envisaged that by 31st March 2004 all eligible agricultural borrowers will be covered under Kisan Credit Cards Scheme. However, due to some constraints, impediments and operational difficulties, the lofty objective could not be fulfilled.

The Indian Banking system has been playing a vital role in supporting and financing small scale industries and village industries, handlooms, power looms, sericulture and rural handicrafts. Until the nationalization of banks, however, this role was quite minimal. Since nationalization, the era of regulated and directed credit stared and commercial banks were brought into the fold of priority sector lending. With the passage of time, the scope of priority sector has expanded to cover various other economic activities contributing to poverty alleviation and creation of employment opportunities.

While the small scale industrial unit is clearly defined in terms of value of investment in plant and machinery, the definition of medium industry is of recent origin. Credit assistance provided by commercial banks of SSI sector is treated as part of credit to priority sector in which banks are expected to deploy 40 per cent of their total credit.

Not only is credit to SSI sector accorded priority, it is also provided at a concessional rate of interest; the element of concessionality is linked to the size of a loan and the priority accorded to it. Credit in the form of terms loans as well as working capital is one of the crucial inputs for the development of the SSI sector. The institutional structure for the flow of credit to the sector comprises of two institutions at the apex level, *viz.*, Small industrial Development Banks of India (SIDBI) and National Bank of Agriculture and Rural Development (NABARD). The primary credit institutions are commercial Banks and state Financial Corporation.

While large companies have recourse to the capital market, the SSI units because of their size and organizational structure, cannot approach this market. There is a need to formulate special schemes to assist the SSI sector units for entering high technology and high risk areas. Other measures needed to increase the flow of finance and tackle the problem of capital inadequacy are fixing norms for working capital/inter-institutional co-ordination, coordinated lending of term loans, working capital etc.

The institutional structure providing both financial and non-financial series is well diversified, ably specialized and closely integrated. With the emergence of SIDBI, the financial institutional structure has been further strengthened. In totality, there has been a phenomenal increase in the financial services to Rural Industrialization.

BANK CREDIT TO SHGS

In terms of improving the outreach of the rural formal banking system, NABARD's major success has been through the SHG-Bank linkage programme. A series of research studies indicated the needs for alternative delivery mechanism. Over the time, it has come to be known as Micro Finance. Microfinance is a useful tool in building the capacity of the poor in management of sustainable self employment activities, besides providing other financial services like savings, housing, consumption credit, insurance cover, etc. The Mission of NABARD is to link one million SHGs with the overall banking system by the year 2008, facilitating access of 100 million rural poor to formal credit system. In the context of up scaling the micro finance programmes in terms of coverage as well as innovative products, studies are going on.

The micro finance concept has captured the imagination of a wide range of stakeholders resulting in an amazingly large number of formal and non-formal bodies pertaining with NABARD over a period of last decade. The saving-led SHG-Bank Linkage Programme initiated by NABARD in 1992 as a pilot project for linking 500 SHGs to banks, has now been recognized as the largest and fastest growing microfinance programme in the world. Cumulatively, 1,079,091 SHGs have been provided with bank credit as on 31st March 2004.

The national policy of microfinance should emphasise on encouraging initiatives and participation of different type of institutions in micro finance, bringing the micro finance sector with the formal banking channels.

Only study of the impact of the programme was conducted in 2002, covering 115 members from 60 SHGs in three backward states *viz.* Chattisgarh, Orissa and Jharkhand. The socio-economic conditions of the members were compared between pre and post SHG situations to quantify the impact. The findings of the study showed significant increases in the assets (30 per cent) structure. Annual savings increased from ₹ 952 to ₹ 1863 registering twofold increase.

There was remarkable improvement in social empowerment of SHG members in terms of self confidence, involvement in decision making, better communication, etc. Besides, repayment performance was found to be much better.

RURAL GODOWN

Storage plays an important role in agriculture. About 8-10 per cent produce is lost during the post harvest storage. If not stored in proper and scientific way, a part of the produce goes waste. The role of rural godowns in this regard can hardly be over-emphasised. Foodgrains are stored for consumption, for payment in kind of labour, feed, seed and year to year reserves. The prime purpose in an expectation of increase in their price and supply to customers during the marketing year. Rural godowns play an important role in storage of agriculture produce. Along with the grains produced by the cultivators, the purchased produce from traders, fertilizers and cotton bales can also be stored.

Being a credit cum subsidy scheme, farmers are also attracted to it for avoiding distress sale. Subsidy under the scheme is linked to institutional credit and is available only to such projects as are financed by commercial banks, cooperative banks and Regional Rural Banks. Loans to entrepreneurs from banks for construction/renovation/expansion of godown etc. would have an adequate long term repayment period. Assistance under the scheme shall be a available on capital cost of construction of go down only. Banks can aggressively finance this scheme. Banks will however be free to finance in addition to storage, allied activities like consumer shops, agriclinics, weighing, grading, packaging and quality certification, warehousing etc. to meet various requirements of the farmers.

Some of the new avenues of Rural Finance which have immense potential in the countryside can be underlined as follows:

1. Minor Irrigation- Drip Irrigation and Sprinkler Irrigation
2. Land Development and Water Management
3. Farm Pond scheme
4. Plantation and Horticulture
5. Cultivation of Medicinal plants, spices and other new crops
6. Organic farming
7. Processing of fruits and vegetables
8. Processing of spices
9. Promoting Dairy Cooperatives for women.

In addition to the above, the Banks need to introduce customer-friendly products. Likewise, a line of credit against the valuation of agriculture land with flexibility to activise the same for acquiring fixed assets, working capital requirements, consumption needs, etc.

Marketing of various deposit and credit schemes by displaying posters at Panchayat Office, primary schools, government hospitals will facilitate smooth flow of rural finance. Rescheduling, the business hours of rural branches to 2 to 3 cash hours is one of the ways to create opportunities for increased flow of finance as more time can be devoted to marketing of schemes, contacting people for canvassing loan proposals, recovery, renewal of documents etc.

In the ultimate analysis, organizing village meets for creating awareness about facilities available with the bank, safety, liquidity of funds, various deposits and advances schemes can go a long way in finetuning the rural finance outlets.

REGIONAL RURAL BANKS

Regional rural banks came into the picture in the year 1975 with a view to providing banking services to rural masses and extending financial assistance to the weaker and underprivileged sections of the society. During the last 27 years, *i.e.*, 1975 to 2002, a rapid growth in number of banks/ branches, deposit/ credit and functions was witnessed. Table 6 presents the major indicators of growth of regional rural banks in some selected years. Originally, 12 districts were covered under rural banks, but by the year 2002, 484 districts were covered. Some discerning facts about the rural banks are as follows:

- Annual increase in branch expansion during the period 1990 and 2002 was (-) 0.05 per cent.
- Accumulated loss of rural banks increased by 267.78 per cent during the period 1990 and 2002.
- Number of loss making banks by the year 2002 was 40, which was 20.41 per cent of the total.
- During the period 1980 and 1991, the annual growth in deposit and advances of rural banks were 217.89 per cent and 122.96 per cent respectively, but the same during the period 1991 and 2002 were 72.06 per cent and 38.73 per cent respectively.
- Credit Deposit ratio, in 1975, was 50.00 per cent, it increased to 70.86 per cent in 1991 but it came down to 41.76 per cent in 2002.
- The annual increase in the disbursement of loans/advances to agriculture sector during the period 1982 and 1990 was 54.17 per cent and the same had come down to 12.36 per cent during the period 1990 and 2002.

Table presents the resource mobiisation of regional rural banks in some selected years. During the period 1980 and 1991, the annual growth in deposits and advances were 217.89 per cent and 122.96 per cent respectively, but the same, during the period 1991 and 2001, were 72.06 per cent and 38.73 per cent respectively. The credit deposit ratio had also come down from 121.79 per cent of 1980 to 70.86 per cent in 1991 and 41.76 per cent in 2002.

Table. Resource mobilization of regional rural banks in some selected years

Year	Resource Total Deposits	Mobilization Total Advances	(Rs. Crore) CD Ration (%)
1975	0.20	0.10	50.00
1980	199.83	243.38	121.79
1991	4989.24	3535.35	70.86
2002	44539	18598	41.76

Source: NABARD, Statistical Reports Institutional Development Department (RRBs Division0, various issues and Regional Rural Banks, Key Statistics, NABARD Publication

Table. Purpose-wise disbursements of Loans and Advances of Regional rural banks

(Rs. Crores)

Sl. No.	Category	1982	1985	1990	2002
1	Agriculture Sector Short term crop loans Term Loans for Agrl. & Alhed Activities Sub-Total	108,64 (18.83) 338,20(41.27) 346,84 (60.10)	264.16 (18.77) 551.40 (39.17) 815 (57.94)	620 (18.42) 1230(34.55) 1850(51.97)	3812 (36.06) 782 (7.40) 5494 (43.46)
	Non-Agriculture Sector Rural Artisanst, village and Cottage industries etc. Retail trade, self-employedetc.	 30.63 (5.31) 124,70 (21.61)	 79.90 (5.68) 366.00 (26.0)	 280 (7.86) 1100(30.90)	 305 (2.89) 1279 (12.10)
2	Other loans	74.94 (12.98)	146.21 (10.39)	330 (9.27)	4393 (41.56)
	Sub-total	230,27 (39.90)	592.11(42.06)	1710 48.03)	5977 (56.54)
	Total	577.11 (100.00)	1407.67(100.00)	3560 (100.00)	10571 (100.00)

Note: Figures in parenthesis are percentages to total

Purpose-wise break up of 12 RRBs is not included for the year 200-01

Source: Compiled from Report on trends and progress of Indian Banking, various issues and Indian Bank's Association, Performance Highlights of Banks, various issues.

Purpose-wise disbursement of loans/advances of rural banks had also shown a disturbing picture. Whereas the share (of loans) under non-agriculture sector has been increasing over the years, the share under agriculture sector has been decreasing. Table presents the purpose-wise disbursements of loans and advances of regional rural banks.

CHALLENGES

The banking sector, which emerged from the money lending business, was in private sector in past, moved to public sector in 1969 and at present, it is distancing from the rural society due to stringent financial reforms. The proposed move of government to reduce its stake in banks from 51 to 33 per cent, may lead to partial/full privatisation of banks with a wide gap between banks and rural poor.

Though cooperatives were the oldest financial institutions dealing with rural banking, their health is deteriorating due to poor governance, lack of professionalism, low capital base, mounting overdue, high non-performing assets and high cost of credit. In spite of a wide network of branches, the cooperatives have not been able to mobilize resources locally and are depending more on higher credit institutions. Their own funds and deposits are much less and borrowings are much greater. They are supposed to extend loans to farmers and other rural people to raise unutilized resources of local areas for productive use. They have not succeeded in this endeavour.

Of late, commercial banks have been distancing from rural lending. Many bankers view rural lending as non-pfofitable and risky venture. The thrust areas of change are in compliance with the International prudential norms, competition from foreign banks and coming up of new generation banks. The reform process has changed the mode of rural lending, *i.e.*, directed lending to business driven lending, and affected the rural banking business driven lending, and affected the rural banking business in the country. Rural credit extended by commercial banks has not grown at the same pace as total banks credit. Though the RRBs were rural banking by design, they seem to shy away from financing the agriculture sector. Their credit deposit ratio has come down sharply from 70.86 per cent in 1991 to 41.76 per cent in 2002 indicating a diversion of funds from lending to investment.

CONCLUSION

The deceleration in agriculture growth is a worrying factor. If there is no turn around, achieving the targeted growth of 7-8 per cent would be difficult. The annual rate of agricultural growth decelerated sharply from 4.7 per cent in Eighth Five Year Plan to only 2 per cent in Ninth Five Year Plan. In 1993-94, the growth in agriculture was as high as 9 per cent. Between 1995 and 1998, the growth rate fell from 3.8 per cent to 1.8 per cent. But the growth in agriculture in the year 2003-04 has been just around 1 per cent. The targets can be achieved only if agricultural growth is at least around 4 per cent, which warrants certain hard decisions.

Recent self-help group (SHG) programme, Kisan Credit Card movement and other related programmes of the government have brought about a change in the mindset of millions of farmers/villagers of our country. The SHG-bank linkage programme in particular has proved its efficacy in reaching and banking the un-reached with lower transaction cost and better repayment performance. The traditional mode of cultivation is slowly changing and the cropping habit is moving in favour of commercial crops. Further, rural non-farm sector as a supplementary source of living is gaining significance. These changes, if continued in a sustained manner, would definitely bring prosperity to village economy in general and agriculture sector in particular.

Under such a situation, acceleration in agricultural growth would not be a distant goal, if it were supported by large flow of rural credit. Necessary legal and institutional changes relating to governance, regulation and functioning of cooperative banks and regional rural banks and also attitudinal change of commercial banks must be addressed for financing agriculture and rural sector, which would not impinge on the viability or compromise o prudential norms.

CONSOLIDATION OF REGIONAL BANKS

The issue of consolidation of banks has acquired the foremost importance with regard to banking sector reforms in the recent past. The Finance Minister Mr. P. Chidambaram said the government would put in place an environment that will be conducive to mergers and acquisition of banks. It was important the Public Sector Commercial Banks (PSCBs) grow in scale and muscle, so that they can compete effectively those banks that operate globally.

Even since independence, the policy of the government of India as well as the Reserve Bank of India (RBI) has been to provide rural credit through institutions so as to relieve the rural credit through institutions so as to relieve the rural poor from the clutches of moneylenders. The setting up of RRBs is one of the milestones on the path of the institutionalizing rural credit in India.

RRBs are specialized rural financial institutions for catering to the credit needs of the rural sector. Even though the RRBs are providing better services to the rural poor, they have only limited resources and concentrate on a small geographical area. This is the time of globalization. In the globalised world, the Indian banks face competition from the foreign banks. The RRBs face competition from other PSCBs and also from private sector banks. It created undue completion among the banks under the same ownership.

Taking these factors into account and against this background, this article attempts to present the future scenario of the working of RRBs in India. The working group, with Sri M. Narsimham as the chairperson, was appointed by the government of India in 1975 to review the system of rural credit. The working group recommended establishing state sponsored, regionally based and rural –oriented banks. In the light of the recommendations of the group, the government passed the Regional Rural Banks ordinance in 1975. The ordinance was later replaced by the Regional Rural Banks Act, 1976.

Generally, the RRBs are sponsored by scheduled commercial banks. Some private banks have also sponsored these rural banks. The state co-operative banks are also permitted to sponsor RRBs in consultation with RBI.

The purpose of setting up the RRBs is to prepare and develop a rural economy through disbursement of credit and other accommodations, especially to small and marginal farmers, agricultural labourers, artisans and small entrepreneurs. The RRBs are expected to combine the local feel and the low cost of co-operative on the one hand managerial competence of the commercial banks on the other.

RRBs are empowered to extend all banking activities under clause (b) of section 5 of the Banking Regulation Act. 1949 and can also undertake one or more types of business described in sub-section (1) of section 6 of the same Act.

PROFILE OF RRBS

There are 186 RRBs operating in 26 states across 518 districts with a network of 14,446 branches as on March 31,2004. The majority of the branches of RRBs is located in rural areas.

Profile to RRBs (As on March 2005)	
Total No. of RRNs	196
No. of RRBs that made profit	167
Deposits	Rs. 62143 crore
Borrowings	Rs. 5524 crore
Investments	Rs. 23200 crore
Total Assets	Rs. 77866 crore
Outstanding Advance	Rs. 32871 crore
Operating Profit	RS. 1009 Core
Net Profit	Rs. 750 Crore

LEGAL PROVISION REGARDING CONSOLIDATION

Under section 23 A of Regional Rural Banks Act, 1976 the Central Government after consultation with the National Bank of Rural Development (NABARD), concerned state government and sponsoring banks can, in the public interest, amalgamate two or more Regional Rural Banks by notification in the official gazette.

Therefore RRB can be amalgamated with another RRB only.

NEEDS FOR CONSOLIDATION

The said consolidation of banks does not refer to the merger of weak banks with strong banks. Instead, it means a merger of two banks, even tow large banks or two strong banks to be a mega as well as strong entity in order to absorb the shocks and survive in the difficult times.

The Narasimham Committee on Banking Reforms, in its report given during 1991, suggested that the banks should be restructured creating 3 to 4 large banks of international character and 8 to 10 national level banks with a network of branches throughout the country.

In India, there are 196 RRBs operating in 26 states covering only 518 districts, averaging three districts per bank. Most of the RRBs have the network of below 50 branches. For this small coverage geographical area a separate entity is not necessary.

Consolidation will not only provide sound financial position but also a large branch network throughout the country, the large clientele base, large resources and bigger growth in terms of assets as well as business figures.

Consolidation will help to utilize the funds effectively for regional balanced rural development. Consolidation of RRBs has further become important due to the following reasons:

- Unhealthy competition among banks under the same ownership
- Expansion of Branches
- Regional imbalance
- Computerization/Installation of ATMs/Networking/Core Banking solutions.

Today, the banking is technology based. All the banks are not in position to revamp themselves using the latest technology available in the banking sector. As far as the RRBs are concerned, each of them covers a limited geographical area, the technology based banking like core banking, networking, ATMs etc. is feasible unless and otherwise they are merged in the possible way.

THE VISION

Consolidation that could be thought in the case of the credit structure of RRBs is discussed in this paragraph. The RRBs can be consolidated in the following ways.

- By merging with commercial Banks
- By merging with Co-operative Credit Structure
- By merging with other RRBs.

In India, the Public Sector Commercial Banks play a vital role in the banking sector. It fulfills needs of the Majority. Generally the RRBs are sponsored by these PSCBs to cater to the credit needs of the rural poor. The system of rural credit is always beset by repayment problem and high cost. RRBs are no exceptions this. The PSCBs have sound financial capacities while the RRBs enjoy a very good network capacity while the RRBs enjoy a very good network in rural credit. Therefore, the RRBs can be merged with sponsor bank or some other PSCBs in order to strengthen the rural credit system.

The institutional credit system in rural India consists of commercial banks, co-operative Banks and RRBs. Among others, the role of co-operative Bank and RRBs in rural credit is dominant. Therefore, in order to broaden the network of rural credit structure, the merger of RRBs with cooperatives can be made. The cost of management of such restructured system will be considerable less than that of the present system. Operational efficiency will also improve. Only question before the consolidation of the RRBs and co-operative Banks is the legal perspective. If we find a solution of this, it will certainly improve the quality of rural credit.

At present, there are 196 Regional Rural Banks operating in India. Every RRB follows its own strategy and plans. It created undue variations among RRBs. In today's connected world, banks will have to be competitive in order to face the challenges and leverage the opportunities. To make the RRBs competitive, the RRBs could be consolidated by merging all RRBs in India.

The vision discussed above, gives the detailed view about the consolidation of RRBs. Today it is difficult to think about mergers of RRBs with public sector commercial Banks or Co-operative Banks. Given the existing legal position a RRB can be merged with another RRB. The RRB is the best mode to serve rural people. These could be consolidated without loosing their basic objectives. Therefore, it is suggested to amalgamate all RRBs in India and create a single superpower Regional Rural Bank covering all parts of the Country.

RELATIVE MERITS OF TRADE CREDIT AND BANK CREDIT

You have already read about trade credit and bank credit. You also know that trade credit is extended by the supplier for a limited period to facilitate purchases. Bank credit is obtained from banks and can be utilised for any purpose.

The relative merits of trade credit and bank credit are as follows:

- Trade credit is available only with purchase of raw material or finished goods. It serves a limited purpose. But bank credit can be utilised by the borrower for any purpose that he may have in view.
- In case of trade credit, payment has to be made after the expiry of credit period. However in case of bank credit repayment after a certain period is not compulsory. The arrangement may be continued.
- No security is required to avail of trade credit. Banks generally ask for some security while advancing credit.
- Interest is not payable in case of trade credit, provided payments are made within the credit period. Interest has to be paid on bank credit in all circumstances.
- The terms and conditions of trade credit vary according to the custom and usage of trade. Bank credit is granted on the terms and conditions which generally are the same for all types of business.

- In case of cash credit, the amount of credit is placed in a separate account of the borrower. Overdraft limit is generally granted to an existing account of the customer.
- The amount of credit in case of cash credit depends upon the value of securities offered. But overdraft limit is decided on the average balance of the customer in his account.
- Overdraft is granted without the security of tangible assets. But for cash credit security of tangible assets is an essential requirement.

TYPES OF SECURITIES REQUIRED FOR BANK CREDIT

Loans and advances are granted by bank on personal security of the borrower as well as on the security of some tangible assets, besides the standing of the firm.

Thus securities against bank credit may be of two types:

1. Personal security
2. Security of tangible assets.

Personal security means the credit-worthiness of the borrower. Banks judge the credit-worthiness of the borrower on the basis of his financial soundness and past dealings with the bank.

The following tangible assets are accepted by banks for extending shortterm finance:

- *Moveable goods*: Stock of raw materials and finished goods are accepted by banks as security against bank credit. In case of non-payment, these goods are sold and money is recovered by banks.
- *Shares and stock*: Shares and stock that are quoted on a recognised stock exchange are accepted as security against bank credit. The borrower is required to deposit the share certificate alongwith a transfer deed signed by him.
- *Documents of title to goods*: Bill of lading, Railway Receipts (RR), Goods Receipt (GR), Warehouse warrant are various documents which are recognised as documents of title to goods. To secure credit from bank, the borrower may deposit any of these documents with bank after duly endorsing the same in favour of the bank. This enables the bank to deal with the goods in case of default in repayment.
- *Fixed deposit receipts*: It is a receipt issued by bank as evidence of fixed deposit made by the customer. Banks grant loan on the security of this receipt. The interest charged on loan is higher than the interest allowed on deposit. Banks normally grant loan upto 90 per cent of the value of such receipts.

- *Life insurance policies*: Banks extend credit on the basis of life insurance policy upto the amount of surrender value of such receipts.
- *Jewellery or precious metals*: This type of security may be offered to borrow money for private as well as for business purposes. Proprietary concerns sometimes offer jewellery or other precious metals to obtain credit.
- *Other securities*: Besides the assets and documents, banks also accept National Savings Certificate (NSC), Indira Vikas Patra (IVP), Kisan Vikas Patra (KVP) to grant short-term credit.

MERITS AND DEMERITS OF CUSTOMERS' ADVANCES AS A SOURCE OF SHORT-TERM FINANCE

Customers' advance refers to advance made by the customer against the value of order placed. It is, thus, a part payment of the value of goods to be supplied later.

Merits

- *Interest free*: Amount offered as advance is interest free.Hence funds are available without involving financial burden.
- *No tangible security*: The seller is not required to deposit any tangible security while seeking advance from the customer. Thus assets remain free of charge.
- *No repayment obligation*: Money received as advance is not to be refunded. Hence there are no repayment obligations.

Demerits

- *Limited amount*: The amount advanced by the customer is subject to the value of the order. Borrowers' need may be more than the a amount of advance.
- *Limited period*: The period of customers' advance is only upto the delivery goods. It can not be reviewed or renewed.
- *Penalty in case of non-delivery of goods*: Generally advances are subject to the condition that in case goods are not delivered on time, the order would be cancelled and the advance would have to be refunded along with interest.

ADVANTAGES AND DISADVANTAGES OF INSTALLMENT CREDIT AS A SOURCE OF SHORT-TERM FINANCE

As you have already studied in this stage, installment credit is a system under which a small payment is made at the time of taking possession of the goods and the remaining amount is paid in installments. Installment money is inclusive of interest. Advantages and disadvantages of this system are given below.

Advantages

- *Immediate possession of assets*: Delivery of assets is assured immediately on payment of initial installment (down payment).
- *Convenient payment for assets and equipments*: Costly assets and equipments which cannot be purchased due to inadequacy of long-term funds can be conveniently purchased on payment by instal-ments.
- *Saving of one time investment*: If the value of asset or equipment is very high, funds of the business are likely to be blocked if lumpsum payment is made. Installment credit leads to saving on one time investment.
- Facilitates expansion and modernisation of business and office Business firms can afford to buy necessary equipments and machines when the facility of payment in installments is available. Thus, expansion and modernisation of business and office are facilitated by installment credit.

Disadvantages

- *Committed expenditure*: Payment of installment is a commitment to pay irrespective of profit or loss in the business.
- *Obligation to pay interest*: Under installment credit system payment of interest of obligatory. Generally sellers charge a high rate of interest.
- *Additional burden in case of default*: Sellers sometimes impose stringent conditions in the form of penalty or additional interest, if the buyer fails to pay the installment amount.
- *Cash does not flow*: Like trade credit, installment credit facilitates the purchase of asset or equipment. It does not make cash available which can be utilised for all needful purposes.

BENEFITS AND DRAWBACKS OF FINANCE FROM COOPERATIVE BANKS

Benefits

- Loans from co-operative banks are easily available to farmers and small businessmen involving minimium formalities.
- Co-operative banks provide a convenient means of borrowing. Loans are generally granted at a lower rate of interest.

- Sometimes co-operative banks organise training programmes for members to familiaries them with the various avenues of business and regarding proper utilisation of loan money.
- Being a member of a cooperative bank, the borrower can participate in the management and also share in the profits of the society.
- Co-operative loans create a sense of thrift and self-reliance among the low income group.
- Loans are generally given for productive purposes and that helps to develop the financial and social status of the people.

Drawbacks

- Loan from co-operative banks is available only to members.
- Co-operative banks find it difficult to ensure repayment of loan money due to inadequate information about the need and utilisation of funds by the borrower. There is little scrutiny of the repaying capacity of the loan seeker at the time of granting loan.
- Inadequate resources and lack of trained personnel for management have restricted the spread of co-operative banking facilities.
- Co-operative banks depend largely on the support of the Government. Therefore Government rules and regulations sometime create hurdles for the borrowers.
- Credit from co-operative banks is available only for limited purposes.

Bibliography

Abha Lakshmi Singh, Irfan Sabir and Sarfraj Asghar: *Rural Women : Work and Health*, The Women Press, 2005.

Arun Kumar Singh and Shashi Singh: *Rural Women Workforce : The Changing Socio-Economic Scenario*, Regal Publication, Delhi, 2009.

B. Suguna: *Empowerment of Rural Women Through Self Help Groups*, Discovery Publication, Delhi, 2006

B.N. Singh: *Rural Women and Education*, Vista International Publication, Delhi, 2006.

Babita Agrawal: *Rural Women in Indian Economy*, ABD Publication, Delhi, 2008.

Bhola Nath Ghosh: *Rural Women Leadership*, Mohit Publication, Delhi, 2002.

J. N. Mishra and Keshav Chandra: *Rural Women and Women Empowerment*, Surendra Publications, Delhi, 2012.

J.N. Mishra: *Rural Women and Education*, Surendra Publications, Delhi, 2011.

Jawahar Lal Gupta: *Rural Women and Development in India*, RBSA Publication, Jaipur, 2011.

Jaya Arunachalam and U Kalpagam: *Rural Women in South Asia*, Rawat Publication, Delhi, 2007.

Jitendera Ahirrao: *Entrepreneurship and Rural Women in India*, New Century Publications, Delhi, 2013.

Krishna Chandra Pradhan and Aswini Kumar Mahapatro: *Rural Women from Darkness To Light*, Atlantic Publication, Delhi, 2011.

Krishna Chandra Pradhan: *Rural Women : Issues and Options*, Sonali Publication, Delhi, 2008.

M.A. Sudhir and A. Balakrishnan: *Empowerment of Rural Women Labour Force*, Anmol Publication, Delhi, 2002

Madhuri Nath: *Rural Women Workforce in India*, B R Publication, Delhi, 2003.

Manoharlal Tomar: *Rural Women and Panchayati Raj*, A.K. Publications, Delhi, 2013.

Meenu Agrawal: *Rural Women Workers in India's Unorganized Sector*, New Century Publications, Delhi, 2012.

N. Lalitha: *Rural Women Empowerment and Development Banking*, Kanishka Publication, Delhi, 1997.

Poonam Vats: *Political Participation and Attitudinal Transformation of Rural Women*, Abhijeet Publication, Delhi, 2004.

Punam Kumari: *Rural Women at Work*, Classical Publication, Delhi, 2001.

Reema Mukherjee: *Rural Women Empowerment*, Adhyayan Publication, Delhi, 2008.

S. Maria John, R. Jeyabalan and S. Krishnamurthy: *Rural Women Entrepreneurship*, Discovery Publication, Delhi, 2004.

S. Mookiah: *Rural Women In Informal Sector*, Pointer Publication, Delhi, 2012.

S.B. Verma, Shiw Kumar Jiloka and Kumari Jyoti Kushwah: *Rural Women Empowerment*, Deep and Deep Publication, Delhi, 2006.

S.N. Pattanaik: *Rural Women Panchayati Raj and Development*, Arise Publishers, Delhi, 2010.

Seema Bhattacharya: *Rural Women Panchayatiraj and Development*, Mohit Publications, Delhi, 2011.

Sharmistha Bhattacharjee: *Rural Women and Their Quality of Life*, Pointer Publication, Delhi, 2007.

Tripta Tikaniya and Sudershan Mehta: *Productive Resources and Rural Women Empowerment*, Swastik Publication, Delhi, 2009.

U Kalpagam and Jaya Arunachalam: *Rural Women and Development in India : Issues and Challenges*, Rawat Publication, Delhi, 2008.

Urmila Devi: *Rural Women And Media*, Swastik Publications, Delhi, 2010.

Index

H

I

K

L

M

N

O

P

Q

R

S

T

U

V

W